Inside the Crystal Ball

Inside the Crystal Ball

How to Make and Use Forecasts

Maury Harris

WILEY

For general information on our other products and services or for technical support, please contact our Customer Care Department within the United States at (800) 762-2974, outside the United States at (317) 572-3993, or fax (317) 572-4002.

Wiley publishes in a variety of print and electronic formats and by print-on-demand. Some material included with standard print versions of this book may not be included in e-books or in print-on-demand. If this book refers to media such as a CD or DVD that is not included in the version you purchased, you may download this material at http://booksupport.wiley.com. For more information about Wiley products, visit www.wiley.com.

Library of Congress Cataloging-in-Publication Data
Harris, Maury.
  Inside the crystal ball : how to make and use forecasts / Maury Harris.
    pages cm
  Includes index.
  ISBN 978-1-118-86507-1 (cloth) – ISBN 978-1-118-86517-0 (ePDF) –
ISBN 978-1-118-86510-1 (ePub)
  1. Economic forecasting. 2. Business cycles. 3. Forecasting. I. Title.
  HB3730.H319 2015
  330.01'12—dc23

                                               2014027847

Printed in the United States of America.

10 9 8 7 6 5 4 3 2 1

Contents

Acknowledgments

A long and rewarding career in forecasting has importantly reflected the consistent support and intellectual stimulation provided by my colleagues at the Federal Reserve Bank of New York, the Bank for International Settlements, PaineWebber, and UBS. Senior research management at those institutions rewarded me when I was right and were understanding at times when I was not so right. My colleagues over the years have been a source of inspiration, stimulation, criticism, and encouragement.

Special thanks are addressed to my professional investment clients at PaineWebber and UBS. Thoughtful and challenging questions from them have played a key role in my forming a commercially viable research agenda. Their financial support of my various economics teams via institutional brokerage commissions has always been much appreciated and never taken for granted in the highly competitive marketplace in which economic forecasters practice their trade.

For this book, the efforts on my behalf by my agent Jeffrey Krames, who led me to John Wiley & Sons, were essential. At Wiley, the editorial and publications support provided by Judy Howarth, Tula Batanchiev, Evan Burton, and Steven Kyritz were extremely helpful.

And the guidance provided by my editorial consultant Tom Wynbrandt has been absolutely superb, as was the tech savvy contributed by Charles Harris. Also, thanks are due to Leigh Curry, Tom Doerflinger, Samuel Coffin, Drew Matus, Sheeba Joy, Lisa Harris Millhauser, and Greg Millhauser, who reviewed various chapters.

Most importantly, it would been impossible for me to complete this project without the steady support, encouragement, and editorial acumen provided by Laurie Levin Harris, my wife of 44 years. The year of weekends and weekday nights spent on this book subtracted from quality time we could have spent together. I always will be most grateful for her unwavering confidence in me and her creation of a stimulating home environment essential for the professional accomplishments of myself and our two children, Lisa Harris Millhauser and Charles.

Introduction

What You Need to Know about Forecasting

Everybody forecasts—it is an essential part of our lives. Predicting future outcomes is critical for success in everything from investing to careers to marriage. No one always makes the right choices, but we all strive to come close. This book shows you how to improve your decision-making by understanding how and why forecasters succeed—and sometimes fail—in their efforts. We're all familiar with economists' supposed ineptitude as prognosticators, but those who have been successful have lessons to teach us all.

I have been fortunate to have had a long and successful career in the field of economic forecasting, first at the Federal Reserve Bank of New York and the Bank for International Settlements, and then, for the majority of my working life, on Wall Street. Often I am asked about so-called tricks of the trade, of which there are many. People want to know my strategies and tactics for assembling effective forecasts and for convincing clients to trust me, even though no one's forecasts, including my own, are right all of the time. But most often, people ask me to tell them what they need to know in simple and accessible language.

They want actionable information without having to wade through dense math, mounds of complicated data, or "inside-baseball" verbiage.

With that need in mind, *Inside the Crystal Ball* aims to help improve anyone's ability to forecast. It's designed to increase every reader's ability to make and communicate advice about the future to clients, bosses, colleagues, and anyone else whom we need to convince or whom we want to retain as a loyal listener. As such, this book shows you how to evaluate advice about the future more effectively. Its focus on the non-mathematical, judgmental element of forecasting is an ideal practitioners' supplement to standard statistical forecasting texts.

Forecasting in the worlds of business, marketing, and finance often hinges on assumptions about the U.S. economy and U.S. interest rates. Successful business forecasters, therefore, must have a solid understanding of the way the U.S. economy works. And as economic forecasts are a critical input for just about all others, delving deeper into this discipline can improve the quality of predictions in fields such as business planning, marketing, finance, and investments.

In U.S. universities, economics courses have long been among the most popular elective classes of study. However, there is an inevitable division of labor between academicians, who advance theoretical and empirical economic research, and practitioners.

My professional experience incorporates some of the most significant economic events of the past 40 years. I've "been there, done that" in good times and in bad, in stable environments and in volatile ones. One of the most valuable lessons I learned is that there is no substitute for real-world experience. Experience gives one the ability to address recurring forecasting problems and a history to draw on in making new predictions. And although practice does *not* make perfect, experienced forecasters generally have more accurate forecasting records than their less seasoned colleagues.

In my career, I have witnessed many forecasting victories and blunders, each of which had a huge impact on the U.S. economy. Every decade saw its own particular conditions—its own forecasting challenges. These events provide more than historical anecdotes: They offer fundamental lessons in forecasting.

At the start of my career as a Wall Street forecaster, I struggled, but I became much better over time. According to a study of interest rate forecasters published by the *Wall Street Journal* in 1993, I ranked second in accuracy among 34 bond-rate forecasters for the decade of the 1980s.[1] *MarketWatch,* in 2004, 2006, and again in 2008 ranked me and my colleague James O'Sullivan as the most accurate forecasters of week-ahead economic data. In the autumn of 2011, Bloomberg News cited my team at UBS as the most accurate forecasters across a broad range of economic data over a two-year period.[2] Earning these accolades has been a long and exciting journey.

When I first peered into the crystal ball of forecasting I found cracks. I had joined the forecasting team in the Business Conditions Division at the Federal Reserve Bank of New York in 1973—just in time to be an eyewitness to what would become, then, the worst recession since the Great Depression. As the team's rookie, I did not get to choose my assignment, and I was handed the most difficult economic variable to forecast: inventories. It was a trial by fire as I struggled to build models of the most slippery of economic statistics. But it turned out to be a truly great learning experience. Mastering the mechanics of the business cycle is one of the most important steps in forecasting it—in any economy.

A key lesson to be learned from the failures of past forecasters is to avoid being a general fighting the last war. Fed officials were so chastened by their failure to foresee the severity of the 1973–1975 recession and the associated postwar high in the unemployment rate that they determined to do whatever was necessary not to repeat that mistake. But in seeking to avoid it, they allowed real (inflation-adjusted) interest rates to stay too low for too long, thus opening the door to runaway inflation. My ringside seat to this second forecasting fiasco of the 1970s taught me that past mistakes can definitely distort one's view of the future.

By the 1980s, economists knew that the interest-rate fever in the bond market would break when rates rose enough to whack inflation. But hardly anyone knew the "magic rate" at which that would occur. With both interest rates and inflation well above past postwar experience, history was not very helpful. That is, unless the forecaster could start to understand the likely analytics of a high inflation economy—a topic to be discussed in later chapters.

The 1990s started with a credit crunch, which again caught the Fed off guard. A group of U.S. senators, who had been pestered by credit-starved constituents, were forced to pester then–Fed Chair Alan

Greenspan to belatedly recognize just how restrictive credit had become.[3,4] That episode taught forecasters how to evaluate the Fed's quarterly Senior Loan Officer Opinion Survey more astutely. Today the Survey remains an underappreciated leading indicator, as we discuss in Chapter 9.

The economy improved as the decade progressed. In fact, growth became so strong that many economists wanted the Fed to tighten monetary policy to head off the possibility of higher inflation in the future. In the ensuing debate about the economy's so-called speed limit, a key issue was productivity growth. Fed Chair Greenspan this time correctly foresaw that a faster pace of technological change and innovation was enhancing productivity growth, even if the government's own statisticians had difficulty capturing it in their official measurements. Out of this episode came some important lessons on what to do when the measurement of a critical causal variable is in question.

A forecasting success story for most economists was to resist becoming involved in the public's angst over Y2K: the fearful anticipation that on January 1, 2000, the world's computers, programmed with two-digit dates, would not be able to understand that we were in a new century and would no longer function. Throughout 1999, in fact, pundits issued ever more dire warnings that, because of this danger, the global economy could grind to a halt even before the New Year's bells stopped ringing. Most economic forecasters, though, better understood the adaptability of businesses to such an unusual challenge. We revisit this experience later, to draw lessons on seeing through media hype and maintaining a rational perspective on what really makes businesses adapt.

Forecasters did not do well in anticipating the mild recession that began in 2001. The tech boom, which helped fuel growth at the end of the previous decade and made Alan Greenspan appear very astute in his predictions on productivity, also set the stage for a capital expenditure (capex) recession. Most economists became so enthralled with the productivity benefits of the tech boom that they lost sight of the inevitable negative consequences of overinvestment in initially very productive fields.

Perhaps the largest of all forecasting blunders was the failure to foresee the U.S. home price collapse that began in 2007. It set into motion forces culminating in the worst recession since the Great Depression—the Great

Recession. Such an error merits further consideration in Chapter 4, focusing on specific episodes in which forecasters failed.

By now, it should be clear that experience counts—both for the historical perspective it confers and for having addressed repetitive problems, successfully, over a number of decades. In reading this book, you will live my four decades of experience and learn to apply my hard-learned lessons to your own forecasting.

The book begins by assessing why some forecasters are more reliable than others. I then present my approach to both the statistical and judgmental aspects of forecasting. Subsequent chapters are focused on some long-standing forecasting challenges (e.g., reliance on government information, shifting business "animal spirits," and fickle consumers) as well as some newer ones (e.g., new normal, disinflation, and terrorism). The book concludes with guidance, drawn from my own experience, on how to have a successful career in forecasting. Throughout this volume, I aim to illustrate how successful forecasting is more about honing qualitative judgment than about proficiency in pure quantitative analysis—mathematics and statistics. In other words, forecasting is for all of us, not just the geeks.

Notes

1. Tom Herman, "How to Profit from Economists' Forecasts," *Wall Street Journal*, January 22, 1992.

2. Timothy R. Homan, "The World's Top Forecasters," *Bloomberg Markets*, January 2012.

3. Alan Murray, "Greenspan Met with GOP Senators to Hear Concerns About Credit Crunch," *Wall Street Journal*, July 11, 1990.

4. Paul Duke Jr., "Greenspan Says Fed Poised to Ease Rates Amid Signs of a Credit Crunch," *Wall Street Journal*, July 13, 1990.

Chapter 1

What Makes a Successful Forecaster?

It's tough to make predictions, especially about the future.

—Yogi Berra

I t was an embarrassing day for the forecasting profession: Wall Street's "crystal balls" were on display, and almost all of them were busted. A front-page article in the *Wall Street Journal on* January 22, 1993, told the story. It reported that during the previous decade, only 5 of 34 frequent forecasters had been right more than half of the time in predicting the direction of long-term bond yields over the next six months.[1] I was among those five seers who were the exception to the article's smug conclusion that a simple flip of the coin would have outperformed the interest-rate forecasts of Wall Street's best-known economists. Portfolio manager Robert Beckwitt of Fidelity Investments, who compiled and evaluated the data for the *Wall Street Journal*, had this to say about rate forecasters: "I wouldn't want to have that job—and I'm glad I don't have it."

Were the industry's top economists poor practitioners of the art and science of economic forecasting? Or were their disappointing performances simply indicative of how hard it is for anyone to forecast interest rates? I would argue the latter. Indeed, in a nationally televised 2012 ad campaign for Ally Bank, the Nobel Prize winning economist Thomas Sargent was asked if he could tell what certificate of deposit (CD) rates would be two years hence. His simple response was "no."[2]

Economists' forecasting lapses are often pounced on by critics who seek to discredit the profession overall. However, the larger question is what makes the job so challenging, and how can we surmount those obstacles successfully. In this chapter, I explain just why it is so difficult to forecast the U.S. economy. None of us can avoid difficult decisions about the future. However, we can arm ourselves with the knowledge and tools that help us make the best possible business and investment choices. That is what this book is designed to do.

Grading Forecasters: How Many Pass?

If we look at studies of forecast accuracy, we see that economic forecasters have one of the toughest assignments in the academic or workplace world. These studies should remind us how difficult the job is; they shouldn't reinforce a poor opinion of forecasters. If we review the research carefully, we'll see that there's much to learn, both from what works and from what hinders success.

Economists at the Federal Reserve Bank of Cleveland studied the 1983 to 2005 performance of about 75 professional forecasters who participated in the Federal Reserve Bank of Philadelphia's Livingston forecaster survey.[3] We examine their year-ahead forecasts of growth rates for real (inflation-adjusted) gross domestic product (GDP) and the consumer price index (CPI). (See Table 1.1.)

If being very accurate is judged as being within half a percentage point of the actual outcome, only around 30 percent of GDP growth forecasts met this test. By the same grading criteria, approximately 39 percent were very accurate in projecting year-ahead CPI inflation.

Table 1.1 Accuracy of the Year-Ahead Median Economists' Forecasts, 1983–2005

Grade(*)	Proportion of Forecasts within ...	GDP Growth	CPI Inflation
A	0.5 percentage point	30.4%	39.1%
B	0.5–1 percentage point	21.7	30.4
C	1–1.5 percentage points	17.4	21.7
D	1.5–2 percentage points	8.7	8.7
E	2–2.5 percentage points	13.0	0.0
F	2.5–3 percentage points	8.7	0.0

*Assigned by the author.
SOURCE: Michael F. Bryan and Linsey Molloy, "Mirror, Mirror, Who's the Best Forecaster of Them All?" Federal Reserve Bank of Cleveland, *Economic Commentary*, March 15, 2007.

We give these forecasters an "A." If we award "Bs" for being between one-half and one percentage point of reality, that grade was earned by almost 22 percent of the GDP growth forecasts and just over 30 percent of the CPI inflation projections. Thus, only around half the surveyed forecasters earned the top two grades for their year-ahead real GDP growth outlooks, although almost 7 in 10 earned those grades for their predictions of CPI inflation. (We should note that CPI is less volatile—and thus easier to predict—than real GDP growth.)

Is our grading too tough? Probably not. Consider that real GDP growth over 1983 to 2005 was 3.4 percent. A one-half percent miss was thus plus or minus 15 percent of reality. Misses between one-half and one percent could be off from reality by as much as 29 percent. For a business, sales forecast misses of 25 percent or more are likely to be viewed as problematic.

With that in mind, our "Cs" are for the just more than 17 percent of growth forecasts that missed actual growth by between 1 percent and 1.5 percent, and for the 22 percent of inflation forecasts that missed by the same amount. The remaining 30 percent of forecasters—those whose forecasts fell below our C grade—did not necessarily flunk out, though. The job security of professional economists depends on more than their forecasting prowess—a point that we discuss later.

The CPI inflation part of the test, as we have seen, was not quite as difficult. Throughout 1983 to 2005, the CPI rose at a 3.1 percent annual rate. Thirty-nine percent of the forecasts were within half a percent of

Table 1.2   Probability of Repeating as a Good Forecaster

GDP GROWTH

Probability of Remaining Better Than the Median Forecast after ...	Observed (%)	Expected* (%)
One success	48.7	49.4
Two successes	44.4	49.4
Three successes	38.7	48.6
Four successes	27.6	48.9

INFLATION

Probability of Remaining Better Than the Median Forecast after ...	Observed (%)	Expected* (%)
One success	46.8	49.3
Two successes	43.5	49.0
Three successes	45.9	48.7
Four successes	35.3	48.6

*Proportion expected assuming random chance.
SOURCE: Michael F. Bryan and Linsey Molloy, "Mirror, Mirror, Who's the Best Forecaster of Them All?" Federal Reserve Bank of Cleveland, *Economic Commentary*, March 15, 2007.

reality—as much as a 16 percent miss. Another 30 percent of them earned a B, with misses between 0.5 and 1 percent of the actual outcome, or within 16 to 32 percent of reality. Still, 30 percent of the forecasters did no better than a C.

In forecasting, as in investments, one good year hardly guarantees success in the next. (See Table 1.2.) According to the study, the probabilities of outperforming the median real GDP forecast two years in a row were around 49 percent. The likelihood of a forecaster outperforming the median real GDP forecast for five straight years was 28 percent. For CPI inflation forecasts, there was a 47 percent probability of successive outperformances and a 35 percent probability of beating the median consensus forecast in five consecutive years.

Similar results have been reported by Laster, Bennett, and In Sun Geoum in a study of the accuracy of real GDP forecasts by economists polled in the *Blue Chip Economic Indicators*—a widely followed survey of professional forecasters.[4] In the 1977 to 1986 period, which included what was until then the deepest postwar recession, only 4 of 38 forecasters beat the consensus. However, in the subsequent 1987 to 1995 period, which included just one mild recession, 10 of 38 forecasters outperformed the consensus. Interestingly, none of the forecasters who outperformed the consensus in the first period were able to do so in the second!

Perhaps even more important than accurately forecasting economic growth rates is the ability to forecast "yes" or "no" on the likelihood of a major event, such as a recession. The Great Recession of 2008 to 2009 officially began in the United States in January of 2008. By then, the unemployment rate had risen from 4.4 percent in May of 2007 to 5.0 percent in December, and economists polled by the *Wall Street Journal* in January foresaw, on average, a 42 percent chance of recession. (See Figure 1.1.) Three months earlier, the consensus probability had been 34 percent. And it wasn't until we were three months into the recession that the consensus assessed its probability at more than 50 percent.

The story was much the same in the United Kingdom (UK). By June of 2008 the recession there had already begun. Despite this, none of the two-dozen economists polled by Reuters at that time believed a recession would occur at any point in 2008 to 2009.[5]

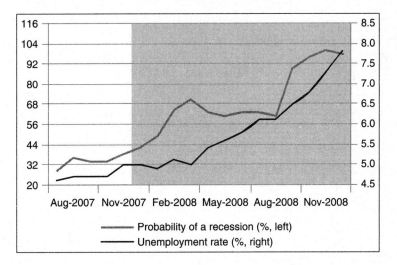

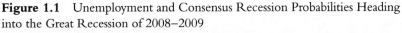

Figure 1.1 Unemployment and Consensus Recession Probabilities Heading into the Great Recession of 2008–2009
Source: Bureau of Labor Statistics, The Wall Street Journal.
Note: Shaded area represents the recession.

In some instances, judging forecasters by how close they came to a target might be an unnecessarily stringent test. In the bond market, for example, just getting the future direction of rates correct is important for investors; but that can be a tall order, especially in volatile market conditions. Also, those who forecast business condition variables, such as GDP, can await numerous data revisions (to be discussed in Chapter 5) to see if the updated information is closer to their forecasts. Interest-rate outcomes, however, are not revised, thereby denying rate forecasters the opportunity to be bailed out by revised statistics. Let's grade interest rate forecasters, therefore, on a pass/fail basis, where just getting the future direction of rates correct is enough to pass.

Yet even on a pass/fail test, most forecasters have had trouble getting by. As earlier noted, only 5 of the 34 economists participating in 10 or more of the semiannual surveys of bond rates were directionally right more than half the time. And of those five forecasters, only two—Carol Leisenring of Core States Financial Group and I—made forecasts that, if followed, would have outperformed a simple buy-and-hold strategy employing intermediate-term bonds during the forecast periods. According to calculations discussed in the article, "buying and holding a basket of intermediate-term Treasury bonds would have produced an average annual return of 12.5 percent—or 3.7 percentage points more than betting on the consensus."[6]

In their study of forecasters' performance in predicting interest rates and exchange rates six months ahead, Mitchell and Pearce found that barely more than half (52.4 percent) of Treasury bill rate forecasts got the direction right. (See Table 1.3.) Slightly less than half (46.4 percent) of the yen/dollar forecasts were directionally correct. And only around a third of the Treasury bond yield forecasts correctly predicted whether the 30-year Treasury bond yield would be higher or lower six months later.

Although it is easy to poke fun at the forecasting prowess of economists as a group, it is more important to note that some forecasters do a much better job than others. Indeed, the best forecasters of Treasury bill and Treasury bond yields and the yen/dollar were right approximately two-thirds of the time.

Some economic statistics are simply easier to forecast than others. Since big picture macroeconomic variables encompassing the entire U.S.

Table 1.3 Percentages of 33 Economists' Six-Month-Ahead *Directional* Interest Rate and Exchange Rates Forecasts That Were Correct

Forecast Variable	Average (%)	Top Forecaster (%)	Worst (%)	Period
Treasury bill rate	52.4	65.2	23.8	1982–2002
Treasury bond yield	33.3	65.2	26.9	1982–2002
Yen/dollar	46.4	66.7	38.5	1989–2002

SOURCE: Karlyn Mitchell and Douglas K. Pearce, "Professional Forecasts of Interest Rates and Exchange Rates: Evidence from the *Wall Street Journal's* Panel of Economists," North Carolina State University Working Paper 004, March 2005.

economy often play a key role in marketing, business, and financial forecasting, it is important to know which macro variables are more reliably forecasted. As a rule, interest rates are more difficult to forecast than nonfinancial variables such as growth, unemployment, and inflation.

If we'd like to see why this is so, let's look at economists' track records in forecasting key economic statistics. Consider, in Table 1.4, the relative difficulty of forecasting economic growth, inflation, unemployment and interest rates. In this particular illustration, year-ahead forecast errors for

Table 1.4 Relative Year Ahead Errors of Forecasters versus "Naive Straw Man"

Forecast Variable	Worst	Best	Median	% of Forecasts Beating Straw Man
Short-term interest rate	1.67%	0.95%	1.20%	92
Long-term interest rate	1.57	0.89	1.20	83
Unemployment rate	2.71	0.63	0.97	31
CPI inflation rate	1.11	0.38	0.54	3
GNP growth	2.09	0.78	0.99	48

NOTE: Short-term and long-term interest rates and unemployment rates are relative to a hypothetical no-change straw man forecast. CPI and GNP growth rates are relative to a same-change straw man forecast.
SOURCE: Twelve individual forecasters' interest rate forecasts, 1982–1991; other variables, 29 individual forecasts, 1986–1991, as published in the *Wall Street Journal*.
Stephen K. McNees, "How Large Are Economic Forecast Errors?" *New England Economic Review*, July/August 1992.

these variables are compared with forecast errors by hypothetical, alternative, "naive straw man" projections. The latter were represented by no-change forecasts for interest rates and the unemployment rate, and the lagged values of the CPI and gross national product (GNP) growth. Displayed in the table are median ratios of errors by surveyed forecasters relative to errors by the "naive straw man." For example, median errors in forecasting interest rates were 20 percent higher than what would have been generated by simple no-change forecasts. Errors in forecasting unemployment and GNP were about the same for forecasters and their naive straw man opponent. In the case of CPI forecasts, however, the forecasters' errors were only around half as large as forecasts generated by assuming no change from previously reported growth.

There are many more examples of forecaster track records, and we examine some of them in subsequent chapters. While critics use such studies to disparage economists' performances, it's much more constructive to use the information to improve your own forecasting prowess.

Why It's So Difficult to Be Prescient

Because so many intelligent, well-educated economists struggle to provide forecasts that are more often right than wrong, it should be clear that forecasting is difficult. The following are among the eight most important reasons:

1. **It is hard to know where you are, so it is even more difficult to know where you are going.**

    The economy is subject to myriad influences. At each moment, a world of inputs exerts subtle shifts on its direction and strength. It can be difficult for economists to estimate where the national economy is headed in the present, much less the future. Like a ship on the sea in the pre-GPS era, determining one's precise location at any given instant is a difficult challenge.

    John Maynard Keynes—the father of Keynesian economics— taught that recessions need not automatically self-correct. Instead, turning the economy around requires reactive government fiscal policies—spending increases, tax cuts and at least temporary budget deficits. His "new economics" followers in the 1950s and 1960s took that conclusion a step further, claiming that recessions could be headed off by proactive, anticipatory countercyclical monetary and fiscal policies. But that approach assumed economists could foresee trouble down the road.

Not everyone agreed with Keynes' theories. Perhaps the most visible and influential objections were aired by University of Chicago economics professor Milton Friedman. In his classic address at the 1967 American Economic Association meeting, he argued against anticipatory macroeconomic stabilization policies.[7] Why? "We simply do not know enough to be able to recognize minor disturbances when they occur or to be able to predict what their effects will be with any precision or what monetary policy is required to offset their effects," he said.

Everyday professional practitioners of economics in the real world know the validity of Friedman's observation all too well. In Figure 1.2, for example, consider real GDP growth forecasts for a statistical quarter that were made in the third month of that quarter— after the quarter was almost over. In the current decade, such

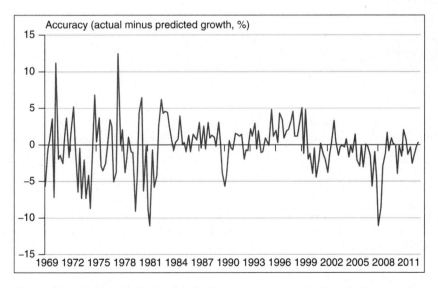

Figure 1.2   In the Final Month of a Quarter, Forecasters' Growth Forecasts for That Quarter Can Still Err Substantially

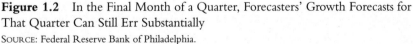

SOURCE: Federal Reserve Bank of Philadelphia.

projections were 0.8 percent off from what was reported. (Note: This is judged by the mean absolute error—the absolute magnitude of an error without regard to whether the forecast was too high or too low.) Moreover, these "last minute" projections were even farther off in earlier decades.

Moving forward, we discuss how the various economic "weather reports" can suggest winter and summer on the same day! Let's note, too, that some of the key indicators of tomorrow's business weather are subject to substantial revisions. At times it seems like there are no reliable witnesses, because they all change their testimony under oath. In later chapters we discuss how to address these challenges.

2. History does not always repeat or even rhyme.

Forecasters address the future largely by extrapolating from the past. Consequently, prognosticators can't help but be historians. And just as the signals on current events are frequently mixed and may be subject to revision, so, too, when discussing a business or an economy, are interpretations of prior events. In subsequent chapters, we discuss how to sift through history and judge what really happened—a key step in predicting, successfully, what will happen in the future.

The initially widely acclaimed book, *This Time Is Different: Eight Centuries of Financial Follies* by Carmen Reinhart and Kenneth Rogoff, provides a good example of the difficulties in interpreting history in order to give advice about the future.[8] Published in 2011, the book first attracted attention from global policymakers with its conclusion that, since World War II, economic growth turned negative when the government debt/GDP ratio exceeded 90 percent. Two years later, other researchers discovered calculation errors in the authors' statistical summary of economic history. Looking for repetitive historical patterns can be tricky!

3. Statistical crosscurrents make it hard to find safe footing.

Even if the past and present are clear, divining the future remains challenging when potential causal variables (e.g., the money supply and the Federal purchases of goods and services) are headed in opposite directions. However, successful and influential forecasters must avoid being hapless "two-handed economists" (i.e., "on the one hand, but on the other hand").

Moreover, one's statistical coursework at the college and graduate level does not necessarily solve the problem of what matters most when signals diverge. Yes, there are multiple regression software packages readily available that can crank out estimated regression (i.e., response) coefficients for independent causal variables. But, alas, even the more advanced statistical courses and textbooks have yet to satisfactorily surmount the multicollinearity problem. That is when two highly correlated independent variables "compete" to claim historical credit for explaining dependent variables that must be forecast. As a professional forecaster, I have not solved this problem but have been coping with it almost every day for decades. As we proceed, you will find some helpful tips on dealing with this challenge.

4. Behavioral sciences are inevitably limited.

There have been quantum leaps in the science of public opinion polling since the fiasco of 1948, when President Truman's reelection stunned pollsters. Nevertheless, there continue to be plenty of surprises ("upsets") on election night. Are there innate limits to humans' ability to understand and predict the behavior of other humans? That was what the well-known conservative economist Henry Hazlitt observed in reaction to all of the hand wringing about "scientific polling" in the aftermath of the 1948 debacle. Writing in the November 22, 1948, issue of *Newsweek*, Hazlitt noted: "The economic future, like the political future, will be determined by future human behavior and decisions. That is why it is uncertain. And in spite of the enormous and constantly growing literature on business cycles, business forecasting will never, any more than opinion polls, become an exact science."[9]

In other words, forecast success or failure can reflect "what we don't know that we don't know" (generalized uncertainty) more than "what we know" (risk).

5. The most important determinants may not be measureable.

Statistics are all about measurement. But what if you cannot measure what matters? Statisticians often approach this stumbling block with a dummy variable. It is assigned a zero or one in each examined historical period (year, quarter, month, or week) according to whether the statistician believes that the unmeasurable variable was active or dormant in that period. (For example, when explaining U.S. inflation history with a regression model, a dummy variable might be used to identify periods when there were price controls.) If the dummy variable in an estimated multiple regression equation achieves statistical significance, the statistician can then claim that it reflects the influence of the unmeasured, hypothesized causal factor.

The problem, though, is that a statistically significant dummy variable can be credited for anything that cannot be otherwise accounted for. The label attached to the dummy variable may not be a true causal factor useful in forecasting. In other words, there can be a naming contest for a dummy variable that is statistically sweeping up what other variables cannot explain. There are some common sense approaches to addressing this problem, and we discuss them later.

6. **There can be conflicts between the goal of accuracy and the goal of pleasing a forecaster's everyday workplace environment.**

Many of the most publicly visible and influential forecasters—especially securities analysts and investment bank economists—have job-related considerations that can influence their advice about the future. It is ironic that financial analysts and economists whose good work has earned them national recognition can find pressures at the top that complicate their ability to give good advice once the internal and external audience enlarges.

Many Wall Street economists, for instance, are employed by fixed-income or currency trading desks. Huge amounts of their firms' and their clients' money are positioned before key economic statistics are reported. This knowledge might understandably make a forecaster reluctant to go against the consensus. And, as we discuss shortly, there can be other work-related pressures not to go against the grain as well.

Are trading desks' economists' forecasts sometimes made to assist their employers' business?

It is hard, if not impossible, to gauge how much and how frequently forecasts are conditioned by an employer's business interests. However, it can be observed that certain types of behavior are consistent with the hypothesis that forecasts are being affected in this manner. For instance, the economist Takatoshi Ito at the University of Tokyo has authored research suggesting that foreign exchange rate projections are systematically biased toward scenarios that would benefit the forecaster's employer. He has attached the label "wishful expectations" to such forecasts.[10]

What is the effect of the sell-side working environment on stock analysts' performance?

In order to be successful, sell-side securities analysts at brokerage houses and investment banks must, in addition to performing their analytical research, spend time and effort marketing their research to their firms' clients. In buy-side organizations, such as pension funds, mutual funds, and hedge funds, analysts generally do not have these marketing responsibilities. Do the two different work environments make a difference in performance? The evidence is inconclusive.

For instance, one study funded by the Division of Research at the Harvard Business School examined the July 1997 to December 2004 period and reached the following conclusions: "Sell-side firm analysts make more optimistic and less accurate earnings forecasts than their buy-side counterparts. In addition, abnormal returns from investing in their Strong Buy/Buy recommendations are negative and under-perform comparable sell-side recommendations."[11]

There is a wide range of performance results within the sell-side analyst universe. For example, one study concluded that sell-side securities analysts ranked well by buy-side users of sell-side research out-performed lesser ranked sell-side analysts.[12] (Note: This study, which was sponsored by the William E. Simon Graduate School of Business Administration, reviewed performance results from 1991 to 2000.)

How does media exposure affect forecasters?

To see how the working environment can affect the quality of advice, look at Wall Street's emphasis on "instant analysis." Wall Street economists often devote considerable time and care to preparing economic-indicator forecasts. However, within seconds—literally, seconds—after data are reported at the normal 8:30 A.M. time, economists are called on to determine the implications of an economics report and announce them to clients.

Investment banks and trading firms want their analysts to offer good advice. But they also want publicity. They're happy to offer their analysts to the cameras for the instant analysis prized by the media. The awareness that a huge national television audience is watching and will know if they err can be stressful to the generally studious and usually thorough persons often attracted to the field of economics. Keep this in mind when deciding whether the televised advice of an investment bank analyst is a useful input for decision making. (Note: Securities firms in the current, more regulation-conscious decade generally scrutinize analysts' published reports, which should make the reports more reliable than televised sound bites.)

7. Audiences may condition forecasters' perceptions of professional risks.

John Maynard Keynes famously said: "Practical men, who believe themselves to be quite exempt from any intellectual influences, are usually the slaves of some defunct economist." Forecasters subconsciously or consciously risk becoming the slaves of their intended audience of colleagues, employers, and clients. In other words, seers often fret about the reaction of their audience, especially if their proffered advice is errant. How the forecaster frames these risks is known as the *loss function*.

In some situations, such pressures can be constructive. The first trader I met on my first day working as a Wall Street economist had this greeting: "I like bulls and I like bears but I don't like chickens." The message was clear: No one wants to hear anything from a two-handed economist. That was constructive pressure for a young forecaster embarking on a career.

That said, audience pressures might not be so benign. Yet they are inescapable. The ability to deal with them in a field in which periodic costly errors are inevitable is the key to a long, successful career for anyone giving advice about the future.

8. Statistics courses are not enough. It takes both math and experience to succeed.

To be sure, many dedicated statistics educators are also scholars working to advance the science of statistics. However, teaching and its attendant focus on academic research inevitably leaves less time for building a considerable body of practical experience.

No amount of schooling could have prepared me for what I experienced during my first week as a Wall Street economist in 1980. Neither a PhD in economics from Columbia University nor a half-dozen years as an economist at the Federal Reserve Bank of New York and the Bank for International Settlements in Basel, Switzerland had given me the slightest clue as to how to handle my duties as PaineWebber's Chief Money Market Economist.

At the New York Fed, my ability to digest freshly released labor market statistics, and to write a report about them before the close of business, helped trigger an early promotion for me. But on PaineWebber's New York fixed-income trading floor, I was expected to digest and opine on those same very important monthly data no more than five minutes after they hit the tape at 8:30 A.M.

There were other surprises as well. In graduate school, for example, macroeconomics courses usually skipped national income accounting and measurement. These topics were regarded as simply descriptive and too elementary for a graduate level academic curriculum. Instead, courses focused on the mathematical properties of macroeconomic mechanics and econometrics as the arbiters of economic "truth." On Wall Street, however, the ability to understand and explain the accounting that underlies any important government or company data report is key to earning credibility with a firm's professional investor clients. In graduate school we did study more advanced statistical techniques. But they were mainly applied to testing hypotheses and studying statistical economic history, not forecasting per se.

In short, when I first peered into my crystal ball, I was behind the eight ball! As in the game of pool, survival would depend on bank shots that combined skill, nerve, and good luck. Fortunately, experience pays: More seasoned forecasters generally do better. (See Figure 1.3. The methodology for calculating the illustrated forecaster scores is discussed in Chapter 2.)

In summation, then, it is difficult to be prescient because:

- Behavioral sciences are inevitably limited.
- Interpreting current events and history is challenging.

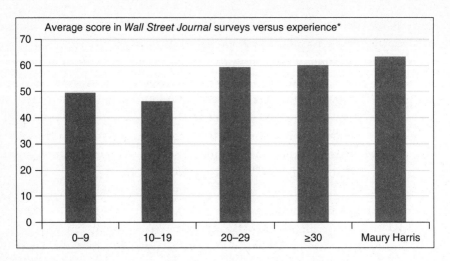

Figure 1.3 More Experienced Forecasters Usually Fare Better

*Number of surveys in which forecaster participated.

SOURCE: Andy Bauer, Robert A. Eisenbeis, Daniel F. Waggoner, and Tao Zha, "Forecast Evaluation with Cross-Sectional Data: The Blue Chip Survey," Federal Reserve Bank of Atlanta, Second Quarter, 2003.

- Important causal factors may not be quantifiable.
- Work environments and audiences can bias forecasts.
- Experience counts more than statistical courses.

Bad Forecasters: One-Hit Wonders, Perennial Outliers, and Copycats

Some seers do much better than others in addressing the difficulties cited earlier. But what makes these individuals more accurate? The answer is critical for learning how to make better predictions and for selecting needed inputs from other forecasters. We first review some studies identifying characteristics of both successful and unsuccessful forecasters. That is followed in Chapter 2 by a discussion of my experience in striving for better forecasting accuracy throughout my career.

What Is "Success" in Forecasting?

A forecast is any statement regarding the future. With this broad definition in mind, there are several ways to evaluate success or failure. Statistics texts offer a number of conventional gauges for judging how close a forecaster comes to being right over a number of forecast periods. (See an explanation and examples of these measures in Chapter 2.) Sometimes, as in investing, where the direction of change is more important than the magnitude of change, success can be defined as being right more often than being wrong. Another criteria can be whether a forecaster is correct about outcomes that are especially important in terms of costs of being wrong and benefits of being right (i.e., forecasting the big one.)

Over a forecaster's career, success will be judged by all three criteria—accuracy, frequency of being correct, and the ability to forecast the big one. And, as we see, it's rare to be highly successful in addressing all of these challenges. The sometimes famous forecasters who nail the big one are often neither accurate nor even directionally correct most of the time. On the other hand, the most reliable forecasters are less likely to forecast rare and very important events.

One-Hit Wonders

Reputations often are based on an entrepreneur, marketer, or forecaster "being really right when it counted most." Our society lauds and rewards such individuals. They may attain a guru status, with hordes of people seeking and following their advice after their "home run." However, an impressive body of research suggests that these one-hit wonders are usually unreliable sources of advice and forecasts. In other words, they strike out a lot. There is much to learn about how to make and evaluate forecasts from this phenomenon.

In the decade since it was published in 2005, Phillip E. Tetlock's book *Expert Political Judgment—How Good Is It? How Can We Know?* has become a classic in the development of standards for evaluating political opinion.[13] In assessing predictions from experts in different fields, Tetlock draws important conclusions for successful business and economic forecasting and for selecting appropriate decision-making/ forecasting inputs. For instance:

"Experts" successfully predicting rare events were often wrong both before and after their highly visible success. Tetlock reports that "When we pit experts against minimalist performance benchmarks—dilettantes, dart-throwing chimps, and assorted extrapolation algorithms, we find few signs that expertise translates into greater ability to make either 'well-calibrated' or 'discriminating' forecasts."

The one-hit wonders can be like broken clocks. They were more likely than most forecasters to occasionally predict extreme events, but only because they make extreme forecasts more frequently.

Tetlock's "hedgehogs" (generally inaccurate forecasters who manage to correctly forecast some hard-to-forecast rare event) have a very different approach to reasoning than his more reliable "foxes." For example, hedgehogs often used one big idea or theme to explain a variety of occurrences. However, "the more eclectic foxes knew many little things and were content to improvise ad hoc solutions to keep pace with a rapidly changing world."

While hedgehogs are less reliable as forecasters, foxes may be less stimulating analysts. The former encourage out-of-the-box thinking. The latter are more likely to be less decisive, two-handed economists.

Tetlock's findings about political forecasts also apply to business and economic forecasts. Jerker Denrell and Christina Fang have provided such illustrations in their 2010 *Management Science* article titled "Predicting the Next Big Thing: Success as a Signal of Poor Judgement."[14] They conclude that "accurate predictions of an extreme event are likely to be an indication of poor overall forecasting ability, when judgment or forecasting ability is defined as the average level of forecast accuracy over a wide range of forecasts."

Denrell and Fang assessed the forecasting accuracy of professional forecasters participating in *Wall Street Journal* semi-annual forecasting surveys between July 2002 and July 2005. (Every six months at the start of January and July around 50 economists and analysts provided six-month-ahead forecasts of key economic variables, such as GNP, inflation, unemployment, interest rates, and exchange rates.) Their study focused on the overall accuracy of forecasters projecting extreme events, which were defined as results either 20 percent above or below average forecasts. For each forecaster, they compared overall accuracy for all of the forecast variables with the accuracy of each forecaster's projections of the defined extreme events.

Forecasters who were more accurate than the average forecaster in predicting extreme outcomes were less accurate in predicting all outcomes. Also, the prognosticators who were comparatively more accurate in predicting extreme outcomes had extreme outcomes as a higher percentage of their overall forecasts. In the authors' assessment, "Forecasting ability should be based on all predictions, not only a selected subset of extreme predictions."

What do these results tell us about the characteristics of forecasters with these two different types of success? Denrell and Fang offer the following four observations:

1. Extreme outcomes are, by definition, less likely than all outcomes. Therefore, extreme outcomes are more likely to be successfully predicted by forecasters who rely on intuition or who emphasize a single determinant than by those forecasters extrapolating from a more comprehensive sense of history.

2. Forecasters who happen to be correct about extreme outcomes become overconfident in their judgment. The authors cite research indicating that securities analysts who have been relatively more accurate in predicting earnings over the previous four quarters tend to be less accurate compared to their peers in subsequent quarters.[15]

3. Forecasters can be motivated by their past successes and failures. Forecasters with relatively bold past forecasts may be tempted to alter their tarnished reputations with more bold forecasts. (Denrell and Fang cite research by Chevalier and Ellison and by Leone and Wu.[16,17]) On the other hand, successful forecasters might subsequently move closer to consensus expectations in order to avoid the risk of incorrect bold forecasts on their reputations and track records. (The authors cite research by Pendergrast and Stole.[18]) In other words, in the world of forecasting both successes and failures can feed on each other.

4. Some forecasters may be motivated to go out on a limb if the rewards for being either relatively right or highly visible with such forecasts are worth taking the reputational risk of building up a bad track record with many long shots that don't pan out. This may be especially so if forecasters perceive that they will be more commercially successful with the attention garnered by comparatively unique projections. However, Denrell and Fang cite research suggesting that securities analysts are more likely to be terminated if they make bold and inaccurate forecasts.[19]

Who Is More Likely to Go Out on a Limb?

It can be dangerous for a forecaster to go out on a limb too often, especially if the proverbial limb usually gets sawed off. But why do some forecasters make that choice? Do we know who they are, so that we can consider the source when hearing their forecasts?

Researchers have examined popular, well-publicized forecast surveys to identify who is most likely to go against the grain and what are the consequences of doing so. Among the studied forecaster surveys have been those appearing in *The Blue Chip Economic Indicators,* the *Wall Street Journal,* and *Business Week.*

Karlyn Mitchell and Douglas Pearce have examined six-month-ahead interest rate and foreign exchange rate forecasts appearing in past *Wall Street Journal* forecaster surveys.[20] They asked whether a forecaster's employment influenced various forecast characteristics. Specifically, they compared forecasters employed by banks, securities firms, finance departments of corporations, econometric modelers, and independent firms.

Their research indicated that *economists with firms bearing their own name deviated more from the consensus than did other forecasters of interest rates and foreign exchange rates.* In the authors' view, such behavior could have been motivated by the desire to gain publicity. (Note: Large sell-side firms employing economists and analysts have the financial means for large advertising budgets and are presumably not as hungry for free publicity.)

While Mitchell and Pearce studied the *Wall Street Journal* surveys, Owen Lamont examined participants in *Business Week's* December surveys of forecasts for GDP growth, unemployment, and inflation in successive years.[21] His statistical results indicated that *economists who own their consulting firms are more likely to deviate from the consensus and are relatively less accurate in forecasting growth, unemployment, and inflation.* His findings indicated to him that some forecasters are "optimizing the market value of their reputations" instead of "acting to minimize mean squared error."

David Laster, Paul Bennett, and In Sun Geoum reviewed U.S. real GDP forecast behavior of economists participating in *Blue Chip Economic Indicator* surveys in the 1976 to 1995 period.[22] They conclude that "forecasters' deviations from the consensus are related to the types of firms for which they work" and illustrate that "professional forecasting has a strong strategic component." Studying mean absolute deviation (MAD) from the consensus, they report that "independent forecasters with firms bearing their own names tend to make unconventional forecasts." (See Table 1.5.)

Table 1.5 Average Forecast Deviations from Consensus GDP Growth Forecasts 1977–1996

Forecasters' Employer	Average Deviation from Consensus (Basis Points)
Industrial corporation	37
Bank	41
Econometric modeler	43
Securities firm	52
Independent forecaster	82

SOURCE: David Laster, Paul Bennett, and In Sum Geoum, "Rational Basis in Macroeconomic Forecasts," Federal Reserve Bank of New York Research Papers, July 1996.

Consensus Copycats

Sticking with the consensus forecast is the opposite of going out on a limb. One motivation for doing so is that there's safety in numbers. Some forecasters might think that they'll never be fired when they are wrong if so many others also were incorrect. *But is it wise to copy the consensus?*

When the economics profession is criticized for inaccurate forecasts, the judgments reflect comparisons of actual outcomes to consensus forecasts. But the reason for copying consensus economic forecasts is that *the consensus average of all forecasts usually outperforms any individual forecaster.*[23]

Why? Because when we consider all forecasts, we incorporate more input information than is represented in any individual pronouncement. Also, the averaging process can iron out individual forecasters' biases. In addition to their relative accuracy, consensus economic forecasts also have the advantage of often being free of charge and time-saving. However, relying on consensus forecasts does have some important drawbacks:

- First, consensus economic growth forecasts almost always fail at critical turning points in the business cycle—especially when heading into a recession.[24] For companies and investors, not being prepared for a recession can often turn success into failure.
- Second, if one's objective is to outperform one's peers, sticking with the consensus is not the recipe for such relative success. Students of forecasting approach this issue from the perspective of herding.

Consider the results of one study of the characteristics of competing forecasters in the Blue Chip Survey. Two-time winners of the top forecaster award herd to the consensus the least amount, while the most herding is done by nonwinners.[25]

Although it may be sensible for less skilled or infrequent forecasters to mimic the consensus, they often don't. Laster, Bennett, and Geoum also find that nonwinners in the Blue Chip survey herd more often to the forecasts of winners than to the consensus forecast.

Success Factors: Why Some Forecasters Excel

Both successful and unsuccessful forecast histories offer valuable lessons. In subsequent chapters we review many of both. What follows here is an example of what one can learn from studying relatively successful forecasters of U.S. Federal Reserve monetary policy—a key input to all financial forecasting.

European Central Bank (ECB) economists analyzed the accuracy and characteristics of forecasters seeking to predict to what extent the Federal Reserve System, in its Federal Open Market Committee (FOMC) meetings between February 1999 and September 2005, would alter the Federal funds rate target.[26] Specifically, they studied how forecasters' accuracy was related to their education, professional experience, type of employer, and geographic location relative to Washington, D.C., where the FOMC meets. Here's what they learned:

- *Education matters, but you don't need a PhD to be a relatively accurate forecaster of Fed actions.* Forecasters with a master's degree were more accurate than those with other degrees. However, having a PhD was not associated with superior accuracy.
- *A forecaster's geographic location and local environment influence monetary policy forecast accuracy.* Prognosticators working in regions where local economic circumstances—inflation and job growth—deviated most from the national conditions influencing U.S. monetary policy recorded larger errors than others. This finding reminds us that forecasters should ask themselves if their everyday environment is conditioning their judgment. My experience is that investors

and analysts in relatively depressed U.S. regions are sometimes too pessimistic about overall U.S. economic conditions, while residents of comparatively strong regions can be too optimistic.

- *In forecasting, specialized knowledge of institutional behavior complements statistical skills.* Individuals who had worked for the Federal Reserve Board of Governors recorded relatively fewer errors in forecasting Fed policy. During the period studied, monetary policy forecasters often estimated statistical "reaction functions," attempting to assign numerical values to actions the Fed had taken in the past in response to various economic statistics (such as inflation and unemployment). However, the Fed can be influenced by variables that are not easily quantifiable. Moreover, the Fed's response to economic statistics can be altered over time by changes in its internal policy making procedures and FOMC membership.

- *Forecasters with better inflation forecasting records registered superior Fed policy forecasting performance.* Interest rate forecasting can be critical for many business prognostications. Because the behavior of a wide variety of interest rates depends largely on Fed policy decisions, forecasters need to place special emphasis and effort on analyzing and forecasting inflation—a topic to be further discussed in Chapter 11 on interest rate forecasting.

Does Experience Make Much of a Difference in Forecasting?

My personal answer is yes. When I initially served PaineWebber as a money market economist in the early 1980s, my ineptitude in forecasting the direction of bond yields prompted colleagues to teasingly call me "wrong-way Maury." But a decade later, as earlier discussed, I was cited as having one of the most accurate interest rate forecast records on Wall Street.

My affirmative answer also reflects my observations of other forecasters. Consider, in Figure 1.3, a study of prognosticators who participated in the semi-annual *Wall Street Journal* forecast surveys from the mid-1980s through the start of the 1990s.[27] (The methodology for computing the depicted average score is discussed in Chapter 2.) On average, those forecasters who had participated in 20 or more semi-annual surveys out-performed forecasters with less experience.

On this and on almost all economics and forecasting matters, there is inevitably a divergence of professional opinion. For instance, Lamont concludes that as forecasters age, their projections deviate more from the consensus and become less accurate. Mitchell and Pearce, by contrast, find that more experienced forecasters deviate less from the consensus.[28,29] *There should be no doubt that there is much to learn from forecasters' experience, whether or not it improves their accuracy.*

Key Takeaways

1. The track record of consensus forecasts masks considerable variation among forecasters.
2. Consistent outperformance of consensus economic forecasts is rare.
3. Inflation has been easier to forecast than growth.
4. Interest rates are especially difficult to forecast.
5. The inability to know exactly where the economy stands at the time a forecast is made is the main barrier to accurate economic forecasting.
6. Forecasters with above-average accuracy in predicting extreme events exhibit below-average accuracy in predicting all outcomes, and they forecast extreme events more often than the typical prognosticator.
7. Some forecasters are motivated to go out on a limb if, in their minds, the rewards for being relatively right or highly visible are worth the reputational risk of a track record filled with long shots that don't pan out.
8. Unconventional forecasts are more likely to be made by independent forecasters who have their own firms bearing own names.
9. More experienced forecasters usually fare better.

Notes

1. Tom Herman, "How to Profit from Economists' Forecasts," *Wall Street Journal*, January 22, 1993.

2. Tim Nudd, "Ad of the Day: Ally Bank—Nobel Prize-winning economist Thomas Sargent lends his expertise, or not, to Grey's theatrical campaign," *Adweek*, September 17, 2012.

3. Michael F. Bryan and Linsey Molloy, "Mirror, Mirror, Who's the Best Forecaster of Them All?" Federal Reserve Bank of Cleveland, *Economic Commentary*, March 15, 2007.

4. David Laster, Paul Bennett, and In Sun Geoum, "Rational Bias in Macroeconomic Forecasts," Federal Reserve Bank of New York Research Papers, July 1996.

5. Andy Bruce and Anooja Debnath, "Bad Habits Plague Economic Forecasts," *Reuters*, June 29, 2011.

6. Herman, "How to Profit from Economists' Forecasts."

7. Milton Friedman, "The Role of Monetary Policy," *American Economic Review*, March 1968.

8. Carmen Reinhart and Kenneth Rogoff, *This Time Is Different: Eight Centuries of Financial Follies* (Princeton, NJ: Princeton University Press, 2010).

9. Henry Hazlitt, "Pitfalls of Forecasting," *Newsweek*, November 22, 1948.

10. Takatoshi Ito, "Foreign Exchange Rate Expectations: Micro Survey Data," *American Economic Review* (June 1990): 434–449.

11. Boris Groysberg, Paul Healy, Greg Chapman, and Yang Gui, "Do Buy-Side Analysts Out-Perform the Sell-Side?" Division of Research at Harvard Business School, July 13, 2005.

12. Andrew Leone and Joanna Shuang Wu, "What Does It Take to Become a Superstar? Evidence from Institutional Investor Rankings of Financial Analysts," William E. Simon Graduate School of Business Administration—University of Rochester, May 23, 2007.

13. Phillip E. Tetlock, *Expert Political Judgment—How Good Is It? How Can We Know?* (Princeton, NJ: Princeton University Press, 2005).

14. Jerker Denrell and Christina Fang, "Predicting the Next Big Thing: Success as a Signal of Poor Judgment," *Management Science* 56, no. 10 (2010): 1653–1667.

15. G. Hilary and L. Menzly, "Does Past Success Lead Analysts to Become Overconfident?" *Management Science* 52, no. 4 (2006): 489–500.

16. J. Chevalier and G. Ellison, "Risk Taking by Mutual Funds in Response to Incentives," *Journal of Political Economy* 105, no. 6 (1997): 1167–1200.

17. Leone and Wu, "What Does It Take?"

18. Canice Prendergrast and Lars Stole, "Impetuous Youngsters and Jaded Old-Timers: Acquiring a Reputation for Learning," *Journal of Political Economy* 104, no. 6 (1996): 1105–1134.

19. H. Hong, J. Kubik, and A. Solomon, "Securities Analysts' Career Concerns and Herding of Earnings Forecasts," *Rand Journal of Economics* 31 (2000): 122–144.

20. Karlyn Mitchell and Douglas K. Pearce, "Professional Forecasts of Interest Rates and Exchange Rates: Evidence from the *Wall Street Journal's* Panels of Economists," North Carolina State University Working Paper 004, March 2005.

21. Owen A. Lamont, "Macroeconomic Forecasts and Microeconomic Forecasters," *Journal of Economic Behavior & Organization* 48 (2002): 265–280.

22. Laster, Bennett, and Geoum, "Rational Basis in Macroeconomic Forecasts."

23. Andy Bauer, Robert A. Eisenbeis, Daniel F. Waggoner, and Tao Zha, "Forecast Evaluation with Cross-Sectional Data: The Blue Chip Surveys," Federal Reserve Bank of Atlanta, *Economic Review* 88, no. 2 (Second Quarter, 2003): 17–32.

24. Clive W. J. Granger, "Can We Improve the Perceived Quality of Economic Forecasts?" *Journal of Applied Econometrics* 11 (1996): 455–473.

25. Peter J. Ferderer, Bibek Pandey, and George Veletsianos, "Does Winning the Blue Chip Forecasting Award Affect Herding Behavior? A Test of the Reputation Model," March 8, 2004, Macalester College Department of Economics.

26. Helge Berger, Michael Ehrmann, and Marcel Fratzscher, "Geography or Stills: What Explains Fed Watchers' Forecast Accuracy of US Monetary Policy?" European Central Bank Working Paper Series 695 (November 2006).

27. Bauer et al., "Forecast Evaluation with Cross-Sectional Data," 17–32.

28. Lamont, "Macroeconomic Forecasts and Microeconomic Forecasters," 278.

29. Mitchell and Pearce, "Professional Forecasts of Interest Rates and Exchange Rates," 20.

Chapter 2

The Art and Science of Making and Using Forecasts

Ultimately there's no alternative to judgment—you can never get the answers out of some model.

—Lawrence Summers, "What in the World Happened to Economics?" *Fortune*, March 15, 1999, p. 66

W hat are the overall philosophies, habits, and techniques that have enabled me to build a reasonably successful track record during my almost four-decade career in professional forecasting? What have I learned from both the successes and failures of the many economists and securities analysts with whom I have worked? In addressing these questions, my initial focus is on what it takes to achieve good long-run forecasting performance for a wide range of variables. Specific techniques and issues are addressed in subsequent chapters.

Statistics courses are a standard element of every business school curriculum, so most business and financial forecasters share a similar academic training in the discipline. Performance among similarly educated professionals can vary widely, however. With this in mind, I believe it is important to first address one's overall approach to, or philosophy of, forecasting and work habits before assessing the many methodological challenges encountered in making forecasts. In my experience, having an edge in forecasting can have more to do with these nontechnical issues than with a specific educational background.

Judgment Counts More Than Math

Statistics and economics texts can be intimidating if math is not one's favorite subject. But one need not be a highly educated statistician, mathematician, or economist to be successful at the type of everyday forecasting performed by most business managers, securities analysts, and investors. Of more importance are exercising good judgment and being well informed about the forecasting data with which one is working. With the proliferation of readily accessible statistical packages, not much computer savvy is required to perform more advanced calculations and simulations.

Relatively sophisticated statistical techniques can be essential for disentangling cause and effect and for isolating historical impacts of potential causal factors. But such models are often easily accessed on public websites. Instead of reinventing the wheel, most business forecasters and financial analysts should use this research as the initial building blocks for their own forecasting needs.

Large multi-equation econometric models of the U.S. economy have made important contributions to a better understanding of our nation's economic behavior.[1] However, are they really necessary for addressing most everyday forecasting challenges? For instance, one study of the forecasting prowess of large econometric models concluded that "there is no evidence that size or complexity adds or detracts from the forecasting ability of the models."[2] Moreover, becoming more proficient at forecasting does not require mastering the statistical mechanics of large models. The big models enforce needed internal consistency of the interacting elements forecasts (e.g., gross domestic product [GDP] components). But the necessary internal consistency of macroeconomic GDP forecasts, for example, also can effectively be achieved by a few simple rules of thumb that we discuss.

Perhaps the most important lesson from economists' experience with large econometric models is that nonmathematical judgment plays a critical role in making the models perform. Former Treasury Secretary and Harvard University economics professor Larry Summers has observed that "ultimately there's no alternative to judgment—you can never get the answers out of some model."[3] My experience and past studies, comparing pure model versus judgmentally adjusted model forecasts, concur.

When I joined the forecasting team at the Federal Reserve Bank of New York in 1973, I was eager to get my first shot at working with the Fed's then famous Federal Reserve Board of Governors–MIT large-scale econometric model.[4] It had many dozen equations and, at that time, was one of the main "runners" in econometricians' "horse races" to judge which of the multi-equation models performed best. In some senses, it was the most important model because the Federal Reserve System's Federal Open Market Committee (FOMC) used it in setting interest rates and conducting U.S. monetary policy. At each FOMC meeting, the model's forecasts were presented by the director of research to the Federal Reserve Board of Governors, and they played a key role in policymakers' discussions of the economic outlook.

My first peek at what this gigantic model could churn out came when I and other New York Fed forecasting team members received internal documents presenting a multitude of forecasted economic statistics—GDP, industrial production, retail sales, the unemployment rate, wages, and prices. What immediately caught my eye was that for each economic variable, there were both the internal Fed Board staff forecast and an accompanying "add factor." This add factor represented the difference between the internal forecast and the "pure model" for each variable. The latter is what the model forecasted when estimated historical interrelationships between variables were applied to assumptions about exogenous variables (i.e., key forecast drivers, such as monetary and fiscal policies, that are not directly determined in the model). In other words, the Board staff's internal forecasts did not simply pick up the historical statistical relationships between key economic variables. Instead, those relationships were adjusted by the add factor to generate more plausible results, ones that reflected the model users' judgment about what was missing in the statistical model of the variable. For example, if a forecasting equation of the key consumer-spending variable appeared out of whack versus forecasters' a priori expectations, they simply added or subtracted from the forecast to obtain a more plausible forecast. In fact, almost all published forecasts labeled as being generated by a large-scale econometric model are a combination of what the model says when simulated *plus* the forecaster's judgments about what the model could not statistically represent.

Past research indicates that judgmentally adjusted forecasts often are more accurate than pure statistical model forecasts. The latter are unaltered by forecasters' subjective judgments about what is not formally quantified and estimated in a model. (Note: In comparing judgmentally adjusted forecasts to such pure model forecasts, statisticians have often used as state of the art pure econometric models those estimated and publicized by Yale University economics Professor Ray Fair.[5])

Research by Stephen K. McNees—a former economist at the Federal Reserve Bank of Boston—has been a commonly cited source for assessing the way judgmentally adjusted forecasts perform versus pure-model forecasts.[6] He compared the judgmentally adjusted forecasts of four prominent forecasters to what their models would have forecast without such adjustment. McNees reported that 62 percent of judgmentally adjusted forecasts of 21 different macroeconomic variables were more accurate than forecasts generated by pure models alone. The percentages of the time that judgmental forecasts outperformed pure model forecasts varied considerably for different forecast variables. (See Table 2.1.) What is especially important to note is that for some commonly forecast macroeconomic variables, judgmentally adjusted forecasts were frequently more accurate than pure model forecasts.

For economic forecasters, McNees' research is particularly useful for identifying those economic variables that are best forecast through a combination of subjective judgment and statistical models, rather than by relying on statistical models alone. Key financial variables—such

Table 2.1   Impact of Judgment on Forecasting Accuracy

	Forecast Horizon		
	One–Quarter Ahead Judgment Improved (%)	Four–Quarters Ahead Judgment Improved (%)	Eight–Quarters Ahead Judgment Improved (%)
Short-term interest rates	90*	77	60
Long-term interest rates	78*	78	76
Federal deficit	76*	71	56
Consumer prices	76*	72	61
Corporate profits	74*	56	75
Nominal GNP	66*	47	65
Labor compensation	65*	52	58
Consumption	64*	50	60
Residential investment	63	72	60
State and local purchases	61	66	53
Unemployment rate	60	48	50
Business fixed investment	59	51	50
GNP implicit price deflator	59	72	85
Nominal net exports	57	57	50
Narrow money stock	56	58	50
Real GNP	55	50	50
Import price deflator	54	52	56
Productivity	53	59	57
Change in business inventories	46	40	48
Imports	36*	28	44
Total	62*	57	58

*Significantly different from 50 at 90 percent confidence level for one-quarter-ahead forecast. Because the four- and eight-quarter-ahead forecasts are not independent, no statistical test was applied.
SOURCE: Stephen K. McNees, "Man vs. Model? The Role of Judgment in Forecasting," *New England Economic Review* (July/August 1990).

as interest rates, corporate profits, the Federal deficit, and consumer prices—were high on the list of variables best forecast by using more than a statistical model. And when nominal GDP, labor compensation, and consumer spending forecasts were judgmentally adjusted, their accuracy, too, improved significantly.

McNees' results are corroborated by other statisticians' research. For instance, Bunn and Wright, in reviewing the literature on the comparative accuracy of judgmental and pure statistical model forecasts, concluded that, "studies in real world settings do show the validity of judgment." They argue that, "Where expert, informed judgmental forecasts are being used, critical analysis of the evidence suggests that their quality is higher than many researchers have concluded."[7]

How much does judgmentally adjusting forecasts matter?

While judgmentally adjusted forecasts in McNees' studies were more likely to outperform pure statistical model forecasts, by *how much* did they do so? And when judgmentally adjusted forecasts were wrong, did they seriously underperform forecasts conducted with only pure statistical models?

One way to address this question is to compare the overall performance of the two competing forecasting methodologies. McNees did this by comparing the root mean squared errors of the two procedures. (As discussed later in this chapter, the root mean squared error comparison penalizes large errors much more than comparatively small errors.) Using this criteria, the judgmental forecasts were superior on 76 percent of forecast occasions for one-quarter-ahead forecasts, 68 percent of the time for four-quarter-ahead forecasts and 64 percent of time for eight-quarter ahead forecasts.

What's the "rap" against judgmental forecasting?

Studies by social psychologists are replete with examples of individual biases in exercising judgment. It's a concern in economic policy-making just as it is elsewhere. Observations about the failures of group decision making at the Federal Reserve, for example, have prompted questions about the potential effects of hidden biases in the construction of judgmentally adjusted models. To lessen this possibility, we've seen numerous recommendations that monetary policy be based solely on statistical rules that reflect the historical interrelationships between policy variables and the economy. (Note: I disagree with suggestions for a strictly rule-based monetary policy.) In addition to the dangers of hidden biases, another common objection to judgmental forecasting is that it can be too ad hoc, and without convincing rationale for potential forecast users.

However, a good case can be made for blending statistical models incorporating measureable causal variables with judgmental forecasting adjustments for hard-to-quantify causal variables. *A key goal of this book is offer guidance on how and when to blend statistical and judgmental forecasts.*

When should we supplement statistical models with judgment?

The first step in utilizing a forecast model is to select the model with the best historical statistical fit when using causal variables that either need not be predicted or are relatively easy to predict. Naturally, if a model has worked exceptionally well in the past there usually is little reason to judgmentally adjust such forecasts. However, if the model has not always performed well in the past, the application of qualitative judgment may be warranted.

A first step in applying judgment to a statistical forecast is to examine a model's in-sample errors. Attempt to determine what was happening when the model went off track. Often this entails reviewing the history of the period when the model erred. Possible periodic causal factors not picked up by a model's statistical drivers include domestic public policy and political uncertainty surrounding elections, or some international development such as war or a jump in oil prices.

The home price collapse precipitating the sharp 2008 to 2009 recession was a prime example of an instance when forecasters should have been blending judgment with results from statistical models. Real (inflation-adjusted) home price changes in the middle of the past decade were rising much more than suggested by a historical model estimated through 2005. That model correlates real home price changes with a real (inflation-adjusted) rent variable. (See the regression model in Table 2.2 and Figure 2.1.) The model's unusually large and persistent underestimation errors in 2005 should have been a sign to forecasters that the more traditional models were omitting an important independent variable. In this case, standard home price models did not account for the period's very easy subprime lending standards. To be sure, at the time it would have been difficult to measure how much difference in prices was due to these relaxed standards. Nevertheless, the statistical model errors should have signaled to forecasters that it was time to supplement their statistical models with judgment.

Table 2.2   Sample Regression Model of Real Home Resale Price Index Change

(Q1 1988–Q4 2005)

	Real Rent of Primary Residence (Four-Quarter Average)	Constant
Response coefficient	3.3	1.5
T–stat	11.0	3.5
R–squared = .63		

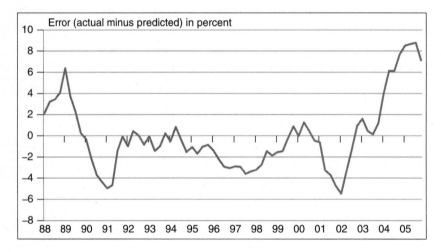

Figure 2.1   Errors from a Standard Home Price Inflation Model
SOURCE: Standard & Poor's, author's calculations.

Habits of Successful Forecasters:
How to Cultivate Them

Far too often I have seen forecasters, especially early in their careers, start from scratch on a new assignment. Doing so can waste valuable time, prevent the forecaster from doing the best possible job, and put deadlines at risk. A more fruitful approach, I believe, is to first review what already has been published about the variable to be forecast. For instance, if one is assigned to forecast demand for a particular component of an automotive engine, a good place to start would be the abundant research on automobile demand.

There are excellent reasons why scholarly research in almost any field begins with a review of the existing literature. It is efficient and allows academic researchers to focus on allocating their time—a valuable, scare resource—where it can best advance knowledge. In the practical world of forecasting, the goal is timely implementation, not originality. A review of academic literature is critical for saving time and being stimulated in thinking about how to approach a forecasting assignment.

Initial Guidance for Preparing Specific Forecasts. One possible starting point for studying more advanced economic research about forecasting a particular economic variable is the *Journal of Economic Literature*—a comprehensive guide to what has been published in economic journals. Articles in scholarly journals, however, may not always be easy to read and understand for persons without more advanced statistical and mathematical backgrounds. But being a successful forecaster does not require advanced math and stat academic pedigrees. The following easily accessible websites offer directories to more academic research and also to generally well-written and easier to understand studies.

Selected U.S. Business Research Sources

Journal of Economic Literature: www.aeaweb.org/jel

National Association of Business Economists *Business Economics*: www.palgrave-journals.com/be/index.html

Bureau of Labor Statistics: www.bls.gov/opub/mlr/subject/a.htm

International Journal of Forecasting: www.forecasters.org/ijf/index.php

Fed-In Print: www.fedinprint.org

Survey of Current Business: www.bea.gov/scb/index.htm

Congressional Budget Office: www.cbo.gov/topics

Federal Reserve Board of Governors: www.federalreserve.gov/econresdata/workingpapers.htm

International Economic Research Sources

International Monetary Fund: www.imf.org/external/research/index.aspx

World Bank: http://worldbank.org/wbsite/external/extdec/0,,menupk:
   47682
Organisation of Economic Co-operation and Development: www
   .oecd.org/newsroom/publicationsandstatistics
European Central Bank: www.ecb.europa.eu/pub/scientific/resbul/
   html/index.en.html
Bank for International Settlements: www.bis.org

How Much Emphasis Should Forecast Users Give to the Gross Domestic Product (GDP)? Forecasters of industry trends and product demands inevitably rely, at least in part, on national economic conditions projections. The question then becomes how much weight to place on such trends. One initial step is to consider statistical correlations between historical industry or product trends and GDP. Table 2.3 provides an example of correlations between the annual growth of nominal (current dollar) GDP and industry shipments. Also displayed are regression coefficients illustrating the percentage change in shipments for each 1.0 percentage point change in GDP.

Correlations with GDP growth usually are higher in durables manufacturing than in nondurables manufacturing. For instance, forecasters of housing-related variables are particularly sensitive to GDP projections as correlations with GDP are relatively high in wood products and furniture and related products.

It is necessary to distinguish between the strength of a relationship, as suggested by a correlation coefficient, and the estimated relationship, as indicated by an estimated regression coefficient. In the example in Table 2.3, a 1.0 percentage point change in nominal GDP is associated with a 2.79 percentage point change in durable goods shipments and a 1.90 percentage point change in nondurable goods shipments.

"Unforced Errors" in Handling Details. Forecasts based on well-reasoned behavioral assumptions still can go awry by failing to adequately consider how historical government or private data on dependent and independent variables are assembled. In the field of economics, one needs to go no further than government statistical agencies' websites to learn about underlying sampling and measurement conventions. These are discussed in Chapter 5.

Table 2.3 Estimated Relationships between Manufacturing Shipments and Nominal GDP Growth (1993–2012)

	Correlation	Regression Coefficient
All Manufacturing Industries	0.73	2.35
Durable goods	0.78	2.79
Wood products	0.79	3.74
Nonmetallic mineral products	0.93	3.37
Primary metals	0.52	3.94
Fabricated metal products	0.77	2.74
Machinery	0.67	2.52
Computers and electronic products	0.72	3.05
Electrical equipment, appliances, and components	0.76	2.67
Transportation equipment	0.59	2.44
Furniture and related products	0.88	3.08
Miscellaneous durable goods	0.64	1.04
Nondurable goods	0.59	1.90
Food products	0.07	0.12
Beverage and tobacco products	0.28	0.65
Textile mills	0.48	1.63
Textile products	0.77	2.67
Apparel	0.67	3.04
Leather and allied products	0.40	1.99
Paper products	0.39	1.22
Printing	0.85	2.03
Petroleum and coal products	0.49	4.84
Basic chemicals	0.65	2.02
Plastics and rubber products	0.77	2.21

SOURCE: Bureau of Economic Analysis, Census Bureau, and author's calculations.

An example of paying attention to detail is forecasting the critical monthly nonfarm payroll statistic. When assessing whether a particular event (e.g., strike or weather) will affect the next payroll number, it is important to consider when during the month the survey is being conducted. The payroll survey is conducted for the two-week pay period including the twelfth day of the month. In addition, forecasters need to consider that employees on a payroll are counted as employed if they are on a payroll at any time during the surveyed pay period. Failure to either know or remember this type of detail is often a reason why the expected effects of the weather on the monthly labor statistics are sometimes much overstated.

Make certain that correct data are being used in analyzing and forecasting. This requirement should be obvious, because the right data is critical for accurate forecasts and a forecasters' credibility. Some of the most embarrassing analytical errors in the field of economics have come from not checking the accuracy of forecasting inputs. And seasoned researchers sometimes delegate data entry to often bright but still inexperienced student research assistants.

For academic economists, one of the most embarrassing kerfuffles of recent years has been the controversy surrounding *This Time Is Different: Eight Centuries of Financial Follies*, a book by Carmen Reinhart and Kenneth Rogoff.[8] It was an instant hit when published in 2011. Economic policymakers and politicians in all corners of the world used it to justify stringent fiscal policy, despite still-high unemployment, because the authors had supposedly demonstrated that, historically, economic growth in advanced economies turned negative when the ratio of government debt to GDP topped 90 percent. Specifically, they cited a −0.1 percent *negative* average growth after that level was exceeded. However, their data, when reviewed and recalculated two years later by economists at the University of Massachusetts, Amherst showed *positive* average growth of +2.2 percent whenever the 90 percent dividing line was breached from below.[9] Apparently, the statistical assistant working with Reinhart and Rogoff had inadvertently omitted some individual country data and coded other data incorrectly.

Unlike Professional Science Journals, Economics Journals Too Often Fail to Check the Statistical Accuracy of Published Research. For example, in reviewing this particular issue, McCullough, McGeary, and Harrison in 2006 stated these sobering conclusions: "Results published in economic journals are accepted at face value and rarely subjected to the independent verification that is the cornerstone of the scientific method. Most results published in economic journals cannot be subjected to verification, even in principle, because authors typically are not required to make their data and code available for verification."[10] In a 2006 survey of 141 economic journals, Vlaeminck reports that only around a fifth of them had articulated data-availability policies for authors.[11]

Kicking the Tires When Choosing Published Statistical Models as Forecast Tools. Published statistical forecasting models are generally abundant. With widely available statistical software, many business managers and analysts have either the individual capability or the staff to reproduce, update, improve, and simulate these models. (For those without such capabilities, published regression sensitivity coefficients can be multiplied by actual or predicted independent—"driver"—variables to obtain a model-based forecast.) However, it can be challenging to judge and select among abundant candidate models. The following criteria, although hardly exhaustive, address some of the most common issues in selecting published models as guides to specific forecasting tasks. Before selecting a model, ask these three questions:

1. Does a model employ contemporaneous or lagged explanatory (independent) variables?

   A model with seemingly impressive high historical statistical accuracy (e.g., R-squared) may not be very useful for forecasting purposes if it uses hard-to-forecast explanatory variables that are contemporaneous with the dependent variable to be forecast. This is often the case with large multi-equation econometric models and models aimed at explaining, rather than forecasting, a variable's behavior. Such models are critical in enabling a forecaster to understand the range of elements that must be considered in producing a forecast. It can be hard to achieve much accuracy, however, if the forecast is contingent on predicting all of the relevant explanatory variables.

   Consequently, when selecting among alternative forecasting models, it can be more practical to use models where the relevant explanatory variable already has occurred. In other words, forecasters should employ models relying on lagged independent, explanatory variables that do not need to be forecast. For instance, this year's reported data on household incomes may do a better job of forecasting next year's product demand than a model relating demand to incomes in the same year. This is especially true if incomes are hard to forecast.

   Using lagged independent variables is especially appropriate if the behavior to be forecast responds with sensible lags to its various drivers. This can be the case, for example, when a firm's overall capital spending budget is not being continually revised during the year, and is a function of the previous year's profits.

Choosing between models with either contemporary or lagged independent explanatory variables can be especially challenging if the following occurs: What if a model using hard-to-forecast con-temporaneous explanatory variables has a much higher R-squared than a model using lagged independent variables? In this case, one option is to consider the typical statistical variance for explanatory variables. Here are the two steps involved:

Step 1: Multiply a model's estimated response coefficients by the upper and lower bounds of an independent variable's likely range (e.g., one-standard deviation on both sides of the typical level or change in the independent variable). The product of these calculations can provide a probable range of forecast outcomes.

Step 2: Compare the range calculated in Step 1 to the range asso-ciated with the model that uses just a lagged independent variable. The latter range might be one standard error on either side of the forecast generated by the model using a lagged independent variable.

Statisticians can offer a variety of ways to perform such a test. Following is a simple example:

Selecting Model A or Model B for Forecasting

Model A (with concurrent independent vairable)

$Y = 2X$, where 2 is the response coefficient

R-squared $= 90\%$

Standard in-sample error $= 0.3Y$

Standard deviation of $X = 0.4Y$

Possible forecast error $= 0.3Y + 2(0.4Y) = 0.38Y$

Model B (with lagged independent variable)

$Y = 1.5X(-1)$, where 1.5 is the response coefficient

R-squared $= 80\%$

Standard in-sample error $= 0.32Y$

Possible forecast error $= 0.32Y$

Table 2.4 There Can Be Substantial Differences between Initially Reported Quarterly Real GDP Growth and the Final Official Revised Estimate

Period	Mean Absolute Difference (%)
Since Q4–1978	1.59
1970–1979	2.33
1980–1989	1.50
1990–1999	1.37
2000–2009	1.28
2010–2013	1.25

SOURCE: Federal Reserve Bank of Philadelphia, author's calculations.

2. Are frequently revised government data driving the forecast?

A government statistic that has historically worked well in explaining and predicting a dependent variable may nonetheless be a poor predictor if it is subject to considerable revision long after being reported. (See in Table 2.4 orders of magnitude for the absolute differences between initially reported real GDP growth and the eventual, final official revision.) For instance, if demand for a product depends on the U.S. real (inflation-adjusted) Gross Domestic Product (GDP), a major forecasting reliability problem might be that the GDP itself is revised frequently—and sometimes considerably well after being initially reported. In Chapter 5 we discuss how to analyze and forecast when having to deal with frequently revised government data.

The point here is that forecasters should check readily available government data on the statistical characteristics of revisions of a government statistic that they are examining as a potential forecast driver. The possible range of such potential revisions should be then multiplied by estimated response coefficients to determine the forecast's sensitivity to revisions of the statistic used as an independent variable. Among the more materially revised major government statistics are the GDP and nonfarm payroll data. On the other hand, major revisions are not a problem for government data such as the unemployment rate, weekly initial claims for state unemployment insurance, and the monthly purchasing agents' data.

3. What is a model's success over different time horizons?

Forecasting models usually become less accurate as projections move further into the future. (See Table 2.5.) In comparing models, therefore, note that some perform better than others over

Table 2.5   Forecast Errors Over Varying Forecast Horizons

	Mean Absolute Error %	Average Error (Actual−Predicted) %
One-Quarter-Ahead Consensus Forecasts		
Since Q4–1968	1.85	−0.23
1970–1979	2.56	−0.76
1980–1989	2.26	−0.04
1990–1999	1.34	0.43
2000–2009	1.61	−0.37
2010–2014	0.92	−0.44
Two-Quarter-Ahead Consensus Forecasts		
Since Q4–1968	2.03	−0.45
1970–1979	2.99	−1.05
1980–1989	2.33	−0.35
1990–1999	1.61	0.50
2000–2009	1.75	−0.79
2010–2014	0.86	−0.44
Three-Quarter-Ahead Consensus Forecasts		
Since Q4–1968	2.15	−0.73
1970–1979	3.29	−1.60
1980–1989	2.20	−0.59
1990–1999	1.64	0.38
2000–2009	1.86	−0.93
2010–2014	1.02	−0.64
Four-Quarter-Ahead Consensus Forecasts		
Since Q4–1968	2.15	−0.79
1970–1979	3.36	−1.74
1980–1989	2.26	−0.71
1990–1999	1.56	0.53
2000–2009	1.80	−1.06
2010–2014	1.02	−0.75

SOURCE: Federal Reserve Bank of Philadelphia, author's calculations.

different time horizons. Therefore, in making and using forecasts, it is important to consider the relevant horizon and to consider changing models in order to select the one most accurate for the time frame in question.

Judging and Scoring Forecasts by Statistics

Forecasters need benchmarks to evaluate the feedback required for critical learning from mistakes. Because forecasters as well as their audiences are consumers of forecasts, both must judge performance. Statisticians typically list the following 10 characteristics of successful forecasts:

1. *Unbiased forecasts*: The average of overforecasts, underforecasts, and absolutely correct forecasts should be zero. This indicates the absence of a directional forecast bias. (Note: The term *bias* also is used to critique forecasters who may be motivated to over- or underforecast. As earlier discussed, such motivations may be job related or political.)

2. *Efficient forecasts*: All useful available information that improves a forecast should be utilized. This is more easily said than done, because forecasters vary in their ability to discover relevant explanatory variables, locate needed information, and perform similar tasks. My experience is that forecasters are not necessarily trained to do the basic research that is essential to successful forecasting. Improving these skills is a recurring topic in this book.

3. *Uncorrelated errors*: Underforecast errors or overforecast in-sample errors should not be grouped together consecutively. This often is a sign of incompletely specified models that repeat the same mistake for a number of successive periods. Identifying the cause of these historical errors (a.k.a. residuals) is critical, with statisticians sometimes urging forecasters to "squeeze the residuals until they talk."

At the same time, a range of *forecast metrics* (i.e., accuracy measures) illustrates how the value of a forecast depends on the various objectives of its producers and consumers.

4. *Mean error:* This is the average forecast error. As discussed earlier, it is a measure of statistical bias, with a zero mean error signifying that a statistical model's forecast errors were directionally unbiased. However, just because forecast errors over time were self-canceling does not indicate a forecasting procedure's usefulness, since individual errors might be quite inaccurate.

5. *Mean absolute error:* This is the average absolute error without regard to its directional sign. In other words, how close did the forecast come to being accurate in each forecast period? Unlike the mean error metric, the mean absolute error metric does not reflect the balance of self-canceling errors. It probably is the most common forecasting metric. Nevertheless, when selecting forecasting models and judging forecaster performance, the mean absolute error does not necessarily represent the most useful forecast.

6. *Root mean squared error:* Squaring gives disproportionately more weight to larger than smaller absolute errors. It is a useful gauge when, for example, a three-percentage-point error is more than three times as costly as a one-percentage-point error.

7. *Standard deviation:* The variation in forecast errors is captured by this statistic. Although a forecaster may have a relatively low average mean absolute error, a wide variation in individual errors signals less reliable forecasts.

8. *Rank:* In comparing forecasters, ranks based on forecasting results are often used. However, rarely reported standard deviations of ranks are important gauges of consistency as well.

9. *Forecast difficulty:* The more volatile the variable, the more difficult, comparatively, to forecast. Thus, when judging a forecaster's overall prowess, more weight should be given to his or her success with harder-to-forecast variables than with the "layups."

10. *Internal consistency:* In evaluating a forecaster's projections of the components used to create a "big picture" (e.g., the U.S. economy), it is helpful to determine if the projections are statistically consistent. This is a way to judge if the forecasts reflect credible reasoning and history, or simply random luck. For instance, there should be a positive correlation of forecast errors for components that have been positively correlated historically. If that is not the case, the

implication is that the forecaster's results reflect random luck versus any logical or historically valid internal system. In economics, a forecaster overestimating inflation while underestimating interest rates should receive a lower score than a forecaster who either overestimated or underestimated both.

Examples of the mean error, mean absolute error, and root mean squared error metrics are illustrated in Table 2.6. This exhibit compares U.S. two-year forecasts made by the Administration (White House Office of Management and Budget), the Congressional Budget Office (CBO), and the Blue Chip consensus survey of professional forecasters.

Table 2.6 Summary Measures of Performance for Two-Year Forecasts (percentage points)

	CBO	Administration	Blue Chip Consensus[1]
Growth in Real Output (1982–2010)			
Mean error	−0.1	0.1	−0.1
Mean absolute error	1.1	1.2	1.1
Root mean square error	1.4	1.6	1.4
Inflation in the Consumer Price Index (1982–2010)			
Mean error	0.2	0.1	0.2
Mean absolute error	0.7	0.7	0.7
Root mean square error	0.8	0.9	0.9
Interest Rate on Three-Month Treasury Bills (1982–2010)			
Mean error	0.6	0.3	0.6
Mean absolute error	1.0	1.1	1.0
Root mean square error	1.4	1.4	1.3
Interest Rate on 10-Year Treasury Notes (1982–2010)			
Mean error	0.4	0.1	0.4
Mean absolute error	0.6	0.8	0.7
Root mean square error	0.7	0.9	0.7

[1] The Blue Chip consensus is the average of approximately 50 private-sector forecasts.
SOURCE: Congressional Budget Office; Office of Management and Budget; and Aspen Publishers, *Blue Chip Economic Indicators*.

The forecast variables are (1) real output (i.e., real GDP growth), (2) consumer price index (CPI) inflation, (3) the three-month Treasury bill rate, and (4) the yield on the 10-year Treasury note in the 1982 to 2010 period.

The mean error (forecast less predicted values) data are mostly positive, indicating forecasts that were too high (upward biased). However, the errors are relatively small (0.1 to 0.2 percentage points) for real output growth and for CPI inflation. For interest rates, though, the overestimates are somewhat higher for CBO and Blue Chip consensus for the three-month Treasury bill rate (0.6 percentage points or 60 basis points) and the 10-year Treasury note yield (0.4 percentage points or 40 basis points). As earlier discussed, interest rates are generally harder to forecast than business-conditions variables, such as real GDP growth.

Mean *absolute* errors, though, indicate that forecasts were less accurate than mean *average* errors—which average overestimates and underestimates—would suggest. For real GDP growth and the three-month Treasury bill rate, mean absolute errors were over a full percentage point.

The highest root mean square errors were for GDP growth. Using this measure, which attaches more weight to relatively large forecast errors, the Administration forecasts were somewhat inferior to projections by the Blue Chip consensus and the CBO.

Tables 2.7 and 2.8 offer a ranking of forecasters by a composite measurement that includes standard deviation, rank, forecast difficulty, and internal consistency metrics. In this particular exercise, the latter two metrics are combined into an average score. (For details, see Eisenbeis et al.) What is being compared is the performance of economists participating in semi-annual forecasts of Gross Domestic Product (GDP) growth, consumer price index (CPI) inflation, two interest rates (Treasury bill and government bonds) and an exchange rate (initially yen/dollar followed by euro/dollar).

In assessing forecasters' performance, note that relatively high average accuracy scores over a number of surveys do not guarantee high ranks in individual surveys. The Blue Chip consensus forecast with the highest average score in Table 2.7 still ranked between 12th and 14th, on average in Table 2.8.

Table 2.7   Average Forecaster Scores (1986–2001)

	Average Score	Current-Year Forecast Average Score	Next-Year Forecast Average Score
Blue Chip Consensus	69.3*** (21.8)	74.7*** (23.2)	63.5** (18.7)
Mortgage Banker Assn. of America	67.1*** (25.9)	73.2*** (26.4)	60.7* (23.8)
Macroeconomic Advisors	66.6** (25.9)	74.2*** (25.4)	58.4 (24.0)
U.S. Trust Company	63.6** (26.0)	68.3*** (25.7)	56.1 (24.8)
Northern Trust Company	62.7** (26.6)	66.0** (26.9)	58.9 (25.7)
Wayne Hummer Investments, LLC	60.6* (25.7)	62.5** (27.5)	58.6 (23.6)
Merrill Lynch	60.1* (26.3)	64.2** (27.2)	55.5 (24.5)
Dean Witter Reynolds & Company	60.0 (30.0)	63.0 (30.7)	56.1 (29.1)
Georgia State University	58.2 (26.3)	59.2 (28.1)	57.2 (24.3)
National City Corporation	56.8 (24.0)	59.4* (25.6)	54.0 (21.9)
Evans Group	56.5 (28.6)	63.4** (28.7)	49.1 (26.7)
Eggert Economic Enterprises, Inc.	56.5 (24.3)	55.6 (27.1)	57.5 (21.1)
DaimlerChrysler AG	56.3 (28.1)	62.8** (28.1)	49.4 (26.3)
DuPont	55.7 (26.0)	59.3* (28.8)	51.9 (22.0)
Bank One	55.3 (30.7)	61.1* (31.1)	48.9 (29.0)
Siff, Oakley, Marks, Inc.	54.8 (27.5)	60.9* (26.4)	48.2 (27.2)
Prudential Financial	54.0 (25.7)	55.7 (28.1)	52.1 (22.7)
U.S. Chamber of Commerce	51.9 (26.7)	54.8 (27.5)	48.7 (25.6)
UCLA Business Forecast	49.9 (28.8)	50.9 (31.5)	48.8 (25.8)
Econoclast	47.5 (27.0)	45.6 (31.0)	49.5 (21.9)
Conference Board	46.4 (29.7)	53.8 (32.1)	38.4* (24.5)
Inforum-University of Maryland	36.6** (26.6)	33.6** (27.1)	39.8* (25.8)

Numbers in parentheses are standard deviations. *, **, and *** represent significance at the 90%, 95%, and 99% confidence levels, respectively, of difference in forecaster's score from 50.0 average score.
SOURCE: Andy Bauer, Robert A. Eisenbeis, Daniel F. Waggoner, and Tao Zha, "Forecast Evaluation with Cross-Sectional Data: The Blue Chip Surveys," Federal Reserve Bank of Atlanta, Second Quarter, 2003.

Table 2.8   Forecaster Ranks (1986–2001)

	Average Rank	Current-Year Forecast Average Rank	Next-Year Forecast Average Rank
Blue Chip Consensus	13.2*** (4.8)	12.4*** (5.1)	13.9*** (4.3)
Mortgage Banker Assn. of America	15.5*** (10.4)	14.3*** (9.9)	16.7** (10.7)
Macroeconomic Advisors	15.5*** (10.8)	13.7*** (9.9)	17.3** (11.5)
Northern Trust Company	17.9** (12.0)	18.3** (11.6)	17.5** (12.4)
U.S. Trust Company	18.5** (12.7)	17.6** (12.0)	20.0* (13.6)
Wayne Hummer Investments, LLC	20.2* (11.3)	21.9 (12.3)	18.3** (9.9)
Merrill Lynch	21.0 (12.4)	21.1 (12.3)	20.9 (12.4)
Georgia State University	21.4 (12.7)	23.1 (13.0)	19.6* (12.2)
DaimlerChrysler AG	21.9 (12.7)	20.5 (12.3)	23.3 (13.0)
National City Corporation	22.4 (11.8)	23.3 (12.3)	21.4 (11.1)
Eggert Economic Enterprises, Inc.	22.4 (12.1)	25.6 (12.0)	19.1* (11.4)
Evans Group	22.4 (13.6)	20.7 (13.2)	24.3 (13.7)
DuPont	22.8 (11.8)	23.4 (12.1)	22.2 (11.5)
Bank One	23.2 (14.9)	21.4 (14.3)	25.1 (15.4)
Siff, Oakley, Marks, Inc.	23.5 (12.8)	23.3 (12.0)	23.7 (13.6)
Prudential Insurance	23.8 (12.7)	26.0 (12.5)	21.3 (12.5)
U.S. Chamber of Commerce	25.3 (11.7)	26.5 (11.1)	23.9 (12.3)
UCLA Business Forecast	26.2 (13.7)	28.0 (13.7)	24.4 (13.5)
Econoclast	27.7 (12.7)	30.5* (12.7)	24.7 (12.0)
Conference Board	29.2 (13.3)	27.2 (13.8)	31.3** (12.5)
Inforum–University of Maryland	31.1** (13.5)	33.9*** (11.9)	28.0 (14.5)

NOTE: Numbers in parentheses are standard deviations. *, **, and *** represent statistical significance versus average forecaster rank at the 90%, 95%, and 99% confidence levels, respectively.
SOURCE: Andy Bauer, Robert A. Eisenbeis, Daniel F. Waggoner, and Tao Zha, "Forecast Evaluation with Cross-Sectional Data: The Blue Chip Surveys," Federal Reserve Bank of Atlanta, Second Quarter, 2003.

Key Takeaways

1. Review earlier research and forecasting models.
2. Understand how the data to be utilized has been prepared.
3. Check accuracy of data entry carefully.

4. Be wary of forecasts requiring frequently revised government data.
5. Determine the ease or difficulty of projecting forecast drivers.
6. Avoid automatically selecting models with best relative in-sample R-squares.
7. Select models with the best success at specifically required forecast horizons.
8. Test model accuracy outside of the sample period.
9. Examine historical model errors to determine if and when nonstatistical judgmental inputs might be useful.
10. Remember that judgmental inputs are often helpful for interest rate forecasts.

Notes

1. For background on the development of model-based forecasting, the interested reader can consult J. Scott Anderson's book titled *Long-Range Forecasting from Crystal Ball to Computer* (New York: John Wiley & Sons, 1985).
2. Ricardo Mestre and Peter McAdam, "Is Forecasting With Large Models Informative? Assessing The Role of Judgment in Macroeconomic Forecasts," European Central Bank Working Paper Series No. 950, October 2008.
3. Lawrence Summers, "What in World Happened to Economics?" *Fortune*, March 15, 1999, 66.
4. Flynt Brayton, Andrew Levin, Ralph Tyron, and John C. Williams, "The Evolution of Macro Models at the Federal Reserve Board," Carnegie-Rochester Conference Series on Public Policy, December 1997, 43–81.
5. Ray C. Fair, *Specification, Estimation, and Analysis of Macroeconomic Models* (Cambridge, MA: Harvard University Press, 1984).
6. Stephen K. McNees, "The Role of Judgment in Macroeconomic Forecasting Accuracy," *International Journal of Forecasting* 6, no. 3 (October 1990): 287–299.
7. Derek Brunn and George Wright, "Interaction of Judgmental and Statistical Forecasting Methods: Issues & Analysis," *Management Science* 37, no. 5 (May 1991).
8. Carmen Reinhart and Kenneth Rogoff, *This Time Is Different: Eight Centuries of Financial Follies* (Princeton, NJ: Princeton University Press, 2010).

9. Michael Ash, Thomas Herndon, and Robert Pollin, "Does High Public Debt Consistently Stifle Economic Growth? A Critique of Reinhart and Rogoff," Political Economy Research Institute, University of Massachusetts, April 15, 2013.

10. Teresa Harrison, Kerry Anne McGeary, and B. D. McCullough, "Lessons from the JMBC Archive," *Journal of Money, Credit and Banking* (June 2006): 1091–1107.

11. Sven Vlaeminck, "Research Data Management in Economic Journals," Open Economics blog, December 7, 2012.

Chapter 3

What Can We Learn from History?

I have but one lamp by which my feet are guided, and that is the lamp of experience. I know of no way of judging the future but by the past.
> —Patrick Henry, Speech in Virginia Convention, St. John's Episcopal Church, Richmond Virginia, March 23, 1775

I don't believe you can be a successful forecaster unless you have a sound grasp of history. I'm not speaking of the statistical history used to generate models; I'm referring to the kind of history that allows you to evaluate current events in the context of an ongoing continuum. What does the past have to do with the future? Plenty.

In this chapter we review some lessons that the history of U.S. business cycles over the past 160 years of modern business cycle accounting hold for forecasters. I also provide commentary on the necessary, nonquantitative history required to process quantitative historical data most effectively.

Let's begin by acknowledging that the past is loaded with relevant lessons for contemporary forecasters. Only a student of the Great Depression of the 1930s, for example, could have begun to understand, beforehand, how financial fragility could trigger an economic contraction as severe as the 2008 to 2009 Great Recession—the worst recession since the 1930s. To predict the following unusually slow business recovery successfully, a forecaster needed to understand what the 1930s experience taught about the practical limits of the Federal government's ability to stimulate recovery. Looking forward, will the Federal Reserve's attempts to accelerate recovery with an unprecedented expansion of its balance sheet eventually lead to greater price inflation? Forecasters cannot go very far with any answer until they understand the roots of the Great Inflation period of the 1970s.

In professional forecasters' unending attempts to obtain better statistical fits for their models, it also helps to be a history buff. My experience is that *historical U.S. economic data used to construct forecasting models can be applied most effectively when they are supplemented with knowledge of what was happening that was important but not reflected in any particular statistic.* For instance, the sharp real gross domestic product (GDP) decline at the end of the 1969–1970 recession was significantly influenced by a large automobile strike. And any model attempting to explain the rise of inflation in the early 1970s must consider the role of 1971–1974 price controls. The shortest U.S. recession, in 1980, can be understood only with knowledge of a temporary, ill-fated credit controls program. With these informational needs in mind, this chapter provides some commentary on the necessary nonquantitative history required to best process purely quantitative historical data.

It's Never Normal

The U.S. economy has experienced many surprising twists and turns throughout its history. Consequently, successful forecast producers and users should always be concerned about *which* history will repeat. The Great Depression of the 1930s was followed by two comparatively mild postwar recessions in 1948–1949 and 1953–1954. However, the 1957–1958 recession was far sharper than its two immediate predecessors. Subsequently, the 1960–1961 and 1969–1970 recessions were mild. But along came the Great Inflation, and the following two recessions in the mid-1970s and early 1980s were the deepest since the Great Depression. They were followed by an around a quarter-of-a-century period that came to be designated as the Great Moderation, with just two comparatively mild recessions and less volatile output growth. However, while many mainstream economists were marveling at what was thought to be a tamer business cycle and debating the accompanying causal factors, the stage was being set in the financial and real estate markets for the Great Recession of 2008–2009. The following years of just slow, fitful growth have now come to be characterized as "The New Normal." Looking ahead, *the considerable variation in the U.S. economy's business cycle history suggests that new normal(s) may not remain normal for very long.*

Clearly, successful forecasters should be keen students of history. As statisticians, they rely on a repetition of certain historical patterns. Moreover, knowledge of history is critical for making the necessary judgmental adjustments required for successfully applying statistical forecasting techniques. How a forecaster thinks the economy works (e.g., Keynesian, monetarist, supply-sider, or some combination of these) is also very important and is discussed in Chapter 6. But historical perspective is often the primary shaper of forecasters' conclusions. A sense of history plays a big role in guiding their selection of independent causal variables and in choosing the statistical models they use to project the past behavior of those variables into forecasts. And when statistical models inevitably fail to fully explain a forecast variable's history, forecasters supplement models' projections with their perceptions of what a broader business and economic history has taught them.

Even after the atypical Great Recession and the also atypical modest business recovery through 2013, forecasters still should not ignore earlier historical trends. Instead, the variations in this history should be a reminder of the economy's propensity for behavioral change. Moreover, history remains an inescapable necessity in understanding how the economy functions—a key to gauging the future.

Numerous characteristics of U.S. economic history remain very relevant for contemporary forecasters. Business contractions, whether labeled as recessions or depressions, are the perhaps the most difficult and critical events to forecast. They entail especially high costs and survival risks for investors and businesses. *Business expansions*, however, are the environment in which forecasters usually operate. *Growth volatility*—a major area of interest before the Great Recession—remains important for forecasters, even though pre-event volatility analyses did not suggest a serious recession on the horizon. Trend growth may be lower after the Great Recession, but the growth volatility surrounding that growth trend remains important for forecasting.

What Does U.S. Economic History Teach about the Future?

Until the Great Recession started in 2008, recessions were becoming less frequent and shorter and business expansions were becoming longer. Over the five decades before the Federal Reserve System was established in late 1913, there were 13 separate business contractions. They ranged in length from 10 to 65 months and the economy was in such periods half (50 percent) of the time. Between the end of World War I and the middle of the century, the economy was contracting 30 percent of the time. Between the early 1950s and the early 1980s, the economy was contracting 20 percent of the time. And the economy was in recession just 7 percent of the time over the following two dozen years.

Table 3.1 summarizes the variety of business history from the middle of the 19th century up until the Great Recession of 2008 to 2009. According to the National Bureau of Economic Research (NBER), there have been 33 business cycles. Each cycle covers an expansion and subsequent contraction of business activity (i.e., trough to trough).

Table 3.1 Business Cycle History (1865–2007) *before* the Great Recession

Period	Number of Contractions	Average Contraction Duration	Average Expansion Duration	Time in Contraction (%)	Frequency of Contractions
1865–1914	13	24 months	25 months	50	3.8 years
1918–1949	8	16 months	36 months	30	3.9 years
1953–1982	7	11 months	46 months	20	4.3 years
1983–2007	2	8 months	106 months	7	12 years

SOURCE: National Bureau of Economic Research.

Table 3.2 presents what has been for forecasters one of the most influential depictions of business cycle history. Starting in the middle of the nineteenth century, the table displays the dates and duration of business cycle expansions and contractions. Such historical information is often used as a start for framing possible business cycle outcomes.

However, it is insufficiently granular for understanding all that happens during business cycles. For deeper insight, one requires detailed GDP component data on a quarterly basis, which is available only for the post–World War II period. Table 3.3 displays magnitudes of change in real (inflation-adjusted) Gross Domestic Product (GDP) and its key components for each listed recession and the initial stages of the subsequent recovery.

Some Key Characteristics of Business Cycles

A business cycle—the upward and downward movements in levels of GDP—are generally measured peak to peak (for expansionary periods) or trough to trough (for recessions). Each cycle is a response to the particular set of conditions prevailing at a given time. In the aggregate, however, business cycles do exhibit three characteristics in common.

1. *Historical odds are low for double-dip recessions,* with one recession quickly following on the heels of the previous downturn. When examining pre– or post–World War II data, one thing that stands out is that the economy has not quickly relapsed into another recession anytime soon after a recession ends. In fact, periods of expansion have generally lasted three years or longer.

   Over the entire 33 business cycles listed in Table 3.2, only three recoveries lasted a year or less. And during the past 90 years only one recovery, in 1980–1981, lasted just a year. (Note: Most economists believe that the short recovery from mid-1980 to mid-1981 represented the final legs of a business expansion starting in early 1975. That expansion was interrupted by the temporary imposition of credit controls—a very atypical business cycle event.) Only one post–World War II recovery (1958–1960) lasted just two years. *Of the dozen postwar recoveries, 10 have lasted at least three years.*

Table 3.2 U.S. Business Cycle Expansions and Contractions

Peaks and Troughs (Quarterly Dates are in Parentheses)		Contraction	Expansion	Cycle (in months)	
Peak	Trough	Peak to Trough (in months)	Trough to Peak (in months)	Trough from Previous Trough	Peak from Previous Peak
	December 1854 (IV)	—	—	—	—
June 1857 (II)	December 1858 (IV)	18	30	48	—
October 1860 (III)	June 1861 (III)	8	22	30	40
April 1865 (I)	December 1867 (I)	32	46	78	54
June 1869 (II)	December 1870 (IV)	18	18	36	50
October 1873 (III)	March 1879 (I)	65	34	99	52
March 1882 (I)	May 1885 (II)	38	36	74	101
March 1887 (II)	April 1888 (I)	13	22	35	60
July 1890 (III)	May 1891 (II)	10	27	37	40
January 1893 (I)	June 1894 (II)	17	20	37	30
December 1895 (IV)	June 1897 (II)	18	18	36	35
June 1899 (III)	December 1900 (IV)	18	24	42	42
September 1902 (IV)	August 1904 (III)	23	21	44	39
May 1907 (II)	June 1908 (II)	13	33	46	56
January 1910 (I)	January 1912 (IV)	24	19	43	32
January 1913 (I)	December 1914 (IV)	23	12	35	36
August 1918 (III)	March 1919 (I)	7	44	51	67
January 1920 (I)	July 1921 (III)	18	10	28	17
May 1923 (II)	July 1924 (III)	14	22	36	40
October 1926 (III)	November 1927 (IV)	13	27	40	41

August 1929 (III)	March 1933 (I)	43	21	64	34
May 1937 (II)	June 1938 (II)	13	50	63	93
February 1945 (I)	October 1945 (IV)	8	80	88	93
November 1948 (IV)	October 1949 (IV)	11	37	48	45
July 1953 (II)	May 1954 (II)	10	45	55	56
August 1957 (III)	April 1958 (II)	8	39	47	49
April 1960 (II)	February 1961 (I)	10	24	34	32
December 1969 (IV)	November 1970 (IV)	11	106	117	116
November 1973 (IV)	March 1975 (I)	16	36	52	47
January 1980 (I)	July 1980 (III)	6	58	64	74
July 1981 (III)	November 1982 (IV)	16	12	28	18
July 1990 (III)	March 1991 (I)	8	92	100	108
March 2001 (I)	November 2001 (IV)	8	120	128	128
December 2007 (IV)	June 2009 (II)	18	73	91	81
Average, all cycles:					
1854–2009 (33 cycles)		17.5	38.7	56.2	56.4*
1854–1919 (16 cycles)		21.6	26.6	48.2	48.9**
1919–1945 (6 cycles)		18.2	35.0	53.2	53.0
1945–2009 (11 cycles)		11.1	58.4	69.5	68.5

*32 cycles

**15 cycles

SOURCE: National Bureau of Economic Research.

Table 3.3 GDP Component Contributions in Recessions and Recoveries

Recession (years)		GDP	Consumer Spending	Residential Invest	Business Fixed Inv.	Final Sales	Domestic Purch.	Federal Govt.	State and Local Govt.	Contributions (Pct. Pts.)	
										Net Exports	Inventories
1953–1954	Recession, % change	−2.4	0.8	2.8	−2.2	−0.9	−2.9	−13.1	9.2	0.5	−1.5
	Recovery, year 1 % change	7.8	7.8	22.8	10.2	6.0	7.9	−9.2	8.9	−0.2	1.8
	Recovery, year 2 % change	2.4	3.0	−9.1	8.7	2.7	2.0	−0.6	2.8	0.4	−0.3
1957–1958	Recession, % change	−3.0	−0.5	−3.7	−11.9	−1.9	−2.1	1.3	6.8	−0.8	−1.0
	Recovery, year 1 % change	9.2	6.5	36.3	8.9	7.1	9.3	1.6	4.7	−0.1	2.1
	Recovery, year 2 % change	2.0	3.4	−9.8	7.5	2.9	1.3	−3.3	3.7	0.8	−0.9
1960–1961	Recession, % change	−0.3	−0.3	−2.7	−3.4	0.6	−0.6	3.8	5.9	0.3	−0.9

	Recovery, year 1 % change	7.6	5.1	11.4	8.5	5.5	8.2	9.7	2.1	-0.6	2.0
	Recovery, year 2 % change	3.6	4.2	6.5	3.8	3.8	3.5	0.3	4.9	0.1	-0.3
1970	Recession, % change	-0.2	1.7	9.4	-4.4	0.8	-0.3	-5.8	4.3	0.2	-0.9
	Recovery, year 1 % change	4.4	5.4	25.2	4.8	4.0	4.7	-7.2	2.8	-0.3	0.4
	Recovery, year 2 % change	6.8	7.3	12.9	11.5	6.3	6.8	-2.7	2.3	0.0	0.5
1974–1975	Recession, % change	-3.1	-0.8	-28.8	-9.4	-1.0	-4.3	2.8	5.4	1.2	-2.1
	Recovery, year 1 % change	6.2	6.3	25.1	2.0	4.6	7.1	1.0	2.9	-0.9	1.5
	Recovery, year 2 % change	3.2	4.5	16.5	9.4	3.4	4.3	0.8	-1.8	-1.1	-0.2
1980	Recession, % change	-2.2	-1.2	-16.0	-4.0	-0.7	-3.8	0.9	-2.8	1.6	-1.5
	Recovery, year 1 % change	4.4	2.3	-4.8	8.8	1.8	5.3	4.9	-1.9	-0.9	2.6

(continued)

Table 3.3 (*Continued*)

Recession (years)	GDP	Consumer Spending	Residential Invest	Business Fixed Inv.	Final Sales	Domestic Purch.	Federal Govt.	State and Local Govt.	Contributions (Pct. Pts.) Net Exports	Inventories
Recovery, year 2 % change	−2.6	1.1	−18.4	−6.4	−1.5	−1.7	3.9	0.8	−0.9	−1.1
1981–1982 Recession, % change	−2.5	2.9	−12.0	−8.0	−0.1	−1.6	6.5	1.6	−1.0	−2.5
Recovery, year 1 % change	7.8	6.4	49.7	10.4	5.9	9.4	2.8	1.1	−1.6	1.9
Recovery, year 2 % change	5.6	4.4	3.7	13.9	5.1	6.6	7.2	5.4	−0.9	0.6
1991–1992 Recession, % change	−1.3	−1.1	−10.7	−3.5	−0.7	−1.8	1.5	1.3	0.5	−0.6
Recovery, year 1 % change	2.9	3.2	14.9	−1.8	2.6	2.7	−2.8	3.0	0.2	0.3
Recovery, year 2 % change	3.3	3.4	7.5	8.7	2.7	3.8	−2.4	0.1	−0.5	0.6

2001	Recession, % change	0.5	2.1	1.5	−6.3	0.9	0.7	3.6	3.3	−0.2	−0.5
	Recovery, year 1 % change	2.0	2.0	8.1	−5.1	1.0	2.8	8.5	1.6	−0.7	1.0
	Recovery, year 2 % change	4.3	3.9	12.6	6.2	4.3	4.3	6.4	−0.8	0.1	0.1
2007–2009	Recession, % change	−4.3	−2.7	−35.7	−18.2	−2.9	−5.8	11.1	1.9	1.5	−1.4
	Recovery, year 1 % change	2.7	2.0	7.0	1.5	1.0	3.4	4.5	−2.4	−0.7	1.7
	Recovery, year 2 % change	1.9	2.6	−6.0	6.4	1.9	1.6	−2.1	−4.2	0.3	0.0
Average*	Recession, % change	−1.8	0.2	−8.9	−7.5	−0.6	−2.1	1.3	4.4	0.2	−1.3
	Recovery, year 1 % change	5.6	5.0	22.3	4.4	4.2	6.2	1.0	2.8	−0.5	1.4
	Recovery, year 2 % change	3.7	4.1	3.9	8.5	3.7	3.8	0.4	1.4	−0.1	0.0

*Average during recessions from 1953 to 2009; 1980 was excluded, as it was an abnormal, short-lived recovery.
SOURCE: Bureau of Economic Analysis.

2. Before the Great Recession and its slow growth aftermath, recessions and subsequent recoveries often were characterized as either U-shaped or V-shaped. The "V" was the most frequent characterization. It represented a sharp recession followed by an also sharp rebound. Of the 10 recessions before the Great Recession, all but the previous two were characterized by initially fast growth rebounds. The initially slower recoveries in the early 1990s recession and again after the 2001 recession followed milder than normal recessions and were frequently characterized as U-shaped.

    The Great Recession and the initially slow and just-partial recovery through 2013 is hard to characterize with a letter from the alphabet. If I had to select a letter, the closest might be a "backward J." Rather than using a letter to describe the Great Recession and its initial aftermath, many observers instead have chosen to label this unusual cyclical episode as the new normal—a topic to be explored in Chapter 7.

3. Postwar recessions often are characterized as mostly being "inventory corrections," although that is a somewhat flawed interpretation. The reason for this characterization is that in Table 3.3 1.3 percentage points of the average 1.8 percent peak-to-trough real GDP decline in postwar recessions has been due to inventory investment reductions. This interpretation has at times led numerous economists to believe that firms' better inventory control was a key to moderating the business cycle. However, it also can be argued that inventory swings themselves reflect cyclical deviations in end-users' goods demands.

National versus State Business Cycles: Does a Rising Tide Lift All Boats?

What has happened in national business cycles is not always a good guide to business cycles in states—an often-important area of consideration for investment and marketing decisions. Table 3.4 presents data on national and state business cycle history from 1939 through 2012.[1] The first column gives the number of recessions in each of the 48 contiguous states

Table 3.4 States in Recession

State	Number of Recessions	Average Monthly Employment Loss as % of Labor Force
Alabama	12	0.08
Arkansas	11	0.08
Arizona	8	0.10
California	9	0.08
Colorado	5	0.09
Connecticut	11	0.11
Delaware	9	0.09
Florida	5	0.13
Georgia	9	0.09
Iowa	10	0.08
Idaho	8	0.11
Illinois	10	0.10
Indiana	13	0.14
Kansas	10	0.11
Kentucky	9	0.09
Louisiana	10	0.08
Massachusetts	11	0.11
Maryland	7	0.09
Maine	10	0.10
Michigan	12	0.14
Minnesota	8	0.09
Missouri	13	0.09
Mississippi	12	0.08
Montana	11	0.09
North Carolina	11	0.09
North Dakota	8	0.04
Nebraska	5	0.08
New Hampshire	7	0.12
New Jersey	7	0.11
New Mexico	5	0.09
Nevada	6	0.15
New York	15	0.08
Ohio	12	0.12
Oklahoma	11	0.08
Oregon	10	0.11
Pennsylvania	14	0.10
Rhode Island	15	0.16
South Carolina	10	0.09

(continued)

Table 3.4   *(Continued)*

State	Number of Recessions	Average Monthly Employment Loss as % of Labor Force
South Dakota	8	0.08
Tennessee	11	0.09
Texas	8	0.07
Utah	7	0.09
Virginia	10	0.07
Vermont	12	0.07
Washington	10	0.09
Wisconsin	13	0.10
West Virginia	13	0.13
Wyoming	6	0.25
United States	12	0.14

Characteristics of recessions and recoveries in each of the 48 contiguous U.S. states used for estimation. Column 2 gives the number of recessions in each state since 1939. Column 3 shows the average employment loss per month of recession, as a percentage of the average size of the labor force over the years 1990 to 2006.
SOURCE: Francis Neville, Laura E. Jackson, and Michael T. Owyang, "Countercyclical Policy and the Speed of Recovery After Recessions," Federal Reserve Bank of St. Louis, Working Paper, October 2013.

since 1939. The second column presents more recently available data on the magnitude of labor market deterioration during the 1990 to 2006 period.

Over the 1939 to 2012 period, there have been a dozen national recessions. However, over that time period researchers have identified just five recessions in Colorado, Florida, Nebraska, and New Mexico. On the other extreme, they have identified 15 recessions in New York and Rhode Island.

What accounts for the varying business cycle differences among states? Part of the answer lies in population shifts that can enable states enjoying relatively large migration inflows (e.g., Florida and Texas) to avoid participation in at least mild national recessions. In some states losing population (e.g., New York, Pennsylvania, and Rhode Island) there have been more recessions than in the country as a whole. Presumably, when there is slow national growth, areas experiencing net out-migration are more likely to be losing output and jobs.

U.S. Monetary Policy and the Great Depression

The most important historical experience for modern business forecasters is the Great Depression of the 1930s. Its depth and duration were so unanticipated by the economics profession that its great thinkers had to go back to the drawing board. Even more than three-quarters of a century later, economists still debate the relative role of various causal factors. A common analytical starting point, however, is U.S. monetary policy.

Before the Federal Reserve System was established at the end of 1913, almost all business downturns were accompanied by financial crises.[2] When news spread about the financial problems of banks' large borrowers, there were runs on bank deposits. (At that time, there was no bank deposit insurance, which was finally established in response to the bank failures at the start of the Great Depression.) On an ad hoc basis, large money center banks would selectively lend to assist failing banks. However, there was no strong, credible and predictable lender of last resort—a central bank.

In reaction to the especially severe Panic of 1907, the National Monetary Commission was created by Congress. Its 1911 report was followed, at the end of 1913, by the Federal Reserve Act. It established a system of regional Reserve Banks to provide more consistent and less uncertain assistance to depository institutions struggling with deposit outflows when large borrowers' financial problems became well publicized. Students of the banking system generally agree that in its early years the Federal Reserve System was a so-called work in progress. There still was not deposit insurance. Also, while there was a more organized lender of last resort system, banks could still be selectively allowed to fail. And the newly adopted system had yet to prove itself to the depositing pubic. In this setting, in the decade and a half following the Fed's creation there were four business contractions before the Great Depression began in the fall of 1929.

Economists generally agree that the Federal Reserve System in its infancy was not always an effective lender of last resort, and it clearly deserves some of the blame for the startling depth of the Great Depression. But opinions still differ as to whether activist New Deal policies helped or hindered the economy in the years after President Franklin Roosevelt initiated them at the start of his first term in 1933. The economy grew during that first term, but hardly enough to make much of a dent in the staggering level of unemployment. From its 24.9 percent peak in 1932, the unemployment rate receded to 14.3 percent in 1937—the start of President Roosevelt's second term. Although improved, the jobless rate still dwarfed its 3.2 percent level in 1929 when the Depression began. Then soon after Roosevelt won reelection, the economy relapsed into a sharp one-year contraction beginning in the spring of 1937, and by 1938 the unemployment rate had risen back to 19.0 percent. When Roosevelt was reelected to his third term in 1940, the unemployment rate was still at a relatively high 14.6 percent. The jobless rate only receded to its pre-Depression levels after the U.S. entry into World War II.

Monetarists lay the blame for the Great Depression squarely on the shoulders of a timid Federal Reserve System, one with weak leadership and a poor understanding of how a more supportive monetary policy could have boosted the economy. Keynesian historians also cite President Roosevelt's diffidence in failing to pursue stimulative tax and spending policies via more aggressive Federal deficit financing. On the other hand, modern day conservatives still place much blame on various activist New Deal policies that, in their opinion, damaged business confidence.

The Ghost of the Great Depression Has Returned to Haunt Business Forecasters

For forecasters, there have been a couple of Great Depression legacies that, at various times, have played influential roles in how they assess potential future outcomes. During the 1950s, memories of the Great Depression were still sufficiently recent to engender caution, especially following the sharp 1957 to 1958 recession. However, in the following decades economists became more influenced by the advent of the so-called New Economics school of thought, which advocated preemptive monetary and fiscal policies to head off serious recessions. Subsequently, though, the two relatively deep and poorly anticipated recessions in the mid-1970s and early 1980s served as a reminder to forecasters that a half century earlier economists failed to predict the Great Depression.

But with just two relatively mild recessions at the start of the 1990s and at the beginning of the past decade, memories of the Great Depression apparently faded and forecasters started to believe in what came to be known as the Great Moderation. However, following the most recent recession, which turned out to be the worst downturn since the 1930s, the subsequent recovery has been uninspiring and incomplete. And forecasters are again haunted by the ghosts of the Great Depression.

This renewed interest in the Great Depression as a potential model for a future economic downturn appears relevant to today's professional forecasters for four reasons.

1. First, potential financial fragility now plays a more prominent role in framing possible outcomes. Financial institutions' utilization of noninsured liabilities (e.g., repurchase agreements) to help finance their assets has exposed them to risks similar to risks posed by runs on banks before deposits were insured.

2. Second, even today, adopted Federal fiscal tax and spending policies are sometimes considered insufficiently stimulative. In the Great Depression, Republican and most Democratic public officials were unfamiliar and uncomfortable with the idea of deficit financing to stimulate the economy. And believers in the recuperative powers of deficit-financed solutions think that the fiscal conservatism of many Congressional Republicans has meant that, just as in the Great Depression, the government has failed to provide sufficient fiscal stimulus.

3. Third, some conservative economists believe that the business community's displeasure with various New Deal programs sapped business confidence and thereby held back the hiring and commercial investment needed for a more rapid recovery. In the recent setting, President Obama's health care policies, mandating employer provision of employees' health insurance, are sometimes cited as injurious to business confidence and expansion.

4. Finally, the widely unanticipated severity of the Great Recession has reminded economists of the difficulty of anticipating such outcomes. Forecasters are now more prone to consider a wider range of outcomes, including the persistently above-normal period of lingering unemployment that characterized the Great Depression.

The Great Inflation Is Hard to Forget

The Great Inflation period of the 1970s is probably not very far behind the Great Depression in shaping how economists, investors, and business planners think about the future. It also marked a most dramatic and critical departure from the earlier historical patterns on which most forecasters' assumptions had been based. And it had profound effects on financial markets as well. Moreover, for modern forecasters, the Great Inflation was personal: an experience lived through by either themselves or their parents. *In the current setting of low price inflation and bond yields, the history of the Great Inflation in the not-too-distant past should be very important for contemplating the future.*

Similar to the middle of the current decade, inflation at the start of the 1960s was not a problem. Then as now, economic policymakers were far more concerned about disappointing growth and jobs. In President Kennedy's first year in office in 1961, the consumer price index (CPI) rose just 1.0 percent. And following the 1960 to 1961 recession, inflation edged just modestly higher. When President Johnson was elected in 1964, the CPI that year only rose 1.3 percent. However, inflation began to accelerate with the escalation of the Vietnam War. The Johnson Administration was politically reluctant to raise taxes to finance what was becoming an unpopular war, and the accompanying fiscal stimulus—via higher defense spending—helped rekindle inflation. In addition, the size of the U.S. armed forces between 1964 and 1968 rose by almost 1 million persons. That represented an incremental 1.25 percent drain on the civilian labor force, came at a time of tightening labor markets, and helped to trigger accelerating wage inflation. In this setting, inflation had accelerated to 4.2 percent by the 1968 Presidential election, its highest level since the Korean War in the early 1950s.

Public dissatisfaction with the Vietnam War, and the higher inflation that accompanied it, helped elect President Nixon to his first term in the fall of 1968. Both the war and inflation continued to fester in the first two years of his administration. By 1971 the President and his advisers were becoming worried about his 1972 reelection prospects. Nixon had started the slow process of disengagement from the war, but the halting progress on that front reflected international considerations beyond the President's control.

However, at home the administration believed that it possessed far more control over its growing domestic inflation problem. CPI inflation had accelerated to 5.5 percent in 1969 and 5.7 percent in 1970. During the period, the annual growth of average hourly wages for private sector nonsupervisory workers accelerated from 4.8 percent during the second term of the Johnson Administration to a 6.1 percent annual pace in the first two years of the incoming Nixon Administration. By the summer of 1971, wages had risen 6.8 percent from a year earlier, while the 12-month change in the CPI was 4.5 percent. Although down from the previous year, it still was around the uncomfortably high level criticized by Present Nixon when campaigning for the presidency in 1968. At the same time, unemployment had been slow to decline after the 1969 to 1970 recession. In June of 1971, the 5.9 percent civilian unemployment rate was still 2.5 percentage points above the 3.4 percent rate when President Nixon was elected in the fall of 1968.

In reaction to this politically worrisome situation, the Nixon Administration surprised the world on August 15, 1971, with the announcement of what came to be known as the New Economic Policy.[3] For the first time in U.S. peacetime history, price controls were announced. A 90-day freeze on wages and prices was followed by Phases One through Four of price control programs that lasted through April of 1974. If that was not already shocking enough, Nixon ordered suspension of the convertibility of the dollar into gold or other reserve assets. In addition, he declared a national state of emergency and imposed a 10 percent surcharge on all U.S. goods imports.

In retrospect, *President Nixon's New Economic Policy only postponed price inflation, but it did result in a temporarily lower unemployment rate.* The jobless rate in November of 1972, when President Nixon was reelected, had fallen to 5.3 percent. Eventually, it fell as low as 4.6 percent in October of 1973. While the CPI 12-month change in November of 1972 had declined to 3.5 percent, a year later it had reaccelerated to 8.4 percent.

To make matters worse for inflation, the Organization of Arab Petroleum Exporting Countries (OAPEC) in October of 1973 declared an embargo on oil shipments to the United States and other nations who had supported Israel in the 1973 Yom Kippur War. That triggered a quadrupling of crude oil prices to around $12 per barrel. In the United States, the price per gallon of regular gasoline soared from

$0.40 per gallon in October of 1973 to $0.56 per gallon by March of 1974. That 40 percent would be equivalent to a $1 rise in retail gasoline prices of around $2.50 per gallon in recent years. Moreover, the embargo was accompanied by widespread gasoline shortages. Although the embargo was lifted in mid–March of 1974, oil and gasoline prices did not recede: members of the Organization of Petroleum Exporting Countries (OPEC) continued to limit production enough to maintain the higher crude oil prices initiated by the embargo.

Inflation relief came only from the 1973 to 1975 recession, which at the time was the deepest since the Great Depression. After rising 11.1 percent in 1974, the CPI slowed to 9.1 percent in 1975 and 5.8 percent in 1976. However, it soon started to reaccelerate after President Carter was inaugurated in 1977. The following year inflation was up to 7.7 percent before the second oil price shock—stemming from the Iranian revolution that began in late 1978—hit. Iran's domestic upheaval resulted in a sharp drop of almost 4 million barrels per day in Iranian crude oil production between 1978 and 1981. Some other OPEC nations initially raised their crude oil production to offset most of the decline from Iran, but in 1980, the Iran-Iraq War began, and a number of Persian Gulf producers started to lower their output. In this setting, between the start of 1979 and the end of 1980, the world price of crude oil soared from around $14 per barrel to more than $35. And CPI inflation accelerated further to 13.5 percent in 1980, when President Carter was defeated for reelection by Ronald Reagan.

The Great Inflation finally was ended by the sharp and protracted 1981 to 1982 recession. It reflected the economy's eventual very negative reaction to the earlier surging oil prices and, more importantly, the high interest rates stemming from an exceptionally stringent Fed monetary policy. By 1983, CPI inflation had tumbled to 3.2 percent. That was more than 1,000 basis points under its peak three years earlier and the lowest annual inflation rate since the mid–1960s.

The Fed's victory over the Great Inflation is widely regarded as one of the most important achievements in the history of modern central banking, which dates back to the 19th century. And it could not have happened without the leadership of Federal Reserve Chairman Paul Volcker. When he was appointed to be Fed Chairman in August of 1979, the 12-month change in the CPI was 11.8 percent. When he departed the Fed after two four-year terms in August of 1987, the CPI in the first half of that year was just 3.0 percent higher than a year earlier.

The history of the Volcker Fed is familiar to most forecasters, investors, and business planners. Among the many books about Volcker's tenure at the Fed, perhaps the most appropriately titled might be William Silber's *Volcker: The Triumph of Persistence*.[4] To accomplish what he did with the means at his disposal required incredible persistence in the face of tremendous public opposition at the time.

Very briefly, here's my take on how Volcker succeeded. These observations reflect my vantage point as the head of the financial markets research division at the New York Fed in the late 1970s and then as PaineWebber's chief economist starting in 1980. (Note: We return to a detailed analysis of the Fed and interest rates in Chapter 11.)

When Volcker became the Fed Chairman in 1979, monetary policy was being conducted primarily via manipulation of the overnight Federal funds rate. That in and of itself was not necessarily a bad policy. However, the Fed was keeping the funds rate very close to CPI inflation, and resulting real (inflation-adjusted) interest rates were not nearly high enough to restrain the economy and inflation. Moreover, the Fed leadership at the time was reluctant to aggressively raise the Fed funds rate as inflation accelerated.

Under Volcker's leadership, the Fed stopped basing its policy on the Fed funds rate. Instead, the Fed started concentrating on controlling the money supply via control of bank reserves. That policy allowed the Fed funds rate to be determined by bank reserve supply and demand. In my view, this permitted real (inflation-adjusted) interest rates to finally rise enough to choke economic growth and inflation. When the economy started tumbling into a deep recession as a result of soaring interest rates two years after Volcker and his new policy arrived, he became very unpopular with politicians and the business community. In 1983, however, as inflation started to recede and the recession finally ended, President Regan rewarded Volcker by appointing him to a second four-year term as Fed Chair. Volcker's persistence in the face of enormous public pain and widespread public opposition paid off.

Although the Great Inflation period ended 30 years ago, three lessons from the experience remain relevant for contemporary forecasters.

1. *When price expectations become embedded in the minds of the public, those minds don't change quickly.* Individuals' behavior can lead to self-fulfilling prophecies. In the case of inflation in the 1970s, consumers' expectations of further inflation generated anticipatory buying that actually augmented the problem. A quarter-century later in Japan, just the opposite occurred. Expectations of lower prices became self-fulfilling as households postponed purchases while they waited for prices to fall. *In the middle of the current decade, forecasters concerned about potential price deflation should pay attention to the fact that households persist in expecting consumer price inflation to hold at just under 3 percent.*

2. *Do not count on the Executive Branch of the U.S. government to quickly correct most major national economic problems.* When confronted with policy options, politicians of both major political parties can be short sighted and pursue politically expedient policy choices. Price controls did not stop inflation. Instead, they only delayed it. The Republican Nixon administration was warned by more conservative Republican economists (e.g., Milton Friedman) that price controls create shortages and fail to address inflation's fundamental monetary and fiscal policy determinants. However, addressing inflation with price controls was politically seductive for politicians. Doing so avoided harder decisions, such as reducing Federal deficits. Moreover, price controls could be applied without Congressional approval. *My experience has been that forecasters can be politically biased and fail to see that their favorite political party, whether Republican or Democrat, can make unwise public policy choices.*

3. *The time it takes for the effects of monetary policy to manifest themselves can frustrate impatient forecasters and observers.* In my experience as a consultant to investors in the early 1980s, I saw that they generally expected the Volcker Fed's anti-inflation monetary policies to deliver results sooner than actually occurred. Likewise, in the middle of the current decade, there probably has been too much pessimism about the ultimate success of the Fed's quantitative easing (QE) policies aimed at stimulating economic growth.

The Great Moderation: Why It's Still Relevant

After the Volcker Fed and the steep 1981 to 1982 recession finally broke the back of inflation, the U.S. economy expanded by a cumulative 129 percent during the next quarter of a century. Two short recessions occurred at the start of the 1990s and again at the beginning of the twenty-first century. However, they were some of the most modest of the postwar downturns. Moreover, U.S. growth was noticeably less volatile than at any other time in the postwar period. And the same could be said for most other developed economies around the globe. (See Tables 3.5 and 3.6.) Had the business cycle been tamed?

Many in the economics profession thought so, and this period came to be known as the Great Moderation. In remarks so titled in early 2004, then-Federal Reserve Board Governor Ben Bernanke hailed the growing body of research documenting diminishing cyclical volatility in domestic output.[5] Initially attracting economists' attention was research on overall national output volatility by Kim and Nelson (1999) and McConnell and Perez-Quiros (2000).[6,7] Less volatility in employment, especially in goods-producing industries, was documented by Warnock and Warnock (2000).[8] Subsequent research by Kim, Nelson, and Piger

Table 3.5   Changes in Volatility of Four-Quarter Growth of Real GDP per Capita in the G7

	Standard Deviation, 1960–1983	Standard Deviation, 1984–2002	Std. Dev. 84–02 divided by Std. Dev. 60–83	Variance 84–02 divided by Variance 60–83
Canada	2.3	2.2	.96	.91
France	1.8	1.4	.71	.51
Germany	2.5	1.5	.60	.36
Italy	3.0	1.3	.43	.19
Japan	3.7	2.2	.59	.35
UK	2.4	1.7	.71	.50
United States	2.7	1.7	.63	.40

NOTES: Entries in the first two columns are the standard deviations of the four-quarter growth in GDP over the indicated time periods. The third column contains the ratio of standard deviation in the second column to that in the first; the final column presents the square of this ratio, which is the ratio of the variances of four-quarter GDP growth in the two periods.

SOURCE: James H. Stock and Mark W. Watson, "Has the Business Cycle Changed? Evidence and Explanations," Federal Reserve Bank of Kansas City, August 2003.

Table 3.6   Changes in Volatility and Cyclical Correlations of Major
Economic Variables

Series	Standard Deviation 1960–2002	Ratio of Standard Deviations, 84–02 to 60–83	Correlation with Four-Quarter GDP Growth	
			60–83	84–02
GDP	2.30	0.61	1.00	1.00
Consumption	1.84	0.60	0.85	0.87
Durables	6.55	0.70	0.76	0.80
Nondurables	1.65	0.62	0.76	0.77
Services	1.17	0.69	0.68	0.71
Investment (total)	10.41	0.79	0.88	0.89
Fixed investment–				
total	6.78	0.79	0.85	0.86
Nonresidential	6.85	0.93	0.75	0.76
Residential	13.25	0.51	0.58	0.57
Inventory investment/				
GDP	0.86	0.83	0.64	0.66
Exports	6.71	0.72	0.30	0.27
Imports	7.25	0.74	0.71	0.68
Government spending	2.46	0.71	0.21	0.25
Production				
Goods (total)	3.65	0.72	0.95	0.95
Nondurable goods	6.98	0.68	0.87	0.89
Durable goods	2.10	0.72	0.64	0.66
Services	1.08	0.74	0.54	0.58
Structures	6.20	0.67	0.80	0.80
Nonagricultural				
employment	1.79	0.71	0.78	0.77
Price inflation (GDP				
deflator)	0.39	0.53	0.16	0.15
90-day T-bill rate	1.73	0.75	0.43	0.39
10-year T-bond rate	1.21	1.10	0.13	0.02

SOURCE: James H. Stock and Mark W. Watson, "Has the Business Cycle Changed? Evidence and Explanations," Federal Reserve Bank of Kansas City, August 2003.

(2003) illustrated that reduced output volatility was broad-based.[9] This global reduction in output volatility was highlighted by Stock and Watson (2003).[10] See Table 3.6.

Why Was There Reduced Growth Volatility during the Great Moderation?

The reasons for reduced growth volatility remain important and should still influence forecasts. Economists studying the Great Moderation identified several determinants. Former Fed Chairman Bernanke has argued that improved monetary policy made an important contribution in damping cyclical volatility. Others have emphasized the role of good luck, such as uninterrupted crude oil supplies and relatively stable energy prices, in avoiding cyclical shocks. In addition, there have been arguments that lesser volatility stems at least in part from structural business changes, such as better inventory control and the growing importance of the less cyclical services sector.

Prior to becoming the Federal Reserve Chairman, and before the Great Recession, Ben Bernanke stated his belief that improved anti-inflation monetary policy under Paul Volcker and then Alan Greenspan played an important role in damping the volatility of economic growth.[11] In his view, less volatile inflation enhanced growth by improving the functioning of markets, enabling easier economic planning and reducing the time and resources that had been focused on hedging inflation risks. This conclusion was just the opposite of what he saw to be earlier monetary policymakers' mistaken belief that there were long-term trade-offs between higher inflation and lower unemployment. He and others also faulted monetary policymakers during the Great Inflation era for not fully appreciating how much Fed policy affected inflation. His reading of history was that when the Fed belatedly focused on tackling inflation, it had to slam on the monetary brakes and thereby aggravated output volatility.

A number of economists also attributed less volatile growth to specific structural changes in the economy. For instance, some argued that overall economic growth became less volatile as the nation's output mix shifted to the less cyclical services sector. Others believed that better

Expansion start date	Expansion end date	Standard deviation
Q2 1961	Q3 1969	2.9
Q1 1971	Q3 1973	4.2
Q2 1975	Q4 1979	4.0
Q4 1980	Q2 1981	6.3
Q1 1983	Q2 1990	2.2
Q2 1991	Q4 2000	1.8
Q1 2002	Q3 2007	1.6
Q3 2009	Q2 2014	1.8

Figure 3.1 Standard deviation of quarterly annual rate % change in Real GDP during recoveries

inventory control was lessening output volatility.[12] Still another some-times cited the economy becoming less energy intensive and thus less sensitive to oil price swings.[13]

And there was also the role of luck during the Great Moderation. Specifically, the economy had not been hit by dramatic rises in foreign oil prices, as had been the case in the early and late 1970s. In addi-tion, there had not been the types of upward food price shocks that had periodically dogged the U.S. economy during the earlier Great Inflation era.

Although the optimism engendered by the Great Moderation ulti-mately proved misplaced, three issues raised in the associated research remain quite relevant for contemporary forecasting purposes.

1. Growth remains less volatile than before the 1984 to 2007 Great Moderation period, but around a lower growth trend. (See Figure 3.1)
2. Some reasons for less volatility remain intact. Among these are fur-ther improving inventory control, more efficient use of energy, and less dependence on fossil fuel imports.
3. Great Moderation enthusiasts overlooked the central bank's effects on asset prices, which can become a source of downside growth risk if allowed to rise too much.

Key Takeaways

1. History is a critical supplement to statistical analysis when searching why models do not fit well in particular periods.
2. The notable variability in the magnitude and length of U.S. business expansions and contractions suggests caution in accepting so-called new normal hypotheses.
3. National and state recession histories can significantly differ.
4. Following the recent severe Great Recession, forecasters are apt to place more weight on the Great Depression experience.
5. The Great Inflation of the 1970s reminds forecasters about the stubborn persistence of inflation expectations.
6. The Great Moderation hypothesis placed too much emphasis on improvement in government antirecession policies.

Notes

1. Francis Neville, Laura E. Jackson and Michael T. Owyang, "Countercyclical Policy and the Speed of Recovery After Recessions," Federal Reserve Bank of St. Louis Working Paper, October 22, 2013.

2. O. M. W. Sprague, *A History of Crises under the National Banking System* (Washington, D.C.: U.S. Government Printing Office, 1910).

3. William N. Walker, "Forty Years After The Freeze," 2011.

4. William Silber, *Volcker: The Triumph of Persistence* (New York: Bloomsbury Press, 2012).

5. Ben Bernanke, "The Great Moderation," February 20, 2004, remarks to the Eastern Economic Association, Washington, D.C.

6. C. J. Kim and C. Nelson, "Has the U.S. Economy Become More Stable? A Bayesian Approach Based on Markov Switching Model of the Business Cycle," *Review of Economics and Statistics* 81, no. 4 (1999): 608–616.

7. M. McConnell and G. Perez-Quiros, "Output Fluctuations in the United States: What has Changed Since the Early 1980s?" *American Economic Review* 90 (2000): 1464–1476.

8. M. V. Cacdac Warnock and Frances Warnock, "The Declining Volatility of U.S. Employment: Was Arthur Burns Right?" Board of Governors of the

Federal Reserve System, International Finance Discussion Paper No. 667, August 2000.

9. C. J. Kim, C. Nelson, and J. Piger, "The Less Volatile U.S. Economy: A Bayesian Investigation of Timing, Breadth and Potential Explanations," Federal Reserve Board International Finance Discussion Paper, August 2001.

10. J. H. Stock and M. W. Watson, "Has the Business Cycle Changed? Evidence and Explanations," Federal Reserve Bank of Kansas City Symposium, "Monetary Policy and Uncertainty," Jackson Hole Wyoming, August 28–30, 2003.

11. Bernanke, "The Great Moderation."

12. S. J. Davis, and J. A. Kahn, "Interpreting the Great Moderation: Changes in the Volatility of Economic Activity at the Macro and Micro Levels," Federal Reserve Bank of New York Staff Report No. 334, July 2008.

13. Anton Nakov and Andrea Pescatori, "Oil and the Great Moderation," Federal Reserve Bank of Cleveland Working Paper 07–17, 2007.

Chapter 4

When Forecasters Get It Wrong

It's almost worth the Great Depression to learn how little our big men know.

—Will Rogers, American humorist

---

earning from the past is critical for human progress. In this chapter we review what forecasters' history, both good and bad, can teach us. We first discuss particularly important events, including the Great Depression, Great Recession, and the turn-of-the-century high-tech revolution with its attendant productivity boom, Y2K computer fears, and the tech crash. Then we examine the characteristics of forecasts made at cyclical turning points.

A key question is, "Has the economics profession learned from its own mistakes?" As discussed in Chapter 3, we economists thought that we would never see anything like the Great Depression again. In fact, the two recessions after the early 1980s were so comparatively mild that some of the finest minds in the profession proclaimed a new era, labeling it the Great Moderation. Much to the chagrin of my profession, the Great Moderation was followed by the Great Recession. About the only fig leaf left was that the Great Recession, bad as it was, was far less severe than the Great Depression. Indeed, economists learned enough from the mistakes made prior to the Great Depression to propose, and then help implement, new government policies that have prevented a repeat.

The Granddaddy of Forecasting Debacles: The Great Depression

As Will Rogers tartly observed, many of the day's leading economic and business thinkers and leaders seemed clueless about the causes of, and cures for, the Great Depression—one of the saddest episodes in our national history. Professor Walter Friedman at the Harvard University School of Business recently reminded us of the intellectual brilliance of that first generation of pre-Depression economic forecasters, luminaries such as Irving Fisher, Roger Babson, and John Moody.[1] Despite their scalding intelligence, they failed to see the big one coming and, when it hit, they were unable to ascertain its depth and duration. At the very least, they remind us that a high level of intelligence and education hardly guarantees success in forecasting. *Why did some of the greatest thinkers in the pre-Depression era miss foreseeing the depth and duration of the Great Depression?* Here's my brief take.

First, so much of forecasting is about repetition of past historical patterns. The pre-Depression economic forecasters were keen students of business slumps and well aware of their tendency to correct, eventually, without government intervention. As the Depression took hold, they concluded that government need not play a major role in stabilizing the economy, since it had eventually self-corrected during business downturns over the previous half century.

Second, around that past repetition of history grew an increasingly flawed body of explanatory theory. Pre-Depression economists mistakenly extended microeconomic theories of markets balancing via flexible prices to their analysis of national aggregate product and labor markets. Falling prices and wages were thought to be necessary for balancing the aggregate demand and supply of national product. In fact, though, falling wages depleted households' purchasing power. Falling prices diminished businesses' confidence, making companies reluctant to invest enough to create and recycle a full-employment level of savings back into the economy.

The lesson drawn from this most painful experience was that business downturns would not necessarily self-correct. This realization opened the door for government intervention. The key interventions— bank deposit insurance, stricter bank regulation and government countercyclical fiscal and monetary policies—were thought to be enough to inoculate the economy from business slumps with the potential to become another Great Depression. And while only some post-Depression recessions (e.g., 1960–1961, 1969–1970, 1991, and 2001) were mild, none came close to approaching the depth and duration of the Great Depression. That is, until the Great Recession of 2008–2009.

The Great Recession: Grandchild of the Granddaddy

How badly did forecasters miss what turned out to be the deepest recession since the Great Depression? New York Fed Economist Simon Potter provides some quantitative perspective on just how surprising the Great Recession was for professional forecasters.[2] He has utilized statistical evidence on the distribution of errors for a range of forecasters during the 1986 to 2006 period (since labeled the "Great Moderation").[3] Based on that statistical distribution, a 2008 real GDP forecast as of October 2007 would be within 1.3 percentage points of the actual outcome 70 percent of the time. Potter notes that in October of 2007 the New York Fed staff forecast was for 2.6 percent real GDP growth in 2008 on a Q4/Q4 basis. That was very near the 2.5 percent consensus forecast reported by the Survey of Professional Forecasters in the final quarter of 2007 for 2008. Thus, repetition of economists' past forecast error patterns suggested a 70 percent probability that 2008 growth would range between 1.2 percent and 3.8 percent. How much did real GDP really change in

2008? The latest official estimate, as of mid-2014, is −2.8 percent—a 5.3 percentage point forecast miss.

Why did the consensus forecast miss the Great Recession by so much? Potter's critique of the New York Fed's forecast failure is representative of much of what has been written about why most economists missed forecasting the depth of the Great Recession. First, there was a widespread failure to understand the extent to which *home prices* were unsustainably high and vulnerable on the downside. Second, there was insufficient understanding of the new forms of *mortgage finance* and their widespread threat to financial stability. Finally, in Potter's words "insufficient weight was given to the powerful *adverse feedback loops* between the financial system and the real economy." Such a dramatic forecasting fiasco has provided important lessons.

Some of the simplest valuation metrics should not be overlooked. To understand why house prices were overvalued by early 2007, one needed to look no further than at publicly available data on housing affordability. Each month the National Association of Realtors publishes a housing affordability index (HAI). (See Figure 4.1.) It reflects three variables: median family income, the median home price, and mortgage rates. By the first quarter of 2007, with home prices rising sharply, the affordability index had fallen to its lowest level in 15 years. One could argue that it had been that low 15 years earlier without disastrous consequences.

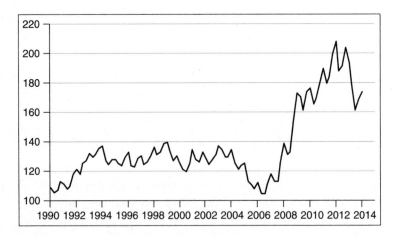

Figure 4.1   Housing Affordability Index (HAI)
SOURCE: National Association of Realtors.

However, the early 1990s marked the start of an economic recovery at a time of considerable pent-up housing demand in the wake of the previous recession. In 2007, when the HAI's low point was reached again, it came after a long boom in housing.

Why did so many forecasters overlook a widely available indicator suggesting potentially lower upcoming prices for homes that had become unusually unaffordable? I think two factors were particularly important. First, although there had been regional home price declines in the United States, there had not been declines in national average current dollar home prices since the Great Depression, more than 70 years in the past. Second, the national home ownership rate had been rising to a comparatively high level, suggesting strong underlying home ownership demand to support prices.

Also widely overlooked were the unusually easy and eventually unsustainable lending parameters for subprime borrowers—a pivotal group sparking demand and boosting home prices. By 2006—the year before home prices peaked—nonprime borrowers (subprime and alt-A) accounted for 39.7 percent of residential mortgage backed security originations, versus 5.8 percent in 1995. (See Table 4.1.) As growing numbers of those borrowers began to default on their loans,

Table 4.1 Residential Mortgage Backed Security Issuance—By Type (% of Total)

Date	Subprime	Alt-A	Nonagency	Agency
1995	5.6	0.2	15.4	84.6
1996	7.0	0.4	15.9	84.1
1997	11.7	1.3	24.5	75.5
1998	8.2	2.3	21.9	78.1
1999	6.7	1.4	17.8	82.2
2000	8.5	2.7	22.1	77.9
2001	6.4	0.8	19.7	80.3
2002	6.6	2.9	22.3	77.7
2003	7.2	2.7	21.6	78.4
2004	19.3	8.4	45.9	54.1
2005	21.6	15.4	55.2	44.8
2006	21.9	17.8	55.9	44.1

SOURCE: *Inside MBS & ABS*, SEC filings and industry surveys.

lenders started to tighten their lending standards, squeezing the supply of available mortgage credit. At the same time, newly wary investors became less willing to buy the loans from lending institutions. The stage was thus set for the first nationwide decline in home prices since the Great Depression.

Why did government policymakers not address the subprime problem in a timely manner? Homeownership has been a highly popular and bipartisan goal for decades. Thus, it was difficult for elected public officials to blow the whistle on rising homeownership. Being a nonelected body, did the Fed have the option, via its regulatory authority, to "take away the punchbowl before the party gets out of hand"? Bank regulation is the jurisdiction of multiple government agencies in addition to the Fed, and it was challenging to mount a coordinated regulatory response to the growing subprime problem.

Moreover, the Fed was under Alan Greenspan's leadership until he retired in February of 2006, and Greenspan was prone to take a noninterventionist tack. At the start of the decade, Fed Governor Edward Gramlich had informally alerted Greenspan to the problem and to the need for coordinated regulatory reform. According to Gramlich: "I would have liked the Fed to be a leader. He (Greenspan) was opposed to it, so I didn't really pursue it." Greenspan was apparently concerned about the potential unintended consequences accompanying added regulatory scrutiny.[4] Governor Gramlich retired from the Fed in August 2005, and he published a study (in June 2007) in which he documented the growing problems of subprime overlending and again recommended regulatory reforms.[5]

Why did most forecasters, also, underestimate the delinquency and sustainability problems of subprime lending?

The political and philosophical reasons that kept policymakers from addressing the subprime problem in a timely manner are both regrettable and understandable. What will be more puzzling to students of history, though, is why private sector investors and forecasters were so slow to recognize the subprime problem and its connection to overpriced residential real estate. The exceptional loosening of lending standards was a matter of public record. Table 4.2 shows selected characteristics for the once popular subprime adjustable rate mortgages (ARMs). Between 2002 and 2006, there were rises in loan/value ratios, "silent seconds"

Table 4.2 Subprime ARM Characteristics

Origination Yr	Loan/Value > 80%	Full Documentation	Silent Seconds*	Interest Only
2002	46.8%	66.9%	3.7%	1%
2003	55.6	63.5	9.9	5
2004	61.1	59.9	19.1	20
2005	64.4	55.9	28.1	32
2006	64.0	54.6	31.0	20

*Estimated assistance from seller or government housing agency for down payment.
SOURCE: Inside Mortgage Finance.

and interest-only loans, and an accompanying decline in full documentation of lending agreements. I think at least part of the problem was that analysts and economists in the financial sector were distracted by the idea of risk diversification in mortgage-backed securities. If these securities were safe investments and perceived as such because of diversification, then there would be fewer concerns about terminating the financing of home buying and the accompanying boom in real estate prices.

The Great Recession: Lessons Learned

1. *Don't ignore simple metrics in assessing bubbles.*
   The Housing Affordability Index (HAI) was clearly signaling affordability risks.
2. *Excessive risk history is too repetitive to ignore.*
   The savings and loan and junk bond debacles in the 1980s, and the tech stock bubble of the late 1990s, should have reminded forecasters that the occasional taking of unwise risk is an enduring human characteristic.
3. *Diversification and risk sharing can be illusory, and they are not necessarily good longer-term insurance policies against financial market instability.*
4. *Timely and rational policy responses to ameliorate deep recession risks should not be assumed.*
   Congress initially refused to adopt the necessary Troubled Asset Relief Program (TARP) in the autumn of 2008. When Congress did subsequently adopt a fiscal stimulus policy in early 2009,

Republicans kept it from being large enough, while Democrats may have spread the stimulus over too long a time frame and, possibly, over too many specific programs.

5. *Individuals in the twenty-first century can still panic as they did during old-fashioned bank runs.*

During the Great Recession, for example, we saw institutions that had loaded up on mortgage-backed securities engage in panic selling. Similarly, early in the recession, we saw employers cut back on employment far more than they usually did for similar drops in demand.

The Productivity Miracle and the "New Economy"

In the 70 years between the between the Great Depression and the Great Recession, a number of challenges offered forecasters the opportunity to be very right or very wrong. Some of the most instructive problems arose near the turn of the century, as forecasters struggled to understand the economic implications of the information technology boom. Though well-schooled in the Schumpeterian concept of "creative destruction through technological innovation," many economists were caught off guard by the speed and pervasiveness of the changes. To be sure, they were familiar with Moore's Law, which states that the computational power of semiconductor chips doubles every 18 months. Still, most forecasters struggled to keep pace with the rapidly developing, often dramatic economic ramifications of the information revolution.

It is hardly a new idea that technological change and innovation enhance productivity. But forecasters must seek to understand when these engines become powerful enough to trigger a meaningful trend in productivity growth. A problem in doing so is the difficulty of measuring the pace of technological change and innovation. *My approach to assessing an accelerating pace of technological change was to gather data on patents and R&D (research and development) activity.* (Figure 4.2 illustrates the positive relationship between patents and labor productivity through the 1990s.)

I began using this methodology in 1997, as economists debated whether productivity growth was speeding up.[6] The nation had

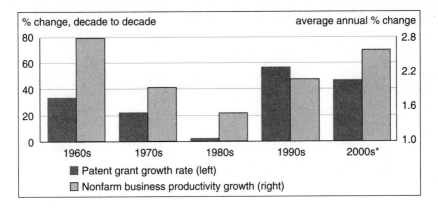

Figure 4.2 Patents and Productivity
*2010–2013 versus 2000–2003
SOURCE: Bureau of Labor Statistics, U.S. Patent Office.

experienced a shallow recession at the start of the 1990s, and had seen only a slow recovery in subsequent economic growth and productivity. Both, however, began to accelerate in the middle of the decade. (See Figure 4.3, later.) Whether this was the beginning of a new trend was an extremely important question, because continued productivity growth would help contain unit production costs, price inflation and, thereby, interest rates.

Within the Fed, the answer to this question would be pivotal in determining the economy's speed limit—how fast it could grow without accelerating inflation. Fed Chairman Alan Greenspan took the position that the technological change spurring improved productivity growth was unlikely to be temporary. As evidence, he cited the history of multiyear waves in technological progress and added recent anecdotal evidence.[7] The ensuing debate about what came to be known as "The New Economy" provides some important lessons for forecasters.

Fed Chair Greenspan spearheaded the 1990s debate about whether technology was boosting productivity. Opposing sides often argued about the believability of the improving productivity statistics. Was productivity being measured properly? Would the early signs of improvement be revised downward with subsequent revisions to annual data? The productivity debate in the second half of the 1990s provides important lessons on making forecasts with imperfect and conflicting inputs.

In internal Fed meetings and via external public statements, Greenspan persistently reiterated his opinion that the economy was entering a new era of faster, technology-led productivity growth. That would mean, he continued, more rapid growth in output than was widely expected, but with less inflation than normally anticipated. With lower inflation, he predicted, there would be less need to tighten Fed interest rates as unemployment fell. There were plenty of skeptics, and they included his internal Fed Board colleagues Alan Blinder and Laurence Meyer.[8]

Some of the pushback came from observers bent on extrapolating trends and pointing out that data available through the middle of the decade had yet to confirm Greenspan's optimism. For instance, in August of 1997, Louis Uchitelle—a widely followed economics reporter for the *New York Times*—stated, "The official broad statistics flatly deny that productivity is rising. Quite the contrary, they show it weaker than ever in the 1990s."[9] From a conceptual perspective, Federal Reserve Board Economist Daniel Sichel published an entire book aimed at debunking anecdotes about companies using new technologies to raise workers' productivity permanently. One of his arguments was that computers could not be making much difference for aggregate productivity because they represented too small a share of the capital stock.[10]

Greenspan, strong in his conviction, did not back off. Though he found it difficult to convince his FOMC colleagues of his productivity thesis, he was successful in limiting their willingness to raise interest rates in an environment with good growth and low price inflation—a key implication of his theory. And by 1999, the official growth and productivity statistics began to validate him. (See Figure 4.3) A year later, in August of 2000, the once skeptical Daniel Sichel was arguing that computers had, in fact, enhanced productivity growth in the second half of the previous decade.[11]

Productivity: Lessons Learned

1. *Simply extrapolating a trend can be a surefire way to end up "behind the curve" and late on a forecast.*

   It is okay for a journalist like Uchitelle to point out that a theory has yet to be proven. However, the job of forecasters and

Fed policymakers is to anticipate what will happen, and to avoid looking at the future through a rear-view mirror.

2. *A logical evolving driver should not be ignored just because it is hard to quantify.*

A periodically faster pace of technological change and innovation has historical precedent and was logical in the context of business developments in the 1990s. My approach—using multiyear patents as a proxy for invention—has admittedly been imperfect. However, it at least allowed me to factor something that is hard to quantify into my forecasts.

I chose to focus on whether a faster rate of technological progress could be identified with statistics in addition to industrial anecdotes. I began to examine data on patent grants.[12] In doing so, I found that there was a sizeable pickup in grants in the 1990s and that, if entire decades were the unit of empirical observation, these patents were positively related to productivity growth. (See Figure 4.3.)

That was enough evidence to persuade me that we were starting to experience a multiyear improvement in productivity growth. However, not everyone was convinced. Skeptics argued that patent grants did not always lead to productivity-enhancing inventions. Moreover, my

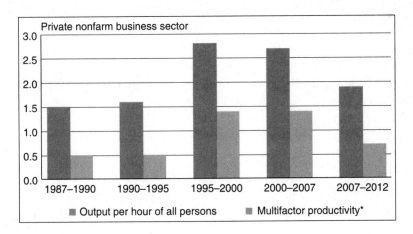

Figure 4.3 Productivity Growth (%)

*Output per unit of combined labor input and capital services.

SOURCE: Bureau of Labor Statistics.

proof—examining a few decades of evidence—did not conform to the traditional regression analysis wherein annual data, for example, would be correlated with some lagged measure of productivity growth.

I acknowledged the problems in interpreting patents. But I reminded the debate's participants and observers that there have always been (and always will be) measurement imperfections and uncertainties in the fields of economics and forecasting. In addition to collecting data, researchers of productivity growth also needed to ask (1) if this current trend had any historical precedent and (2) if it was logically plausible. I answered both questions in the affirmative and was proven correct. In the 1990s, annualized nonfarm business productivity growth accelerated from a 1.6 percent annualized pace in the first half of the decade to a 2.8 percent pace in the latter. (See Figure 4.3, earlier.)

Y2K: The Disaster That Wasn't

At the same time that economists were debating the broader benefits of the technology boom, noneconomists (and some economists, too) were fretting over whether computers might actually harm the economy. Such worries stemmed from the fact that yearly dates in computer programs had been entered as two digits instead of four digits. This happened because early in the computer age, when memory costs were expensive, it made sense to limit the amount of information being stored. Such frugality was no longer necessary, though, because advances in semiconductor chip storage capacity had cut the cost of memory dramatically. However, in the intervening years, the existing body of programs had become stuffed with two-digit year entries. The fear was that, at the turn of the century, those programs would not be able to distinguish between 1900 and 2000, and they would become confused and unable to perform their normal tasks.

Why was this known problem not addressed well before 2000? After all, it was no longer necessary to economize on data entries. However, programs with two-digit yearly dates generally were compatible with programs housing four-digit dates *if* it was not yet 2000. And it would be expensive to rewrite all of the existing body of computer programs having two-digit dates. Until the year 2000 neared, this was a problem for which there was procrastination. Whether computers were programmed with two-digit or four-digit dates, they still could interact until the year 2000 hit.

When the clock struck midnight on December 31, 1999, no one was quite sure what would happen. If the Y2K bug were not eradicated by then, through massive computer reprogramming, would our computers—the ones playing such vital roles in almost every aspect of our daily lives—suddenly stop functioning? If they did, what types of cataclysmic events might ensue? Survivalists made plans to live without telephones, electric power, and the modern supply chains that have come to sustain us. At the other end of the spectrum, some viewed all Y2K warnings as a hoax perpetrated by the information technology industry, which, in this scenario, saw Y2K as a once-in-a lifetime opportunity to sell volumes of Y2K-compliant equipment and software.

To help the public better assess what needed to be done to avert the potential disasters, the United States Senate formed the Special Committee on the Year 2000 Technology Problem.[13] In early 1999, it concluded that large domestic corporations were better prepared than smaller U.S. enterprises and foreign companies. For example, in the U.S. small business sector, the Committee's staff estimated that "over 90 percent of doctors' offices and 50 percent of small and medium-sized businesses had yet to address the problem."

For forecasters, the challenge was daunting. No one really knew to what extent there might be a global computer breakdown. And if there were serious problems in pivotal parts of the economy, how bad would the damage be? Since we had never encountered such a potential problem, there seemed to be no historical guidance.

The response of most economists, myself included, was to consider any Y2K-related economic problems temporary: not serious enough to cause a full-fledged recession. Most of my fellow economists and I were ill equipped to opine on exactly what had to be done to achieve Y2K compliance. So in the absence of computer technology expertise, I used logic and my knowledge of U.S. business history to address the problem. I knew that what usually disrupted the economy were unanticipated events (e.g., oil price surges), rather than problems for which there had been early warnings. I also knew that the American business system was remarkably adaptable and resourceful. If it was going to take a huge amount of money and manpower to solve the Y2K problem quickly, the U.S. had ample reserves of both. Moreover, precisely because a computer failure could be so devastating to an organization, there was a huge incentive to avert the problem. Finally, technology experts were saying that the Y2K problems were solvable, although they questioned the system's ability to mobilize resources quickly enough. Economics, though, is about how a market system goes about accomplishing resource mobilization as input supplies adjust to shifting demands.

As it turned out, the Y2K fears did not materialize. The great majority of economic forecasters made the correct call this time. The real GDP grew at a fast 7.1 percent pace in the final quarter of 1999, with 2 percentage points of that gain coming from accelerating inventory building that partly reflected Y2K-related fears of shortages. Growth did temporarily slow to a 1.2 percent annual rate in the first quarter of 2000, as the earlier precautionary inventory build was reversed, but final demand (GDP less inventory investment) rose at a healthy 4.0 percent annual rate. *The Y2K episode serves as a reminder of how the U.S. economy is geared to mobilize resources in addressing potentially serious supply-side problems if they are signaled far enough in advance.* Avoidance of a recession made economists look smart versus some the gloomy prognosticators from the tech sector. However, our credibility would soon be tested by another technology-related development.

The Tech Crash Was Not Okay

Technology improved productivity in the latter half of the 1990s without falling apart at the end of the decade. However, productivity and Y2K debates distracted the economics profession from more serious consideration of another technology problem: the possibility of overinvestment in technology. Such a concern was on the mind of even the most prominent technology boom enthusiast, Alan Greenspan, when he kicked off the new century with a January 13, 2000, address to the Economic Club of New York.[14]

In his public remarks, Greenspan could sometimes sound like the proverbial two-handed economist (i.e., "on the one hand, but on the other hand"). And he did so then, as he speculated about whether the low inflation-high growth New Economy could persist in the new century. He stated:

> When we look back at the 1990s, from the perspective of, say, 2010, the nature of the forces currently in train will have presumably become clearer. We may conceivably conclude from that vantage point that, at the turn of the millennium, the American economy was experiencing a once-in-a-century acceleration of innovation, which propelled forward productivity, output, corporate profits, and stock prices at a pace not seen in generations, if ever.
>
> *Alternatively, that 2010 retrospective might well conclude that a good deal of what we are currently experiencing was just one of the many euphoric speculative bubbles that have dotted human history.* And, of course, we cannot rule out that we may look back and conclude that elements from both scenarios have been in play in recent years. [italics added for emphasis]

It is always better to alert audiences to alternative scenarios than to only mention your forecast and its rationale. Greenspan's words, just as the new millennium was getting underway, are a case in point. The tech boom soon would begin to unravel. In fact, just two months after Greenspan spoke, the NASDAQ composite stock index—the primary gauge of tech stock prices—peaked. By April it already was 20 percent off its March high and fell a further 40 percent from its peak over the next 12 months. (See Figure 4.4.)

The tech boom was over. Current dollar spending on information processing equipment as a percent of GDP fell from almost 2.9 percent of GDP at the start of the decade and continued declining until the middle of the decade. (See Figure 4.5 and Figure 4.6.) The collapse in tech stock prices and its spillover effects into other markets as well as the swoon in tech spending would push the U.S. economy into a recession in 2001.

As indicated earlier, this, too, was a recession that the consensus was late to see. A couple of factors can help explain why most forecasters failed to foresee the unsustainable nature of the tech boom. First, by the turn of the century more economists were starting to agree that

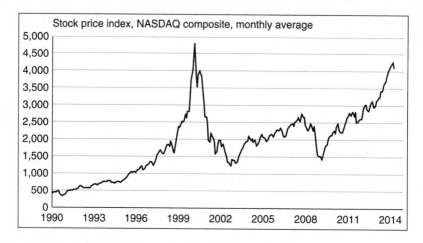

Figure 4.4 NASDAQ Composite Stock Price Index
SOURCE: NASDAQ.

the tech boom was good for productivity and growth. And as long as the incomes from that growth were being pumped back into the economy through spending, overall growth could continue: a so-called virtuous cycle. Second, as the price of information equipment fell, it made sense for firms to utilize technology more intensively. Over the second half of the 1990s, the government's chain price index for information processing equipment was falling at an average annual rate of 10.0 percent—around triple the annual rate of decline in the first half of the decade.

To be sure, there was recognition that Y2K preparations were adding a temporary increase to spending on computer software and hardware, but it was not thought to be significant. For instance, in response to a special question in the Survey of Professional Forecasters conducted in May of 1999, almost 60 percent of the respondents anticipated the various Y2K preparation effects to augment 1999 real GDP growth by 0.1 to 0.5 percent. Around half of the forecasters projected that reversal of these temporary effects in 2000 would impact real GDP growth by between 0.0 and −0.4 percent.[15] The net effect was zero, with the temporary negative effects in 2000 not enough to cause an economy-wide recession.

In retrospect, forecasters overlooked some key considerations. More intensive utilization of high-tech capital goods relative to output

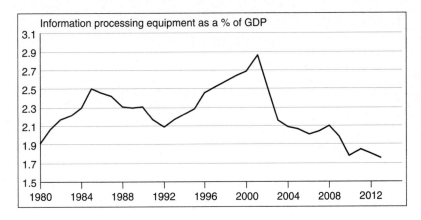

Figure 4.5   Information Processing Equipment as a Share of Nominal GDP
SOURCE: Bureau of Economic Analysis.

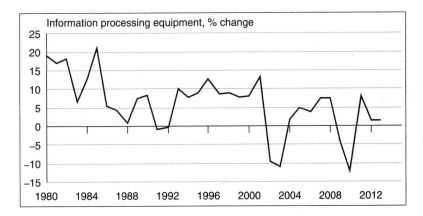

Figure 4.6   Growth of Real Information Processing Equipment
SOURCE: Bureau of Economic Analysis.

and labor input was sensible in light of falling relative prices of capital goods and the very cheap equity capital that came courtesy of NASDAQ investors. However, once a desired ratio of such capital goods to output is achieved, the growth of these capital goods will slow to the growth of output. Moreover, once the NASDAQ started falling in early 2000, equity financing for high-tech ventures was becoming more expensive and less available.

Forecasters at Cyclical Turning Points: How to Evaluate Them

The forecasting community's performance heading into and during recessions is especially important for modern forecasters who want to learn from past mistakes as well as successes. To gauge the community's performance, we shall ask four questions:

1. Did they foresee the recessions coming?
2. Did they know when it hit them?
3. Were they surprised by how much the economy declined?
4. Did they foresee it coming to an end?

In assessing the history, we rely on the archival data maintained by the Federal Reserve Bank of Philadelphia on consensus forecasts of the annualized quarterly growth rates of the real (inflation-adjusted) gross domestic product (GDP) in the Survey of Professional Forecasters (SPF). Conducted in the final month of each quarter ever since 1965, the SPF surveys have covered varying numbers of active forecasters. In the recent 2013 surveys, there were 45 participants. (Note: Before 1992, the size of the economy was measured by the gross national product [GNP] instead of the GDP. GDP is what is produced within the boundaries of the U.S. by both nationals and foreigners. GNP measures what is produced by U.S. citizens at home and abroad.)

Consensus forecasts from the final month of each quarter are compared to initially reported growth data. (See Tables 4.3 through 4.9. In these Tables, "t" is the quarter for which growth is reported and "t−n" is n quarters beforehand.) Subsequently revised statistics for a quarter reflect a more complete sampling of the economy, but comparing initial data to forecasts offers a better perspective on the immediate value of the forecasters' projections to their clients. My experience is that clients who are making timely business and investment decisions cannot afford to delay until the government provides revised data. Instead, part of a forecaster's job is to interpret initially reported data on a variety of related indicators in order to help clients make those difficult decisions. (Note: In Chapter 5, we discuss differences between initially reported and revised national economic data. Although such differences can at times be substantial, they generally do not change the story

Table 4.3 The Comparatively Mild 1969–1970 Recession Looks Somewhat Worse Than It Actually Was, as the Sharp Q4(70) Real GDP Decline Reflected an Auto Industry Strike. In the Last Month of the Initial Two Negative Quarters, the Consensus Was That There Had Been Weak but Not Negative Growth

1969–1970 Recession	Initially Reported GDP (%)	Consensus Forecasts (%)				
		t	t−1	t−2	t−3	t−4
Q4-1969	−0.1	0.2	1.9	2.4	4.2	4.0
Q1-1970	−1.6	0.7	0.3	1.4	1.5	0.0
Q2-1970	0.3	−0.6	0.3	0.6	2.4	0.0
Q3-1970	1.4	2.8	2.8	2.1	2.5	0.0
Q4-1970	−3.3	−1.3	2.2	3.1	4.5	3.1

SOURCE: Federal Reserve Bank of Philadelphia and Bureau of Economic Analysis.

Table 4.4 The Severe 1973–1975 Recession Reflected the Earlier Surge in Oil Prices and Significant Overall Price Inflation, Which Raised Interest Rates and Reduced Purchasing Power. The Initial Negative Quarter Was Anticipated a Quarter Earlier (i.e., t−1) and the Second Negative Quarter Was Anticipated Two Quarters in Advance (i.e., t−2)

1973–1975 Recession	Initially Reported GDP (%)	Consensus Forecasts (%)				
		t	t−1	t−2	t−3	t−4
Q4-1973	1.3	1.4	1.6	3.1	3.3	4.2
Q1-1974	−5.8	−2.1	−0.3	2.3	3.6	4.0
Q2-1974	−1.2	−0.3	−0.5	−0.6	2.7	3.1
Q3-1974	−2.9	0.3	1.9	2.3	2.1	3.5
Q4-1974	−9.1	−4.3	1.2	3.6	3.7	2.7
Q1-1975	−10.4	−5.5	−1.7	2.7	3.9	4.0

SOURCE: Federal Reserve Bank of Philadelphia and Bureau of Economic Analysis.

Table 4.5 The Brief but Sharp 1980 Recession Was Mainly Due to Higher Interest Rates, an Earlier Jump in Oil Prices and a Temporary Credit Control Program. The Only Negative Quarter Was Anticipated Two Quarters Earlier

1980 Recession	Initially Reported GDP (%)	Consensus Forecasts (%)				
		t	t−1	t−2	t−3	t−4
Q1-1980	1.1	0.0	−4.0	−1.5	1.0	2.4
Q2-1980	−9.1	−5.1	−2.5	−2.8	2.6	1.2
Q3-1980	1.0	−3.8	−3.6	−0.7	1.7	3.6

SOURCE: Federal Reserve Bank of Philadelphia and Bureau of Economic Analysis.

Table 4.6   The Severe 1981–1982 Recession Mostly Was Due to an Especially Stringent Anti-Inflation Monetary Policy. This Downturn's Beginning and Depth Were Not Well Anticipated

1981–1982 Recession	Initially Reported GDP (%)	Consensus Forecasts (%)				
		t	t−1	t−2	t−3	t−4
Q3-1981	−0.6	0.0	2.1	2.9	3.5	4.9
Q4-1981	−5.2	−3.4	2.1	3.3	3.8	4.2
Q1-1982	−3.9	−2.9	−1.1	3.5	4.1	4.6
Q2-1982	1.7	0.1	2.7	3.3	4.0	2.9
Q3-1982	0.8	1.6	3.4	4.4	5.4	4.3
Q4-1982	−2.5	1.1	2.4	4.1	4.7	4.5

SOURCE: Federal Reserve Bank of Philadelphia and Bureau of Economic Analysis.

Table 4.7   The Shallow Recession at the Start of the 1990s Had Its Roots in a Commercial Real Estate Crash and an Accompanying Bank Credit Crunch. Forecasters Had Been Expecting Weak but Not Negative Growth Beforehand

1990–1991 Recession	Initially Reported GDP (%)	Consensus Forecasts (%)				
		t	t−1	t−2	t−3	t−4
Q3-1990	1.8	1.4	2.5	2.4	2.4	4.0
Q4-1990	−2.1	−1.4	0.8	1.9	2.7	2.3
Q1-1991	−2.8	−1.9	−0.9	0.8	2.9	2.2

SOURCE: Federal Reserve Bank of Philadelphia and Bureau of Economic Analysis.

Table 4.8   The Very Mild 2001 Recession Was a Product of a Pullback in an Overheated Tech Sector

2001 Recession	Initially Reported GDP (%)	Consensus Forecasts (%)				
		t	t−1	t−2	t−3	t−4
Q1-2001	2.0	0.8	3.3	3.0	2.6	2.8
Q2-2001	0.7	1.2	2.2	3.2	2.7	2.6
Q3-2001	−0.4	1.2	2.0	3.3	3.3	3.2
Q4-2001	0.2	−1.9	2.8	2.6	3.7	3.2

SOURCE: Federal Reserve Bank of Philadelphia and Bureau of Economic Analysis.

Table 4.9 The Very Severe 2008–2009 Recession—the Great Recession—Was Due to a Crash in Real Estate Values and the Accompanying Strong Negative Spread Effects in the Financial Sector. Forecasters Were Caught Off Guard

2007–2009 Recession	Initially Reported GDP (%)	Consensus Forecasts (%)				
		t	t−1	t−2	t−3	t−4
Dec-2007	0.6	1.5	2.7	2.9	3.2	2.9
Mar-2008	0.6	0.7	2.2	2.7	2.9	3.1
Jun-2008	1.9	0.2	1.3	2.3	2.9	3.0
Sep-2008	−0.3	1.2	1.7	2.8	2.7	2.7
Dec-2008	−3.8	−2.9	0.7	1.8	2.8	2.8
Mar-2009	−6.1	−5.2	−1.1	1.6	2.3	3.1
Jun-2009	−1.0	−1.5	−1.8	0.8	2.1	2.5

SOURCE: Federal Reserve Bank of Philadelphia and Bureau of Economic Analysis.

about critical business cycle turning points heading into, and then exiting, recessions.)

Forecasting Recessions

The forecasting profession does not have a particularly strong track record when it comes to seeing recessions before they occur. Sometimes, in fact, we forecasters fail to recognize a recession even when we're in one.

A fair question to ask is, "How far in advance have professional forecasters anticipated the first negative real GDP growth quarter in recessions?"

The answer is that *in none of the last seven recessions for which SPF forecast data are available did the consensus forecast a first negative real GDP growth quarter by more than two quarters.* And only once—in the short but sharp 1980 recession—did the consensus forecast the first negative growth quarter two quarters in advance (i.e., t−2 in Table 4.5.) The sharp initially reported 9.1 percent annualized rate of real GDP decline in Q2 (1980) was one of the steepest quarterly contractions in the postwar period. What helped prompt the relatively early recession forecast in Q4 (1979) was the earlier discussed August of 1979 adoption by the incoming Volcker Fed of a new anti-inflation monetary policy focusing on bank reserves and the monetary aggregates instead of the Federal funds rate. Between August and December—the last month of a quarter when the SPF is conducted—home mortgage interest rates surged from a monthly average of around 11 percent to almost 13 percent—close to three percentage points above year-earlier levels.

Realizing You Are in a Recession

It would seem easier to know if a recession has started than to forecast one in advance. But this is not always the case. If we compare estimates made in the final month of a quarter to the initially reported growth for that quarter, we see that in only three (1973 to 1975, 1980, and 1990 to 1991) of the seven most recent recessions did a consensus forecast made in the first quarter of negative real GDP growth correctly predict negative growth.

Have downturns been worse than expected during recessions?

In the last seven postwar recessions, the deepest quarter of decline was always worse than anticipated by the consensus conducted in the last month of the quarter.

What are the right and wrong lessons from recession forecasting history?

Professional forecasters' struggles to anticipate and gauge the last seven recessions clearly illustrate the difficulty of this particular challenge. Given this history, one good lesson is that a forecaster's clients should, at the very least, be advised of downside risks once the forecaster is reasonably certain that a recession has arrived—a topic to be discussed in a later chapter.

My professional experience during these past seven recessions is that forecasters and policymakers are prone to act as "generals fighting the last war." When I joined the forecasting team at the New York Fed in 1973, the Fed's senior economists misjudged the severity of the 1974–1975 recession partly because the two prior recessions, in the early 1960s and early 1970s, had been comparatively mild. In reaction to the 1974–1975 recession, Fed policymakers were too timid in raising the Fed funds rate to tackle the rising inflation in the latter part of the decade. More recently, I think the two comparatively mild recessions in 1990–1991 and 2001 contributed to the complacency of forecasters both inside and outside the Fed before the Great Recession of 2008–2009.

Because rising oil prices preceded two harsh recessions in the mid-1970s and early 1980s, it is tempting to forecast a recession each time energy prices surge. However, it is important to distinguish between demand-driven energy price rises and the foreign supply-driven energy price jumps before these two business downturns. In the current setting, a less energy-intensive U.S. economy and reduced dependence on oil imports greatly tempers the threat of another recession should energy prices jump—a topic to be more thoroughly reviewed in Chapter 12.

Just because the severity of the Great Recession of 2008 to 2009 was exacerbated by too much financial leverage does not mean that another recession is anywhere near being imminent when credit utilization strengthens. My experience is that some forecasters can overreact to credit build-ups and become too cautious too soon in a business recovery.

Forecasting Recessions: Lessons Learned

1. In only three of the seven most recent recessions did the professional forecaster consensus in the first quarter of negative real GDP growth correctly predict such negative growth.
2. In the last seven recessions, the quarter of deepest real GDP decline has always been worse than estimated by the professional consensus in the last month of that quarter.
3. In none of the last seven recessions did the consensus of professional forecasters anticipate the first negative real GDP growth quarter by more than two quarters.

Key Takeaways

1. Although the forecasting failures heading into the Great Depression and the Great Recession leave us more wary about future economic downside risks, the legacy of such events is public policy reform that should ameliorate subsequent business cycles.
2. The difficulties in projecting the exceptionally favorable productivity developments in the late 1990s are a reminder about the potential for meaningful data revisions and the usefulness of economic history.
3. Although most economists were not misled by Y2K doomsday forecasts, the exceptional focus on this issue distracted attention from the implications of overinvestment in technology.
4. Consensus economist GDP forecasts become less reliable around business cycle turning points.

Notes

1. Walter A. Friedman, *Fortune Tellers* (Princeton, NJ: Princeton University Press, 2013).
2. Simon Potter, "The Failure to Forecast the Great Recession," Liberty Street Economics, Federal Reserve Bank of New York, November 25, 2011.
3. David Reifschneider and Peter Tulip, "Gauging the Uncertainty of the Economic Outlook from Historical Forecasting Errors," Finance and Economics Discussion Series, Federal Reserve Board of Governors, Washington, D.C., November 19, 2007.
4. Greg Ip, "Did Greenspan Add to Subprime Woes? Gramlich Says Ex-Colleague Blocked Crackdown On Predatory Lenders Despite Growing Concerns," *Wall Street Journal*, June 9, 2007.
5. Edward Gramlich *Subprime Mortgages: America's Latest Boom and Bust* (Baltimore, MD: Urban Institute Press, June 2007).
6. Maury N. Harris, "Recent Patent Surge Is Leading Indicator of More Strong Productivity Gains—Patents Are Key Gauge of Technological Change," PaineWebber Economics Group, November 6, 1997.

7. Alan Greenspan, "Remarks at von der Mehden Hall-University of Connecticut," October 14, 1997.

8. Greg Ip and Jacob M. Schlesinger, "Did Greenspan Push His Optimism About the New Economy Too Far?" *Wall Street Journal*, December 28, 2001.

9. Louis Uchitelle, "Measuring Productivity in the 90s: Optimists vs. Skeptics," *New York Times*, August 2, 1997.

10. Daniel Sichel, *The Computer Revolution: An Economic Perspective* (Washington, D.C.: Brookings Institution, 1997).

11. Stephen Oliner and Daniel E. Sichel, "The Resurgence of Growth in the Late 1990s: Is Information Technology the Story?" *Journal of Economic Perspectives* 14 (Fall, 2000): 3–22.

12. Harris, "Recent Patent Surge Is Leading Indicator."

13. The United States Senate Special Committee on the Year 2000 Technology Problem, "Investigating the Impact of the Year 2000 Problem," Summary of the Committee's Work in the 105th Congress, February 24, 1999, Washington, D.C.

14. Alan Greenspan, "Technology and the Economy," remarks before the Economic Club of New York, January 13, 2000.

15. Kevin L. Kliesen, "Was Y2K Behind the Business Investment Boom and Bust?" *Federal Reserve Bank of St. Louis Monthly Review* (January/February 2003).

Chapter 5

Can We Believe
What Washington,
D.C. Tells Us?

F orecasters have no choice but to rely on information from the
nation's capital—Washington, DC. There are several reasons for
this. Government statistics are the raw material for most forecasting models, and projections and analyses by various government organizations can be key inputs shaping thinking about the future. Also, analyses
by Washington, DC–based public policy interest groups and lobbyists are

often influential as well. The challenge for forecasters is to assess the credibility of this information. Government statistics are subject to substantial revisions. And very different answers to the same questions come from the government agencies and organized interest groups inside the Beltway. Thus, forecasters are regularly challenged to sift through the welter of statistics and analyses coming out of Washington, DC and determine what information to trust when assembling their forecasts.

Does the U.S. Government "Cook the Books" on Economic Data Reports?

On the morning of October 5, 2012—just a month before the Presidential election—the financial markets and most forecasters were surprised when the Bureau of Labor Statistics (BLS) reported that the civilian unemployment rate in September had dropped by 0.3 percentage points to 7.8 percent. For supporters of President Barack Obama's presidential reelection campaign, it was good news. When President Obama was inaugurated in January of 2009, the civilian unemployment rate stood at 7.8 percent. Despite the $787 billion in fiscal stimulus embodied in the American Recovery and Reinvestment Act (ARRA) signed by the President in February of 2009, the unemployment kept rising to 10 percent in October of 2009. It subsequently declined slowly, but remained well above the rate it had been when President Obama assumed office—a fact that the Republican challenger Mitt Romney was repeating to the American electorate on an almost daily basis during the 2012 Presidential election campaign. In the eyes of President Obama's supporters, the sharp decline in the September unemployment rate confirmed their confidence and proved that his economic policies were indeed producing results.

However, some Republican supporters of former Massachusetts Governor Romney cried foul. Jack Welch—the former Chairman of the General Electric corporation, charged on Twitter: "Unbelievable jobs numbers … these Chicago guys will do anything … can't debate so change numbers."[1] (Note: President Obama was from Chicago. In the first of three presidential election debates with Governor Romney, the President was widely viewed as having done a poor job.)

Did someone in the Obama Administration really order the BLS to fake the September unemployment rate data to aid President Obama's reelection bid? Members of the Obama Administration were outraged. The Secretary of Labor, Hilda Solis, responded on CNBC soon after Mr. Welch made his allegation that: "It's really ludicrous to hear that kind of statement ... I have the highest regard for our professionals that do the calculus."[2]

While Governor Romney subsequently lost the election, some critics of the Obama Administration persisted in asserting that something had been amiss with the September 2012 unemployment rate report. Just over a year later on November 18, 2013, a headline in the *New York Post* exclaimed: "Census 'Faked' 2012 Election Jobs Report."[3] The Census Bureau had been hired by the Labor Department to conduct the monthly household survey from which the responses are used to calculate the unemployment rate. According to the *Post* business reporter John Crudele, an unnamed source claimed that the Census Bureau either allowed or overlooked employees filling out fake questionnaires in a manner that lowered the unemployment rate. As evidence of a workplace environment that was supposedly conducive to such behavior, Crudele cited the Census Bureau's firing in 2010—two years before the Presidential election—of an employee for turning in faked questionnaires in order to exaggerate to his superiors how many surveys he was able to complete. Crudele's unnamed source claimed that such behavior on the part of other Census employees continued during the 2012 election, and that the Census Bureau failed to report the problem and the earlier firing to the Labor Department.

A week after Crudele leveled his charges, they were challenged by Nelson Schwartz, a business reporter for the *New York Times*.[4] He quoted former Labor Department personnel who said that the size of the monthly household survey sample—54,000—was far too large to be materially affected by a few dozen faked responses. Moreover, for September of 2012 there was other corroborative evidence of stronger job formation from the separate monthly survey of employer payrolls.

I mention this episode because it illustrates the degree of suspicion surrounding the veracity of government economic data. Disappointed securities investors and traders and angry political partisans sometimes have complained to me that some statistic unfavorable to their trading position or political cause has been somehow or other rigged to make economic conditions appear better than they really are. When an inflation statistic is lower than expected by a bearish bond investor, it is not uncommon to hear complaints that the government is trying to hide the true inflation rate for political reasons. Bullish bond investors sometimes assert that the government's reported unemployment statistics are in some sense intentionally rigged so as to understate true unemployment. I characterize such allegations as representing the "conspiracy theory" of government economic statistics.

It is understandable why some observers believe that the U.S. government deliberately alters potentially unfavorable economic reports. This belief probably stems, in part, from investors' experiences with data released by a few foreign governments. Specifically, there have been instances where government budget statistics have been very misleading in countries struggling to maintain investor interest in government debt issues. Or in the case of Mexico during the 1994 debt crisis, there were reporting delays from the Mexican government's usual release schedule for government budget and Treasury cash data. Some observers, too, are somewhat (or more) suspicious of Chinese economic data. Why? There may be incentives for regional government officials to overstate their region's economic activity so as to please senior Communist Party officials in Beijing and obtain more financial aid that is linked to a region's size and economic performance.

With the following possible exception, I do not believe that U.S. economic data are politically manipulated before being released to the public. Government agencies are subject to ever more media scrutiny. In addition, whenever a suspiciously strong data report is issued during an election campaign, politicians are quick to encourage scrutiny by both the media and Congressional investigative staffs. Another consideration is that government statistical agencies are headed by career civil servants who are generally immune from political pressures and who care about their professional reputations.

That said, won't an incumbent President order stepped-up preelection government spending to both stimulate the economy and produce better economic data? Undoubtedly, this happens in many countries. In the United States in 2012, on October 26—just over a week before the November elections were to be held—the Commerce Department reported an unexpectedly large 2.0 percent annualized rise in real GDP growth for the third quarter of 2012. And the especially surprising GDP component was an initially reported sharp 9.6 percent annualized quarterly rise in Federal purchases of goods and services. It accounted for 0.7 percentage points of the overall 2.0 percent real GDP gain.

Did the incumbent Obama Administration order accelerated government spending for political reasons? Critics thought the rise was suspicious. After all, the surprising gain came at a time when existing budget legislation dictated Federal spending restraint. Leading the overall third quarter Federal spending rise was a 13 percent annualized increase in Federal defense spending. It had declined at annualized rates of −7.1 percent in the first quarter of the year and by a further 0.4 percent in the preceding quarter. Then in the fourth quarter such spending tumbled at a 22.2 percent annual pace. The critics contended that the Obama Administration had deliberately held back defense allocations in the previous two quarters so that such spending would stimulate the economy and boost a key economic statistic on the eve of the national elections.[5]

Absent very specific evidence of communications from an administration to Federal agencies either suggesting or ordering such manipulation, such charges are hard to prove. Defense spending is one of the most volatile GDP components on a quarterly growth basis. Also, the third quarter of a calendar year is the final quarter of a Federal fiscal year. And this is a strong incentive for agencies to spend the types of earlier appropriated funds that must be spent or lost before a fiscal year ends.

To What Extent Are Government Forecasts Politically Motivated?

Although I doubt that government officials politically manipulate reported government economic data, I have no doubt at all that the economic data forecasts issued by government agencies are politically motivated at times. As discussed in Chapter 1, there is evidence of private sector forecasts having a strategic element. Biases can reflect the business needs of different employers and the business strategies of independent forecasting firms. Forecasters in the public sector are only human and also can exhibit similar types of strategic behavior. Instead of perceived business needs biasing their forecasts, public sector economists and their forecasts can be influenced by their perceptions of office politics in Washington, D.C.

Cost overruns in the public sector are an all too familiar example of government forecasts going awry. Are some government officials and their staffs strategically motivated to low ball their initial estimates of a proposed program's expenses? This might well have been the case with two major government cost overruns in the administration of President George W. Bush—the start of the Iraq war beginning in 2002 and the Medicare Prescription Drug Improvement Act of 2003. Prior to the U.S. invasion of Iraq in 2002, the Defense Department underestimated the war's costs as well as its troop requirements. Both the Pentagon and Congress acknowledged the subsequent troop shortages two years later.[6] A year after the expanded Medicare prescription drug legislation was adopted, it was revealed that its costs were initially underestimated by around $150 billion.[7]

The strategic rationales for fudging forecasts of future costs should be obvious. A government forecaster might have a personal preference for a particular policy or course of action. Also, just as in the private sector, government forecasters may consider self-preservation, in the form of promotion and job security, when contemplating a forecast at odds with an employer's specific goals. On the other hand, there are reputational issues for public sector forecasters, as there are for their private sector brethren who may also prize their professional integrity. Civil service laws, too, help to protect government employees from undue pressure from their appointed superiors.

In my years (1973–1980) as an economist at the Federal Reserve Bank of New York, I never felt overt pressure from my superiors to tilt my analyses and forecasts in any specific direction. However, after reviewing a report, senior management would decide on the size of the internal distribution list. The short list limited a report's exposure and was ostensibly justified by considerations of other internal persons' interests and their lack of time to read all of the voluminous research being churned out by the staff. However, some of my colleagues confided in me their disappointment at having a hard-researched report go only to the short list.

To better understand public servants' forecasting behavior, political scientists George A. Krause and J. Kevin Corder have proposed the following theory about "bureaucratic inter-temporal decision making."[8] They suggest that, "an agency's forecast optimism is related to the extent to which it discounts future reputation costs associated with bureaucratic incompetence." From this general theory come the following three hypotheses:

1. *Forecast Horizon Hypothesis*: As the forecast horizon increases, the level of forecast optimism will rise.
2. *Static Organizational Stability Hypothesis*: Less stable agencies will produce more optimistic forecasts than more stable agencies for a given forecast horizon.
3. *Dynamic Organizational Stability Hypothesis*: The difference in forecast optimism between less stable and more stable agencies will grow as the forecast horizon increases.

These hypotheses were tested by comparing forecasts by the Office of Management and Budget (OMB) with those of the Social Security Administration (SSA). The forecasts covered real GDP, CPI inflation, and the unemployment rate over a half-dozen forecast horizons in the 1979–2003 period. The OMB director is appointed by the President and works in the Executive Office Building. In the 24 years up through 2005, directors stayed on their job for an average of just over two years. By way of contrast, in the same 1981 to 2005 period, there were only two chief actuaries of SSA. Note that from its inception through 2003, the SSA was part of a cabinet agency and thus relatively insulated from the President. The comparatively shorter tenure of OMB directors suggests that they may not be too concerned about the longer-term consequences of forecasts that go awry, whereas the chief actuary during the sample period was on the job long enough to be held responsible for the consequences of longer-term forecasts.

Krause and Corder report that over six forecast horizons between 1979 and 2003, the OMB produced more optimistic forecasts than the SSA. Moreover, the optimism gap widened as the forecast horizon lengthened. The authors concluded that, "more stable agencies place a premium on minimizing reputation costs." *The three lessons for private sector forecasters and consumers of forecasts are*:

1. Forecasts by government agencies closely aligned with the White House have a tendency toward optimism.
2. According to the research by Krause and Corder, the government forecasts of real GDP growth and the unemployment rate were less optimistic under Democrat than Republican presidencies between 1979 and 2003.
3. Private forecast users should ask themselves if the forecasting economists or securities analysts will be held accountable for their accuracy over longer forecast horizons.

Other research on the forecast bias of government agencies corroborates the Krause and Corder findings over a somewhat longer sample period—1976 through 2008. Robert Krol reports that real GDP forecasts by the OMB are more upward-biased than forecasts by the Congressional Budget Office and the Blue Chip consensus. He argues that this result reflects the OMB being relatively less politically independent.[9]

In addition to being relatively more optimistic, Executive Branch economic forecasts are somewhat less accurate than forecasts by the CBO, Federal Reserve, and private sector economists' consensus. David Reifschneider and Peter Tulip compared the root mean squared errors of various government and private sector forecasts over the 1986–2006 period.[10] In this study, they compared Administration forecasts to those from the CBO, the Federal Reserve Board staff, Federal Open Market Committee members and two private sector consensus forecasts: Blue Chip and Survey of Professional Forecasters. (See Tables 5.1 and 5.2.) For both real GDP growth and CPI inflation, the Administration's root mean squared error was somewhat larger than for the other forecasts.

Though it would appear that Administration forecasts from its OMB are relatively optimistic, the forecasts do not become more optimistic in election years. That, at least, was the conclusion of J. Kevin Corder, who compared OMB forecasts to forecasts by CBO and SSA between 1976 and 2003.[11] The OMB was found to be less independent of White House pressure than was the CBO, which serves both political parties in Congress, and the earlier discussed SSA. He concluded, though: "There is no systematic bias present in any of the forecasts unique to

Table 5.1   Root Mean Squared Prediction Errors for Real GDP[1] Q4/Q4 (Projections Published from 1986 to 2006)

	Projection Period Year			
	Current[2]	Second	Third	Fourth
Winter projections				
Monetary Policy Report FOMC	1.10	—	—	—
Federal Reserve Staff (Greenbook)	1.19	1.39	—	—
Congressional Budget Office	1.26	1.39	1.35[2]	1.43[2]
Administration	1.29	1.48	1.46	1.52
Blue Chip	1.17	1.30	—	—
Survey of Professional Forecasters	1.14	1.31[2]	—	—
Average	1.19	1.37	1.40	1.48

[1] Percent change, fourth quarter of year from fourth quarter of previous year.
[2] Percent change, annual average for year relative to annual average of previous year.
SOURCE: David Reifschneider and Peter Tulip, "Gauging the Uncertainty of the Economic Outlook from Historical Forecasting Errors," Finance and Economics Discussion Series Division of Research and Statistics and Monetary Affairs, Federal Reserve Board, Washington, D.C., 2007–60.

Table 5.2   Root Mean Squared Prediction Errors for the Consumer Price Index[1] (Projections Published from 1986 to 2006)

	Projection Period Year			
	Current[2]	Second	Third	Fourth
Winter projections				
Federal Reserve Staff (Greenbook)	1.00	0.98	—	—
Congressional Budget Office	0.99	0.9	0.80[2]	0.87[2]
Administration—CEA, OMB	1.07	1.05	1.04	1.16
Blue Chip	0.95	0.91	—	—
Survey of Professional Forecasters	0.93	0.98[2]	—	—
Average	0.99	0.96	0.92	1.01

[1] Percent change, fourth quarter of year from fourth quarter of previous year.
[2] Percent change, annual average for year relative to annual average of previous year.
SOURCE: David Reifschneider and Peter Tulip, "Gauging the Uncertainty of the Economic Outlook from Historical Forecasting Errors," Finance and Economics Discussion Series Division of Research and Statistics and Monetary Affairs, Federal Reserve Board, Washington, D.C., 2007–60.

the Presidential election year. Whatever bias is detected in the forecast is evident in each year, independent of the proximity of elections."

Can You Trust the Government's Analyses of Its Policies' Benefits?

If government economic forecasts can be politically biased, can the same be said for government analyses of the probable benefits of its public policy proposals? Yes. That said, forecasters and forecast users frequently rely on such analyses for inputs or baselines. Why? Because evaluating government policies from scratch is time consuming. Doing so often requires considerable resources and a specialized experience in building statistical models. Even if one has the time and skills necessary for independent policy evaluation, it is very hard to avoid being at least somewhat influenced by highly publicized partisan policy debates.

A sensible approach to evaluating government policy analyses is to consider all sides of a policy debate. Typically, any major government policy under consideration is evaluated by the President's Council of Economic Advisers (CEA), Congressional staffs serving Republican and Democratic elected officials, and also by what is supposed to be a bipartisan CBO. The challenge for business persons and investors is to understand conclusions that are sometimes quite disparate. For instance, Republican politicians are more likely to be skeptical of the job creation potential of infrastructure spending than are Democrats. When added funding for infrastructure is adopted, should potential beneficiaries plan on accelerated expansion or remain more cautious with regard to their capital spending and payrolls? Which side of the public debate on this topic should large companies and their public investors believe?

The debate surrounding President Obama's American Recovery and Reinvestment Act (ARRA) of 2009 provides a still relevant and useful study of the challenges involved in evaluating the potential impact of public policies on businesses and the economy. Remember, just a month after President Obama was inaugurated in January of 2009, a Democratic-controlled U.S. House and Senate adopted the ARRA fiscal stimulus legislation. The CBO estimated that the various provisions of the bill added up to $787 billion of fiscal stimulus to be more than 90 percent implemented before the end of fiscal 2012—just a month before the November national elections when President Obama would likely be standing for reelection to another four-year term. According to the CBO, the estimated $787 billion in fiscal stimulus included tax cuts ($212 billion), enhanced spending on mandatory programs such as Medicaid and unemployment benefits ($296 billion), and discretionary spending ($279 billion) in areas such as aid to individuals and investments in infrastructure, energy, health care, and education.

At the outset, the program was controversial with many Republicans and even a number of Democrats. Some Congressional Democrats and their academic advisers regarded the newly adopted stimulus package as being too small, spread out over too many years and too focused on tax cuts. They also asserted that the new Administration's underlying economic assumptions were not pessimistic enough. Therefore, in their view, the economy needed a larger initial dose of stimulus. In addition, these critics contended that the mix of stimulus was too tilted toward tax cuts, which were thought to be less immediately effective than government spending.

At the same time and from the other side, Republican critics and their academic supporters charged that the stimulus package was both too large and poorly designed. Some warned of the longer-term debt service consequences of such massive deficit spending. A few argued that the economy would soon recover on its own without government assistance. If a massive stimulus really was needed, critics believed it should be skewed toward more tax relief instead of Federal spending.

In the academic world, some Nobel Prize-winning economists, such as Paul Krugman and Joseph Stiglitz, complained that the stimulus was too small and represented unwise political compromise on the part of President Obama and Congressional Democrats. And though President Obama claimed broad support from professional economists, approximately 200 of them vented their opposition in a full-page advertisement in the *New York Times* and the *Wall Street Journal* on January 28, 2009. Among the signers were Nobel Prize winners Gary Becker, James. M. Buchanan, Edward C. Prescott, and Vernon L. Smith. They stated that, "to improve the economy, policymakers should focus on reforms that remove impediments to work, saving, investment and production. Lower tax rates and a reduction in the burden of government are the best ways of using fiscal policy to boost growth."[12] Such disagreements among economists reflected both different theories of how the economy would respond to government spending and tax changes, and varying statistical estimates of the effectiveness of such fiscal policy actions.

On a theoretical level, those economists either supporting the stimulus program or thinking that it should have been even larger were mostly working with the basic Keynesian paradigm (to be discussed in Chapter 6). They believed that the size of a fiscal program understated its ultimate positive economic impact stemming from the chain reaction of spending summarized in the Keynesian multiplier concept. The disagreement among them about the necessary size of the program reflected different assessments of just how weak the underlying economy was in early 2009. At the start of the year Christina Romer, who was to become Chair of the Council of Economic Advisers (CEA), and Jared Bernstein, who was to become the top economic adviser to incoming Vice President Joe Biden, estimated that without stimulus the unemployment rate would reach almost 9 percent by early 2010.[13] Instead, the jobless rate peaked at 10 percent in the third quarter of 2009 even after the stimulus program had begun to be implemented. In retrospect, those economists favoring even more fiscal stimulus were reinforced in their beliefs.

However, economists opposing the Obama version of fiscal stimulus believed that the ultimate economic impact of the $787 billion fiscal stimulus would be perhaps a good deal less than $787 billion. In other words, the Keynesian multiplier would be less than 1.0—a sharp contrast to the plan's supporters' belief that the multiplier would be well over 1.0. (Romer and Bernstein assumed cumulative multiplier effects of 1.55 for government purchases and 0.98 for tax cuts.) The critics of the Obama plan made a couple of arguments. Some emphasized what is known among economists as "Ricardian equivalence"—the public would save more in anticipation of the higher future taxes eventually needed to service and repay the ballooning government debt created by the fiscal stimulus. They also stressed the idea that the stimulus and related deficit financing would lead to higher interest rates.

A further source of professional disagreement about the stimulus program was the range of statistical estimates of its impact. (See early 2009 estimates in Table 5.3.) The estimates by CEA and the consensus of private forecasters were similar. However, the CBO chose to highlight a

Table 5.3   Early 2009 Estimates of the Effects of the Recovery Act on the Level of GDP

	Percent				
	2009	2010	2011	2012	2013
CEA: Model Approach	1.1	2.4	1.8	0.8	0.3
CBO: Low	0.4	0.7	0.4	0.1	0.1
CBO: High	1.7	4.1	2.3	0.8	0.3
Average of five private sector forecasters	1.0	2.5	1.7	0.5	—

NOTE: Firm estimates were obtained from and confirmed by each firm or forecaster, and collected in CEA's Ninth Quarterly Report.
SOURCE: Congressional Budget Office, "Estimated Impact of the American Recovery and Reinvestment Act on Employment and Economic Output from October 2012 through December 2012," CEA Ninth Quarterly Report, CEA Calculations.

wide range of estimates reflecting different forecasting methodologies.[14] The highest estimates were derived from *macroeconomic forecasting models*. CBO economists describe them as models that "incorporate relationships among aggregate economic variables that are based on both historical data and economic theory." The lowest estimates are from *time series models*. CBO economists explain them as models that "rely heavily on historical data and place less emphasis on economic theory; they document the historical correlation between fiscal policy and measures of aggregate economic activity." Also considered are *dynamic general-equilibrium (DGE) models* that "rely less on historical data and place greater emphasis on economic theory; such models are labeled dynamic because they focus on how an economy evolves over time."

A further depiction of the variation in estimated fiscal impacts comes from examining the range of estimated multipliers for different types of fiscal stimulus. (See Table 5.4 for such estimates by the CEA and CBO.)

Note: The CEA multipliers show the impact of a permanent change in the component of 1 percent of GDP after 6 quarters, or, equivalently, the cumulative impact of a one-time change of 1 percent of GDP over 6 quarters. The CBO multipliers show the cumulative impact of a one-time change of 1 percent of GDP over several quarters.

When there are many divergent theories and statistical results, how do I judge which inputs to utilize?

In judging research on the economic effectiveness of government policies, I address the following questions: Do underlying behavioral

Table 5.4 Estimated Output Multipliers for Different Types of Stimulus

	CEA	CBO Low	CBO High
Public investment outlays[a]	1.5	0.5	2.5
State and local fiscal relief	1.1	0.4	1.8
Income and support payments[b]	1.5	0.4	2.1
One-time payments to retirees	0.4	0.2	1.0
Tax cuts to individuals	0.8	0.3	1.5
Business tax incentives	0.1	0.0	0.4

[a] Includes transfer payments to state and local government for infrastructure and tax incentives to businesses directly tied to certain types of spending.
[b] Includes such programs as unemployment compensation, COBRA, and SNAP
SOURCE: Congressional Budget Office, "Estimated Impact of the American Recovery and Reinvestment Act on Employment and Economic Output from October 2012 through December 2012," CEA Calculations.

assumptions make sense? Does the analysis recognize potential causation by variables other than those included in the analysis? Who has conducted the research? The first two questions should be asked in judging any research. The last question can be especially important for public and private research originating in Washington, D.C.

1. *Behavioral assumptions.*

Some behavioral assumptions are more palatable than others. For instance, *rational expectations* theorists invoke the earlier discussed Ricardian equivalence theory to claim that fiscal stimulus via government spending on goods and services won't be very stimulative. Their reasoning is that taxpayers will save more as they realize that their future taxes will rise to cover the debt service and repayment necessitated by the fiscal deficits accompanying fiscal stimulus. I find it hard to believe that the general public is that farsighted and so understanding of public finance. That said, I also am skeptical about the assumptions embodied in the relatively new *behavioral economics* theories built on human experiments. This line of thinking sometimes views irrational behavior as the norm. In most instances, though, my experience is that rational, self-interested behavior is a better assumption.

2. *Omitted causal variables.*

Another consideration in evaluating the credibility of any fiscal policy analysis is the extent to which it includes all of the relevant potential causal variables influencing the economy. For example, some politicians claim that the Obama fiscal stimulus program was a failure because the unemployment rate remained relatively high in the first four years after the program's implementation. However, the more appropriate and fairer analysis is to consider how high the unemployment might have risen in the absence of fiscal stimulus in an environment where bank credit was tight and home prices were declining. (Note: Statisticians sometimes label this problem partly as an omitted variable problem.) The claimed statistical effect of an independent variable will be biased if other relevant variables excluded from an analysis are much correlated with the included independent variables.

3. *Reverse causation.*

Does a studied policy only affect the economy or is it partly determined by the economy? For instance, advocates of higher state government spending sometimes cite empirical evidence of large multiplier spread effects on states' GDP from such expenditures. However, part of that positive association reflects the impact of the state economy on state tax collections, which in turn are spent. Statisticians label this situation as an "endogeneity" or "identification" problem. It can be addressed by statistical techniques such as inclusion of instrumental variables in a regression analysis. If you suspect that reverse causation is an issue in studying a policy's potential impact and if the research study under consideration does not identify and address potential reverse causation problems, the conclusions from such a study should be viewed skeptically.

4. *Consider the source.*

In evaluating most research, one can be prejudiced by the author's known ideological and political leanings. In fairness and in the interests of honest inquiry, I try not to judge the validity of an analysis by what I think about the author's politics or previous research. However, in the case of research being done in the highly politicized contemporary environment of advocacy in Washington, D.C., I cannot avoid considering the source. As earlier discussed, forecasts and policy impact analyses published by participants in the Executive branch of government tend to be too optimistic. This was the case with regard to the major tax cuts initiated by

Republican President Ronald Reagan in the 1980s and the more recent stimulus policies enacted during the first term of the Obama Administration.

5. *Whose policy research in Washington, D.C. is the least politically biased?* I most prefer policy research conducted within the politically independent Federal Reserve System. Congressional Budget Office researchers are subject to pressures from both political parties of Congress. That environment can result in evenhanded evaluations but sometimes too cautious conclusions.

The Beltway's Multiplier Mania

Advocates of specific programs, policies, and projects naturally tout potential benefits. Almost always, the projected cost of a proposal is far exceeded by estimated benefits due to spread or multiplier effects. As an economist, I am sometimes asked to judge such estimates. In doing so, I approach these analyses with a good deal of skepticism. This is partly because of some past very disappointing outcomes versus professed benefits, and also because of the methodological challenges entailed in such estimates.

Some instructive examples of the differences between advocates' forecasts and what actually happens come from the world of sports. State and local governments are periodically approached by sponsors of some sporting event and asked for public funding assistance that "will pay for itself and much more" as the event generates sizeable community events. One example is the Super Bowl. For the 32 host cities from 1970 through 2001, economists have estimated that there was an average $93 million in positive personal income impact stemming from these events. According to the researchers performing this particular study, the National Football League typically touts benefits four times larger than their estimated $93 million average income impact.[15] (See further examples of forecasts and actual benefits for some key sporting events in Tables 5.5 and 5.6.)

Sometimes it is not hard to spot such overly optimistic promises. For instance, tourism officials in Denver, Colorado in March of 2005 estimated that hosting a National Basketball Association (NBA) All-Star

Table 5.5   Examples of Mega-Event *ex ante* Economic Impact Studies

Event	Year	Sport	Impact
Super Bowl (Miami)	1999	Football	$393 million
MLB World Series	2000	Baseball	$250 million
NCAA Men's Final Four (St. Louis)	2001	Basketball	$110 million
U. S. Open	2001	Tennis	$420 million
World Cup (Japan)	2002	Soccer	$24.8 billion
World Cup (South Korea)	2002	Soccer	$8.9 billion
World Cup	2006/2010	Soccer	$6 billion; 129,000 jobs
Summer Olympics (Atlanta)	1996	Multiple	$5.1 billion; 77,000 jobs

SOURCE: Victor A. Matheson, "Mega-Events: The Effect of the World's Biggest Sporting Events on Local, Regional, and National Economies." College of the Holy Cross, Department of Economics Faculty Research Series, Paper No. 06–10.

Table 5.6   Examples of Mega-Event *ex post* Economic Impact Studies

Event	Years	Variable	Impact
Super Bowl	1970–2001	Personal Income	$91.9 million
MLB playoffs and World Series	1972–2000	Personal Income	$6.8 million/game
NCAA Men's BB Final Four	1970–1999	Personal Income	down $6.4–$44.2 million
World Cup	1994	Taxable Sales	down $4 billion
Summer Olympics (Atlanta)	1996	Employment	3,500–42,000 jobs

SOURCE: Victor A. Matheson, "Mega-Events: The Effect of the World's Biggest Sporting Events on Local, Regional, and National Economies." College of the Holy Cross, Department of Economics Faculty Research Series, Paper No. 06–10.

Game would bring 100,000 visitors to town.[16] Since the city at that time had only about 6,000 hotel rooms and the sports venue held only 20,000 spectators, it was easy to identify this overestimate. However, most cost-benefit analyses are not so easily dismissed, as we shall see when considering their role in the debates about national economic policies during the first term of the Obama Administration.

Could the American Recovery and Reinvestment Act of 2009 Create or Save over 5 Million Jobs?

Soon after the $787 billion American Recovery and Reinvestment Act (ARRA) was adopted in February of 2009, President Obama's Council of Economic Advisers (CEA) estimated that by the fourth quarter of 2010 this legislation would create 3.5 million jobs. And by the end of 2012—the year in which President Obama would be up for reelection—another 2.0 million jobs would be "saved or created."[17] Note that the President's advisers added "saved" to politicians' normal reference to "created jobs." This change in language partly reflected the fact that a portion of the stimulus package went to states that would otherwise have terminated jobs and trimmed some programs. Adding "saved" would also make it easier, subsequently, to respond to critics who would call the program a failure if the national jobs data did not rise by 3.5 million at the end of 2010. Such language came in handy. By the end of 2010, nonfarm payrolls were *down* by 2.5 million from February of the previous year, when the ARRA legislation was adopted!

How did President Obama's economists ever come up with the 3.5 million jobs estimate in the first place? Simply put, they multiplied the stimulus to be provided over the period ending in Q4 (2010) by an estimated multiplier of the spread effects to the economy. Then they divided this estimated incremental to GDP by $92,000—the estimated annual cost per job created. (Table 5.7 provides a more detailed example of how such calculations are performed.)

Table 5.7 Estimating Annual Jobs From Fiscal Stimulus: An Example

---

Annual jobs from stimulus = (annual fiscal stimulus) divided by jobs per $1 billion of annual stimulus

Annual fiscal stimulus[(*)] = $100 billion per year

Jobs per $1 billion stimulus = 10,000 at estimated $100,000 stimulus cost per job[(**)]

Annual jobs from stimulus = 1,000,000

[(*)]Fiscal stimulus = $50 billion higher Federal outlays and $50 billion lower taxes.
[(**)]$125,000 stimulus cost per job for tax cut with 0.75 GDP multiplier and $75,000 stimulus cost per job for higher outlays with 1.25 GDP multiplier.
SOURCE: Author's calculation.

Table 5.8   Output Effects of a Permanent Stimulus of 1 Percent of GDP

Quarter	Government Purchases	Tax Cuts
1	1.05%	0.00%
2	1.24	0.49
3	1.35	0.58
4	1.44	0.66
5	1.51	0.75
6	1.53	0.84
7	1.54	0.93
8	1.57	0.99
9	1.57	0.99
10	1.57	0.99
11	1.57	0.99
12	1.57	0.99
13	1.57	0.99
14	1.57	0.99
15	1.57	0.99
16	1.55	0.98

SOURCE: Council of Economic Advisers, "Estimates of Job Creation from the American Recovery and Reinvestment Act of 2009," May 2009.

The CEA estimated that government purchases are associated with a higher GDP multiplier than a tax cut. Specifically, a dollar of tax cuts was estimated to raise GDP by $0.66 after a year and by $0.99 after two years. A dollar of government purchases, though, was estimated to raise GDP by $1.44 after a year and by $1.57 after two years. (See Table 5.8.) Tax cuts were estimated to offer less GDP stimulation than similar amounts of government purchases, because it was assumed that relatively more of the tax cut was saved.

Critics of the CEA's calculations believed these GDP multiplier estimates for government purchases were overestimates for four important reasons:

1. The financing of the accompanying fiscal deficits raised the prospects for higher interest rates that would have negative feedback effects on the economy. This is sometimes labeled *crowding out*. Whether borrowing to finance fiscal stimulus raises interest rates will also depend on the behavior of the Federal Reserve. If the

Fed buys some or all of the incremental securities issued to finance a higher Federal budget deficit without selling other securities, it is said that the Fed is monetizing the deficit by expanding its balance sheet. Although such purchases could temporarily maintain relatively high bond prices and keep interest rates low, critics of Fed financing of the Federal deficit argue that the associated money supply expansion will be viewed by investors as being eventually inflationary—a fear that could raise longer-term interest rates.

2. Deficit financing could harm business confidence and therefore investment. This is because business leaders might be philosophically uncomfortable with the idea of the government taking actions that deliberately raise the Federal deficit and debt burden.

3. Households and firms would raise their savings and trim current consumption in anticipation of the future higher taxes required to service a gigantic Federal deficit. This is the earlier discussed Ricardian equivalence theory. Some evidence in support of this behavioral assumption is that voters routinely vote against special project bond proposals.

4. Spending by states and localities is less when Federal monies finance a larger portion of state and local programs. As a recession trims state and local tax receipts, states and localities would be forced to cut spending unless they received added Federal assistance.

Multiplier Effects: How Real Are They?

Any user or maker of forecasts naturally wants to know how much plausibility can be assumed for any given multiplier. As Keynes' followers saw it, the multiplier is the inverse of the sum of the saving rate, the marginal overall tax rate and the marginal propensity to import. (More about the Keynesian multiplier is in Chapter 6.) Plausible assumptions are a 15 percent overall (personal plus business) private saving rate, a 30 percent marginal overall tax rate and a 15 percent marginal propensity to import goods and services. The inverse of their 60 percent sum is 1.67. *Therefore, I am wary of relatively large multipliers much over 1.5.*

Why Are Some Assumed Output and Jobs Multipliers Larger Than Others?

It's because *different types of fiscal stimulus can have varying estimated impacts.* (See Figure 5.1.) For instance, military spending is assumed to have relatively less jobs impact than other types of government spending. This is partly because a portion of the Federal government's military budget is allocated to defense goods, such as aircraft and missiles, whose production is relatively capital intensive. On the other hand, spending on educational services is comparatively labor intensive and therefore spurs a greater number of jobs. Tax cuts are often assumed to have a lower jobs impact than most types of Federal spending, in part because a portion of a tax cut is saved instead of spent.

Multipliers estimated from input-output tables can vary with forecasters' assumptions when they apply the information to a specific forecast. Input-output tables are essentially recipes containing the ingredients for an industry's output. Such tables are often used to trace the effects of spending proposals on the industries and resources that provide whatever is purchased. Sometimes the information is used to estimate specific labor requirements for the various types of Federal spending in fiscal policy

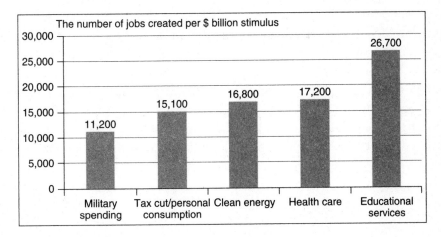

Figure 5.1 Different Impacts for the Same Amount of Initial Fiscal Stimulus
SOURCE: Robert Pollin and Heidi Garrett-Peltier, "The U.S. Employment Effects of Military and Domestic Spending," Department of Economics and Political Economy Research Institute, University of Massachusetts, December 2011.

Table 5.9 Input-Output Estimates of Negative U.S. Economic Impacts of
Potential Spending Reductions in the Budget Control Act of 2011 in Fiscal Years
2012 and 2013 (in Billions of Current Year Dollars)

Sources of Impact	Defense	Non-Defense	Total Impacts
Direct impacts	−$56.7	−$59.0	−$115.7
Total output	−$94.5	−$120.5	−$215.0
Personal earnings	−$46.5	−$62.9	−$109.4
Employment	−1,090,359	−1,047,349	−2,137,708
Direct	−325,693	−420,529	−746,222
Indirect	−282,426	−150,552	−432,978
Induced	−482,240	−476,268	−958,508

SOURCE: Stephen S. Fuller, "The Economic Impact of the Budget Control Act of 2011 on DOD and
non-DOD Agencies," report prepared for the Aerospace Industries Association, Arlington Virginia,
July 17, 2012.

proposals. But the more frequent application is in estimating which
industries and jobs will be affected by spending proposals for a particular
project (e.g., a sports stadium) or program (e.g., infrastructure).[18]

In a standard input–output analysis, three separate effects of a spending proposal are summed to provide an estimate of how it will impact
sales, incomes, and/or jobs. There are *direct impacts* accruing to the
providers of the goods and services being purchased (e.g., construction
firms). There also are *indirect impacts* accruing to the suppliers of goods
and services for the providers (e.g., materials producers). And there
also are *induced impacts* accruing to the suppliers of goods and services
that are purchased by the recipients of the direct and indirect incomes
associated with the project. (Table 5.9 provides an illustration of results
from an input-output study of the potential harm inflicted on output,
incomes, and jobs by the Budget Control Act of 2011.)

Critics of input-output studies argue that the studies often overstate
benefits due to unrealistic assumptions embodied in the input-output
tables used to estimate such benefits.[19] The four most frequently voiced
criticisms are:

1. The output "recipes" assume a fixed proportion of inputs. This is
   an unrealistic assumption as input mixes can be altered in response
   to relative input price changes.[20]

2. Government provided input-output information is often dated. This is a problem in a dynamic economy where technologies and relative prices can rapidly change.

3. Input-output studies can overlook crowding out of resources already being deployed before being diverted to the proposed project.

4. Such studies also overlook financing implications. For instance, a community may exhaust its borrowing capabilities by financing a project that prevents other projects from being financed.

Why Government Statistics Keep "Changing Their Mind"

Although some forecasters object to what can seem like slanted official policy analyses coming out of Washington, almost everyone in the profession is frustrated at times by the periodically large official revisions of already-released information from the government's statistical mills. Realistically, not much can be done to remedy this problem. It is therefore incumbent on forecasters to understand and cope with the reality.

On the first Friday of every month, the investment world is riveted to the Bureau of Labor Statistics' (BLS) monthly report on the previous month's labor market conditions. Investors know that the global stock, bond, and foreign exchange markets can suddenly move quite dramatically in response to either unexpectedly good or bad news. However, while a report containing unexpected news can evoke sharp market responses, just a month later that same report can be revised so significantly that those initial responses are more than reversed. Such temporary swings in stock and bond prices are of little consequence for the broad economy. But major changes in U.S. monetary and fiscal policies in response to economic information are not apt to be reversed quickly, even if the information on which those changes were based is substantially revised subsequently.

Consider the initially available job market information on September 13, 2012, when the Fed announced its QE3 monetary policy. At the time, the adoption of QE3 was considered a major step in U.S.

monetary policy. After increasing its balance sheet and adding reserves to the banking system (i.e., "quantitative easing" or QE) during the QE1 and QE2 programs, between June 2011 and mid-2012 the Fed had stopped expanding its balance sheet. However, as the economic recovery started to look more fragile, the Fed decided to begin expanding its balance sheet again.

The monthly jobs data were perhaps the most important factor conditioning the Fed's reappraisal of the recovery's strength before announcing QE3 on September 13, 2012. On September 7 the BLS had reported that nonfarm payrolls in August had risen by a disappointing 96,000—well under the consensus forecast of 135,000. Moreover, the reported job gains for the previous two months were revised downward. The initially reported 163,000 July increase was revised down to 141,000, and the initially reported 80,000 June rise was now reported as just a 45,000 increase.

However, on October 5—just three weeks after the Fed's decision to launch QE3—when the BLS reported a 114,000 gain in September payrolls it also revised the initially reported 96,000 August increase to a 114,000 rise and the earlier downward revised July increase of 141,000 was revised up to 192,000. Subsequently when a 171,000 October payroll rise was reported on November 2, the initially reported 96,000 August gain was revised up for a second time to a 192,000 increase— 96,000 jobs *above* the level reported on the eve of the Fed's decision to launch QE3.

This is not to say that the Fed would never had undertaken QE3 had it known that the August data was really so much stronger than initially reported. However, if that information had been in hand, the decision probably would not have come until later in the year or at the start of 2013 and possibly could have entailed a smaller magnitude of monthly securities purchases.

Fiscal policy history has also been influenced by initially reported data that were substantially revised later. In one particular case, it was GDP data. When Congress passed the $787 billion ARRA on February 17, 2009, some critics argued that it should have been even larger considering the economy's weakness. At the end of January, the Commerce Department had reported that real GDP in the fourth quarter of 2008 had fallen at a 3.8 percent annual rate. A month later at the end of February—two weeks *after* the ARRA was passed—the Commerce Department revised its estimate of the fourth quarter of 2008 real GDP decline to −6.2 percent. By the summer of 2011, the Commerce Department was estimating that the real GDP in the fourth quarter of 2008 had fallen at an annual rate of 8.9 percent—more than twice as fast as the initially reported 3.8 percent decline. Had Congress and President Obama had a more accurate gauge of the depth of the evolving recession, the initial fiscal package could have been larger and more stimulative.

These two episodes where data revisions might have impacted important national economic policies both reflect unusually large revisions. That said, they still serve as a reminder of the inevitable risks accompanying investment and business decisions relying on initially reported government data. Although the two episodes illustrate abnormally large revisions, the typical revisions to jobs and real GDP growth data still are large enough to merit caution when evaluating and extrapolating from the early reports issued on these critical data points.

The reasons for such revisions are access to more complete information with the passage of time. (See Boxes 5.1 and 5.2.) These revisions are a fact of life about which not much can be done. However, it is important to consider their potential magnitudes and directions.

The mean and mean absolute revisions for real GDP are displayed in Table 5.10 for the 1983 through 2009 period. Between the first (advance) and latest estimate, the mean absolute revision was 1.3 percent. However, there was no strong directional bias to the revisions, with the mean revision between the first and latest estimate being +0.2 percent.

As depicted in Table 5.11, for monthly nonfarm payroll changes, the mean absolute net revision from the initial estimate to the final estimate in the current decade has been 47,000. The mean revision of 40,000 indicates that, on average, revisions tended to show better job growth than initial estimates. In the current decade, when through 2014 there

Table 5.10   Quarterly Real GDP Growth Revisions (1983–2009)

Mean Absolute Revisions				Average Revisions			
1st–2nd	1st–3rd	2nd–3rd	1st–latest	1st–2nd	1st–3rd	2nd–3rd	1st–latest
0.5%	0.6%	0.2%	1.3%	0.1%	0.1%	0.0%	0.2%

SOURCE: Bureau of Economic Analysis.

Table 5.11   Monthly Nonfarm Payroll Change Revisions (000)

	Mean Absolute Revisions			Average Revisions		
	Second Minus First	Third Minus First	Net Revisions	Second Minus First	Third Minus First	Net Revisions
1970–79	59	63	99	11	26	49
1980–89	56	72	93	−10	7	−10
1990–99	39	52	95	8	26	49
2000–09	34	48	75	3	5	−15
2010–13	28	42	47	10	28	40

SOURCE: Bureau of Labor Statistics.

had yet to be a recession, the positive mean revision probably reflected, at least partly, more thorough sampling that included more small firms, which typically prosper in a recovery. On the other hand, in a recession, when credit tends to be relatively tight for smaller firms, initial estimates are likely to overstate the final number, which will include more small firms.

Box 5.1: How Does BLS Revise Monthly Payroll Data?

"The estimate of employment change is based on a monthly survey of about 560,000 worksites, selected to represent the millions of businesses throughout the country. (For simplicity, we refer to worksites as businesses even though many individual businesses provide data for multiple worksites.) In the survey sample, businesses report the total number of people who worked or received pay during the pay period that includes the 12th of the month. Although BLS uses a variety of methods to gather these reports as quickly as possible, many businesses do not have their payroll data ready to report by the scheduled date that BLS initially releases the data. In 2012, for example, the average collection rate at the time of the initial release was 73.1 percent.

"The initial estimate of job change for a month is based on the growth or loss of jobs at the businesses that have reported their data. Generally, BLS assumes that the employment situation at businesses that had reported is representative of the situation at those that had not yet reported. BLS continues to collect outstanding reports from the businesses in the sample as it prepares a second and then a third estimate for the month. With each subsequent estimate, more businesses have provided their information. In 2012, the average collection rate at the time of the third estimate for a month was 94.6 percent."

Source: Excerpts from Thomas Nardane, Kenneth Robertson, and Jill Hatch Maxfield, "Why Are There Revisions to the Jobs Numbers?" Bureau of Labor Statistics, *Beyond the Numbers* 2, no. 17 (July 2013).

Box 5.2: How Does BEA Revise GDP?

"BEA revises the NIPA estimates for two related reasons. First, the NIPAs serve a multitude of purposes, some of which require frequent and immediately available estimates and others of which require consistent, long-term time series. Second, much of the source data that BEA uses to prepare the estimates are part of statistical programs that provide, over time, more complete or otherwise better coverage—for example, monthly surveys that are superseded by an annual survey that is drawn from a larger sample or that collects more detailed information. To address this implicit tradeoff between estimates that are the most timely possible and estimates that are the most accurate possible, BEA has developed a release cycle for the NIPA estimates. This cycle progresses from current quarterly estimates, which are released soon after the end of the quarter and which are based on limited source data, to comprehensive-revision estimates, which are released about every 5 years and which incorporate the most extensive source data available.

"For GDP and most other NIPA series, the set of three current quarterly estimates are released on the following schedule. 'Advance' estimates are released near the end of the first month after the end of the quarter. Most of these estimates are based on initial data from monthly surveys for either 2 or 3 months of the quarter; where source data are not yet available, the estimates are generally based on previous trends and judgment.

"'Second' and 'third' quarterly estimates are released near the end of the second and third months, respectively; these estimates incorporate new and revised data from the monthly surveys and other monthly and quarterly source data that have subsequently become available. The current quarterly estimates provide the first look at the path of U.S. economic activity.

"Annual revisions of the NIPAs are usually carried out each summer. These revisions incorporate source data that are based on more extensive annual surveys, on annual data from other sources, and on later revisions to the monthly and quarterly source data, and they generally cover the three previous calendar years. These revised NIPA estimates improve the quality of the picture of U.S. economic activity, though the overall picture is generally similar to that shown by the current quarterly estimates.

"Comprehensive revisions are carried out at about 5-year intervals and may result in revisions that extend back for many years. These estimates incorporate the best available source data, such as data from the quinquennial U.S. Economic Census. Comprehensive revisions also provide the opportunity to make definitional, statistical, and presentational changes that improve and modernize the accounts to keep pace with the ever-changing U.S. economy."

Source: Excerpts from Bureau of Economic Analysis, "Sources and Methods of U.S. National Income and Product Accounts," Chapter 1, pp. 9–10, February 2014.

Living with Revisions

I handle the revisions challenges in two ways. First, when a typically highly revised independent variable is used as a statistical driver of a forecast, I factor its potential revisions into the range of possible errors in the forecast of the dependent variable. Second, in assessing where the economy stands at any point in time, I use conceptually similar variables to corroborate the economy's status. For instance, I compare the growth of real GDP with the behavior of the manufacturing and non-manufacturing Institute for Supply Management (ISM) business gauges. With payrolls I compare them to the unrevised ISM reports on jobs, with weekly reported initial claims for state unemployment insurance, and the Automatic Data Processing job data.

Key Takeaways

1. U.S. government-produced economic data are assembled and reported in a politically independent fashion.
2. The Executive branch of the Federal government can try to influence preelection data reports via timing government expenditures.
3. Forecasts by the President's Council of Economic Advisers tend to be more optimistic relative to forecasts by other government agencies and private sector forecasters.
4. For assessing policy issues, the researchers in the Federal Reserve System are a good source of politically independent analysis.
5. Key statistical checks on the veracity of public policy studies are omitted variables and reverse causation.
6. Beware of estimated policy multiplier output effects much above 1.5.
7. Input-output studies of benefits from proposed policies and individual infrastructure projects are prone to overstatement.

> **8.** Revisions to key GDP and jobs data are large enough to merit caution when extrapolating implications of these key driver variables.
>
> **9.** When handling data subject to sometimes large revisions, look for corroborative data.

Notes

1. Jack Welch (@jackwelch), October 5, 2012.

2. Rachel Weiner, "Jack Welch Accuses Obama of Cooking Jobs Numbers," *Washington Post*, October 5, 2012.

3. John Crudele, "Census 'Faked' 2012 Election Jobs Report," *New York Post*, November 18, 2013.

4. Nelson D. Schwartz, "Political Questions About the Jobs Report," *Economix* blog, November 20, 2013.

5. "Did Obama Manipulate Q3 GDP To Create His Election Victory?" *Economic Policy Journal*, January 30, 2013.

6. Thomas Shanker, "Reserve System Needs Change, Military Experts Believe," *New York Times*, July 4, 2004, www.nytimes.com/2004/07/04/national/04RESE.html.

7. *The Economist*, "Poor George: The Case for Pessimism About the President's Prospects," [Lexington—371] (June 26, 2004): 38.

8. George A. Krause and J. Kevin Corder," Explaining Bureaucratic Optimism: Theory and Evidence from U.S. Executive Agency Macroeconomic Forecasts," *American Political Science Review* 101, no. 1 (February 2007).

9. Robert Krol, "Comparing the Real GDP Forecast Accuracy and Loss Functions of Government Agencies," California State University, Northbridge, October 25, 2011.

10. David Reifschneider and Peter Tulip, "Gauging the Uncertainty of the Economic Outlook from Historical Forecasting Errors," Federal Reserve Board Finance and Economics Discussion Series, November 19, 2007.

11. J. Kevin Corder, "Managing Uncertainty: The Bias and Efficiency of Federal Macroeconomic Forecasts," 7th National Public Management Conference, Georgetown University, October 2003.

12. "Cato Institute Petition against Obama 2009 Stimulus Plan," http:/cato.org/special/stimulus09/cato_stimulus.pdf.

13. "The Job Impact of the American Recovery and Reinvestment Plan," White House press release, January 10, 2009, analysis provided by Christina Romer and Jared Bernstein.

14. Felix Reichling and Charles Whalen, "Assessing the Short-Term Effects on Output of Changes in Federal Fiscal Policies," Congressional Budget Office Working Paper 2012–08, May 2012.

15. Victor A. Matheson, "Mega-Events: The Effect of the World's Biggest Sporting Events on Local, Regional and National Economies," College of Holy Cross, Department of Economics Faculty Research Series Paper No. 06–10, October 2006.

16. Ibid.

17. Executive Office of the President Council of Economic Advisers, "Estimates of Job Creation from the American Recovery and Reinvestment Act of 2009," May 2009.

18. Cletus C. Coughlin and Thomas B. Mandelbaum, "A Consumer's Guide to Regional Economic Multipliers," *Federal Reserve Bank of St. Louis Review* 73, no. 1 (January/February 1991).

19. Salim Furth, "Research Review: What Can Be Learned from Local Multiplier Estimates?" The Heritage Foundation, Issue Brief No. 4011, August 8, 2013.

20. Rebecca Bess and Zoe O. Ambargis, "Input-Output Models for Impact Analysis: Suggestions for Practitioners Using RIMS II Multipliers," 50th Southern Regional Science Association Conference, New Orleans, Louisiana, March 23–27, 2011.

Chapter 6

Four Gurus of Economics

Whom to Follow?

---

*Practical men, who believe themselves to be quite exempt
from any intellectual influences, are usually the slaves of
some defunct economist.*

—John Maynard Keynes, *The General Theory of Employment,
Interest, and Money* (1936)

In forecasting, judgment is a necessary supplement to statistical techniques. But what factors should condition that judgment? In the field of economic forecasting, the selection of statistical models—and judgmental adjustments to their purely statistical prognostications—can reflect the forecaster's view of what makes the economy tick. For a forecaster, it is therefore important to recognize how one's overall ideas about the economy's workings can influence, and possibly bias, predictions.

Forecast users, too, should consider whether their views on the determinants of economic activity are influencing their selection of the particular macroeconomic forecasts they use in their planning and projections.

In financial market forecasting, I have found it especially helpful to consider how those who participate in the markets think the economy functions—even when I disagree with their ideas. The challenge I faced in forecasting bond yields during the 2009 to 2014 period, when the Federal Reserve System was implementing its quantitative easing (QE) policy, provides a good example. The policy, which aimed to reliquefy the U.S. banking system and reduce Treasury note and bond yields and mortgage rates, entailed the central bank buying huge volumes of U.S. Treasury notes and mortgage-backed securities. Because both the type and size of the program were unprecedented (it eventually cumulated to more than $3 trillion), there was not much in the way of relevant statistical history to guide me.

So in evaluating how QE might affect bond yields, I needed to consider how investors would think about its potential consequences. The Fed's massive securities purchases were injecting huge amounts of bank reserves into the U.S. banking system. From a short-term perspective, it was pretty clear that these actions would reduce interest rates. Almost all investors are familiar with basic Keynesian economic theories, which argue that an increase in bank reserves and related bank deposits (i.e., money supply) will lower rates. However, many investors have also been introduced to monetarism. One of its major tenets is that increases in money supply eventually augment price inflation. Since investors in longer-term, fixed-income securities are naturally concerned about price inflation over time, might Fed actions to boost the money supply actually raise multiyear inflation expectations and longer-term interest rates? In Chapter 11, on interest rate forecasting, we examine how to handle such contradicting possibilities. For the time being, though, the critical point is that you must understand how investors think the economy works in order to forecast their reactions to public policies such as the Fed's QE.

In forming underlying viewpoints on how the modern economy functions, there are many theories from which to choose. Moreover, my experience is that both makers and users of forecasts often change (or at least consider changing) their fundamental views during their careers. For instance, during the booming years of the 1960s, a *Time* magazine

article at the end of 1965 proclaimed "We Are All Keynesians Now."[1]
Two decades later, as the country was heading into what was then the
deepest recession since the Great Depression and President Ronald Rea-
gan proposed tax cuts to stimulate the economy, the St. Louis Federal
Reserve Bank published an article titled "We Are All Supply-Siders
Now."[2]

Four Competing Schools of Economic Thought

In this chapter, we first review the major ideas that shape how economists, businesses, and investors think about future outcomes. The goal
of this exercise is not to advocate any specific idea but, rather, to consider
the relative merits of competing approaches, and to familiarize the
reader with evolving macroeconomic thought. The leading schools are:

1. **Minskyites:** Economic thinking is frequently shaped by perceptions of what has been working recently. With that in mind, we
   begin by reviewing the financial fragility models commonly credited
   to Hyman Minsky. They are popularly perceived to be the framework that best enabled forecasting the Great Recession.
2. **Supply-Siders:** Then we discuss its predecessor in the "what worked
   recently" category—supply-side economics. This theory of economic growth became quite popular in the 1980s when President
   Reagan cut taxes and the economy posted a strong recovery from the
   serious recession at the start of that decade. The tech boom of the
   1990s was also viewed as a type of supply-side economics.
3. **Monetarists:** Before supply-side economics became popular, monetarism had been the theory du jour in the 1970s. The notion that
   the money supply is the key determinant of economic growth and
   inflation is a few centuries old. However, it recaptured the economics profession's attention during the period of rapid inflation in
   the 1970s and the subsequent Fed attempt to combat the problem
   by targeting bank reserves and the money supply.
4. **Keynesians:** Prior to monetarism, the economics of John Maynard
   Keynes was the primary school of thought in the 1950s and 1960s.
   Keynesian economics was commonly seen as the most important set
   of ideas influencing the monetary and fiscal policies that helped to
   moderate the U.S. business cycle in the postwar era.

Minskyites: Should We Keep Listening to Them?

It is understandable that forecasters, planners, and investors are tempted to place more emphasis on what has worked recently. As attention became riveted on the financial crisis accompanying the Great Recession of 2008 to 2009, an article in the November 17, 2008, edition of the *Nation* proclaimed, "We're All Minskyites Now."[3]

That headline acknowledged that, according to some of the disciples of the economist Hyman Minsky (1919–1996), the few economists forecasting the depth of the Great Recession took their cues from Professor Minsky's *financial instability hypothesis* (FIH). In the summer of 2009, the economist Dirk Bezemer—a leading proponent of Minsky's theories—documented the work of a dozen different economists who departed from consensus thinking and predicted that the evolving financial crisis would trigger a serious recession. He concluded:

> Central to the contrarians' thinking is an accounting of financial flows (of credit, interest, profit and wages) and stocks (debt and wealth) in the economy, as well as a sharp distinction between the real economy and the financial sector (including property). In these "flow-of-funds" models, liquidity generated in the financial sector flows to companies, households and the government as they borrow. This may facilitate fixed-capital investment, production and consumption, but also asset-price inflation and debt growth. Liquidity returns to the financial sector as investment of debt services and fees.[4]
>
> It follows that there is a trade-off in the use of credit, so that financial investment may crowd out the financing of production. A second key insight is that, since the economy's assets and liabilities must balance, growing financial markets find their counterpart in a growing debt burden. They also swell payment flows of debt service and financial fees. Flow-of-funds models quantify the sustainability of the debt burden and the financial sector's drain on the real economy. This allows their users to foresee when finance's relation to the real economy turns from supportive to extractive, and when a breaking point will be reached.[5]

Who Was Hyman Minsky?

Unlike the great economists John Maynard Keynes, Milton Friedman, and John Kenneth Galbraith, Hyman Minsky was hardly a household name in the worlds of investment and forecasting. In fact, a 2007 pre–Great Recession article about Minsky in the *Wall Street Journal* was titled, "In Time of Tumult, Obscure Economist Gains Currency."[6] Educated at the University of Chicago and Harvard University, Professor Minsky taught at Brown University, the University of California, Berkeley and Washington University in St. Louis. It was only posthumously during the 1998 Russian debt crisis that the economist Paul McCulley coined the term "Minsky Moment."[7]

What Distinguished Minsky's Theories?

Minsky was a Keynesian economist who, unlike pre-Keynesian classical economists, believed that markets did not naturally self-correct when imbalances developed. Key to Minsky's thinking was his earlier mentioned FIH (financial instability hypothesis). According to this hypothesis, with prosperity comes so-called irrational exuberance on the part of businesses and investors. This sets the stage for investment disappointments and another prerecession financial crisis. Specifically, "Minsky maintained that endogenous economic forces breed financial and economic instability."[8] In other words, after an economy starts to recover from a recession or earlier financial crisis, investors and lenders regain their confidence and start taking on more risk. And with growing confidence and less risk aversion comes more leveraged investments, lending into sectors formerly deemed to be too risky, and increasing financial fragility. When the more risky investments eventually but inevitably turn sour, leveraged lenders and investors experience cash shortfalls that must be addressed by selling less risky and more liquid investments. In this setting, lenders are setting tighter credit standards and asset prices are falling, leading to an exacerbated financial crisis that "feeds on itself" and triggers recession.

While Minsky's description of the financial roots of the business cycle was a familiar history, mainstream economists had trouble accepting FIH. This was partly because of their belief in the well-known and increasingly popular efficient market hypothesis, which maintains that rationality and widespread information will insure that asset markets do not become dangerously overvalued or undervalued. Despite a historical record rife with repetitive cycles of overextended lending institutions and markets, economists and investors apparently believe that improved information availability and processing are a vaccine against lapses of discipline in lending and investing. Minsky, on the other hand, was generally skeptical of financial innovation. Also, in his view, "money manager capitalism" was becoming ever more prevalent. Assets were increasingly managed by institutional investors, who competed against each other and had a shorter-term investment horizon than traditional individual and bank investors did.

Why Were Minskyites Largely Ignored for So Long?

After the Great Recession, some of Minsky's disciples seemed to relish what they saw as vindication of Minsky's pessimistic view of evolving financial systems. Dirk Bezemer has extensively documented the failure of big econometric models at major forecasting institutions to predict the Great Recession. In his view, it was because they ignored Minsky's analytical framework and warnings.[9] It is fair to ask, in retrospect, why most forecasters before the Great Recession failed to build Minsky's pessimistic prognosis into their forecasts.

One answer is that, from the perspective of investors, business planners and forecasters, warnings about the severe consequences of financial overleverage had generally turned out to be somewhat exaggerated in the quarter-century before the Great Recession. To be sure, there were financial crises associated with overextended U.S. savings and loan institutions in the late 1980s, the Asian financial market crash and the failure of the much overlevered Long-Term Capital Management hedge fund in the 1990s. But despite these crises, the recessions at the start of the 1990s and in 2001 were comparatively mild, and the subsequent economic expansions were relatively robust.

Academic economists had additional reasons for ignoring Minsky. He and his followers were so-called institutional economists.[10] For more than a century, their school of thought de-emphasized the role of markets in determining economic outcomes. Instead, they believe that markets are a reflection of an economy's key institutional characteristics (e.g., laws, customs, and industrial organization). Consequently, these economists have often viewed their profession's continued efforts to develop mathemati-cal models of market (and market participants') behavior with disdain. In his 1986 book, *Stabilizing an Unstable Economy*, Minsky stated that "the policy failures since the mid-1960s are related to the banality of orthodox economic analysis . . . . Only an economics that is critical of capitalism can be a guide to successful policy for capitalism."[11]

In the view of academicians, according to Charles Kindleberger—a Minsky follower—Minsky was "a man with a reputation among mon-etary theorists for being particularly pessimistic, even lugubrious, in his emphasis on the fragility of the monetary system and its propensity to disaster."[12] (Note: Professor Kindleberger is well known for authoring the highly influential "Manias, Panics and Crashes: A History of Finan-cial Crises.")[13]

During my career, I have taken institutional-oriented economists' warnings about the growing dangers of financial leverage seriously. I was an undergraduate student at a University of Texas Economics Department that, contrary to convention, emphasized the institutional economists' approach to economic analysis. Consequently, I have been reluctant to ignore forecasts that are based on an understanding of how financial institutions operate, even when these analyses seemed to ignore modern theories of macroeconomic and microeconomic behavior.

In fact, Professor Minsky personally reinforced my thinking when I forecast the 1990 recession. That forecast reflected my research, which highlighted a correlation between bank lending conditions and reces-sions. Specifically, I had studied historical information from the Federal Reserve's Senior Loan Officer Opinion Survey of Bank Lending prac-tices (see the example in Figure 6.1), and my calculations indicated that the net percentage of banks tightening their business lending stan-dards had risen to levels that preceded earlier recessions. I presented this research at a monetary economics seminar at Columbia University in the autumn of 1990. Professor Minsky was in attendance, and he com-mented that the Fed loan officer survey data was a good way to quantify a credit crunch.

Most forecasters, though, generally dismissed the warnings by Min-sky and his followers about the dire consequences of too much leverage. And their reluctance to embrace Minskyite prophecies is understand-able. After all, the two most serious recessions in the mid-1970s and

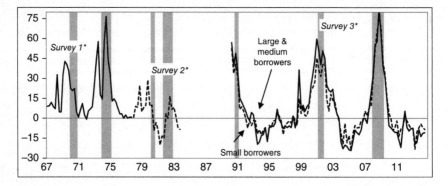

Figure 6.1   The Net Percentage of Banks Tightening Business-Lending Standards* Illustrates the Cyclical Changes in Credit Conditions That Are Key to Minsky's Business Cycle Theory
NOTE: Shaded areas represent recessions.
*Since 1990, banks have been asked about "standards to approve commercial and industrial loans or credit lines" to firms according to size. By contrast, from 1978 to 1983, banks were asked about "standards to qualify for the prime rate," and between 1967 and 1977, about "standards for loans to nonfinancial businesses." The question asked between 1978 and 1983 was considerably narrower than the earlier, more general standards question. From 1984 through 1989 this question was not asked in any manner.
SOURCE: Federal Reserve Board of Governors.

early 1980s could be attributed to surging oil prices and anti-inflation monetary policies. And the comparatively mild 2001 recession could be linked to the collapse of the earlier tech boom. Thus, one could explain most recent recessions by factors other than leverage.

Mainstream economists were aware of the problems accompanying excessive leverage, but they believed these problems could be contained quickly enough to prevent the economy from falling into anything approaching the Great Recession. The savings and loan crisis of the late 1980s had resulted in a credit crunch that was at the root of the 1991 recession. But it was mild by historical standards, partly because of a large-scale, temporary real estate asset purchase program conducted by the government-sponsored Resolution Trust Corporation. And the Federal Reserve had been able to orchestrate a financial industry bailout program following the collapse of the Long-Term Capital Management hedge fund in 1998. Many economists had confidence in the tools at the government's disposal.

Economists had other reasons, too, to discount the very serious potential downside consequences of rising leverage. They had

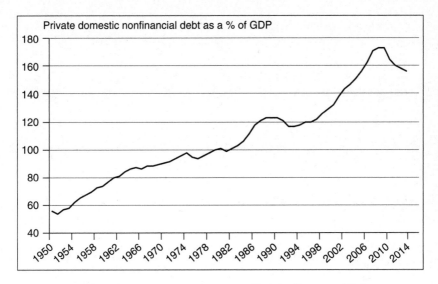

Figure 6.2 There Has Been a Longer-Term Trend of Increased Private Sector Leverage

SOURCE: Federal Reserve Board of Governors, Bureau of Economic Analysis.

been watching private sector leverage increase for almost 60 years (see Figure 6.2). Since the economy was usually expanding and becoming more prosperous during that time, it was not at all obvious if—or when—the level of debt was becoming toxic.

In the household sector, the percentage of families having access to and using credit was rising over time. Did more debt as a percentage of personal income mean there was too much debt per debtor, or was it simply that a greater fraction of the population was using credit? Also, the burden of debt service is partially determined by interest rate levels, and these are quite different at different stages of the business cycle. (Note: The role of debt in forecasting consumer spending will be discussed in far more detail in Chapter 9.)

In the business sector, how much debt was too much debt depended on whether borrowed money was successfully invested in productive assets. In other words, business liabilities needed to be judged, in part, against the size and quality of business assets.

Economists' thinking on overall debt was also conditioned by their acceptance of government deficit financing. It is a key element in the countercyclical tax and spending policies advocated in the often-popular

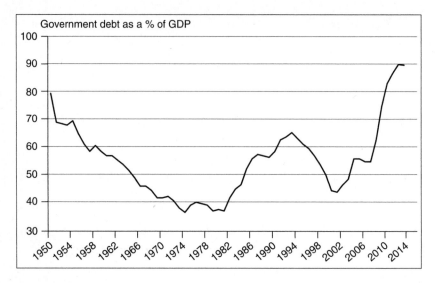

Figure 6.3   Many Mainstream Academic Economists Were Not Particularly
Alarmed by Rising Public Sector Leverage
SOURCE: Federal Reserve Board of Governors, Bureau of Economic Analysis.

Keynesian economics framework. Using Federal deficit financing to
combat recessions was thought to reinvigorate the economy and its
related Federal tax revenues. Public debt also went along with some
economists' ideas on the optimum amount of resources dedicated to the
public sector. Thus, most mainstream economists were not particularly
alarmed by higher public debt as a percent of GDP. (See Figure 6.3.)
In my view, the thought process underlying the economics profession's
approval of public sector debt also shaped how economists viewed
private sector debt. *Whether debt was good or bad for the economy depended
not so much on its quantity but on how the funds were being deployed.*

What Are Minskyites Telling Post–Great Recession Forecasters to Do Differently?

Minsky's followers believe that mainstream economists failed to forecast
the severity of the Great Recession because they did not place enough
emphasis on financial sector leverage. Financial sector debt as a percent
of GDP had been soaring during recent decades. (See Figure 6.4.) When
the Great Recession began in 2008, financial sector debt was two-thirds

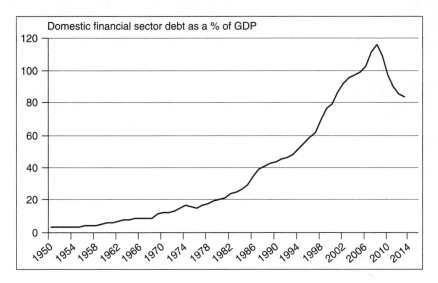

Figure 6.4 Minskyites Focus on Financial Sector Leverage
SOURCE: Federal Reserve Board of Governors, Bureau of Economic Analysis.

the size of overall private domestic nonfinancial debt—double what it had been 20 years earlier.

In order to better reflect the financial sector's role in the overall economy, Minsky disciple Dirk Bezemer has proposed what are known as *accounting* or *flow-of-funds models*.[14] In his words, these models "represent households', firms', and governments' balance sheets and their interrelations."

"More specifically," he added, "the balance sheets of firms, households and governments, and the regulations in the economic system on what sorts of balance sheets are being allowed, co-determine what forms new credit flows can take, how much there can be of it to different sectors (e.g., the finance, insurance and real estate (FIRE) sector versus the real economy), and consequently how the economy will evolve."

Bezemer explains that "Key features of such models include (a) the circular flow of goods and money, (b) a separate representation of stocks (inventories, wealth and debt) and flows (goods, services and funds), (c) explicit modeling of the financial sector as distinct from the real economy, so allowing for independent growth and contraction effects from finance on the economy, (d) non-optimizing behavior by economic

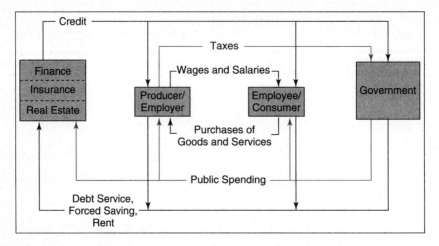

Figure 6.5   A Flow of Funds Accounting Model
SOURCE: Michael Hudson, "The Road to Serfdom: An Illustrated Guide to the Coming Real Estate Collapse," *Harper's*, April 2006.

agents in an environment of uncertainty, and (e) accounting identities (not the equilibrium concept) as determinants of model outcomes in response to shocks in the environment or in policy."[15] A graphical summary cited by Bezemer is reproduced in Figure 6.5.

What Should Forecasters Learn from Minskyites?

Whether forecasters are developing a large-scale mathematical or statistical macroeconomic forecasting model, or aiming to weigh all relevant considerations in forming their judgmental projections, they can benefit from some of the Minskyites' research and analysis. To be sure, economic forecasters almost always consider at least some of the financial issues raised by Minsky and his followers. However, some key elements of the Minskyite analysis distinguish their approach and serve as important reminders for the forecasting community at large.

I believe *one of Minsky's key contributions was his utilization of an institutional economics research approach.* As earlier discussed, this entails focus on how financial institutions evolve and operate, instead of how markets momentarily set prices and clear. For example, consider the mortgage-backed bond fiasco that helped trigger the financial crisis preceding the Great Recession. In retrospect, financial analysts should have devoted more time to understanding how subprime mortgage loans were being originated and then assembled in mortgage asset pools instead of focusing on the pricing of mortgage-backed securities.

- *The flow of funds approach directs attention on the roles of specific types of suppliers and demanders of financial assets.* For instance, what are the characteristics and evolving objectives of specific credit suppliers (e.g., insurance companies, foreign central banks and bond funds)?
- *Remembering historical swings in investor psychology and enthusiasm provides an important perspective on future market values.* At times this analytical emphasis is more important for private securities valuations than traditional earnings estimates are.

That said, there are a few caveats about the Minsky approach to forecasting. First, there are analytical risks of overreacting, as well as underreacting, to leverage trends. My experience is that forecasters who almost always bemoan rising household leverage have often underestimated consumer-spending growth. Second, forecasters' and regulators' scrutiny of financial sector leverage has much improved since the Great Recession. This is partly because Minsky's followers were eventually proven right about the potentially disastrous economic consequences of leverage when it becomes too high and too risky.

Monetarists: Do They Deserve More Respect?

Economists' present interest in the earlier, underappreciated ideas of Hyman Minsky should remind us not to dismiss analytical frameworks simply because they are not in vogue. My experience is that the perception of "what's working nowadays" is sensitive to current events and recent history. As a result, change over time in perceived appropriate paradigms is inevitable. One of my candidates for a macroeconomic theory that was ignored, embraced, ignored again, and now very possibly due for a comeback, is monetarism.

Monetarism—the concept that the money supply is an important leading indicator of economic growth and inflation—is now a few centuries old. Its most influential 20th-century advocate was Professor Milton Friedman. In 1963, he and his colleague Anna Schwartz co-authored

A Monetary History of the United States.[16] In it, they argued that cycles in the U.S. money supply preceded major turning points in the business cycle. Most importantly, Friedman and Schwartz believed that the Great Depression would not have been nearly as serious had the Federal Reserve not allowed a collapse in the money supply.

Academic economists were initially skeptical of the Friedman and Schwartz monetary interpretation of business cycles. Most economists in the postwar period had been educated about Keynesian economics. As we discuss, Keynesians believed that monetary policies on money supply and interest rates were inadequate tools for preventing and addressing recessions. Instead, changes in tax rates and government spending were thought to be more important countercyclical instruments than the Fed's monetary policy.

Monetarism attracted more interest in the late 1960s—and throughout the 1970s—with the dramatic pickup in price inflation. The monetarists linked this rise to money supply increases (see Figure 6.6), and they argued that containing monetary growth was a key to controlling inflation. For reasons that we shall discuss next, many economists remained skeptical about the link between money supply and inflation.

However, one very important economist was much more attuned to monetarism. He was Paul Volcker, the incoming Fed Chairman,

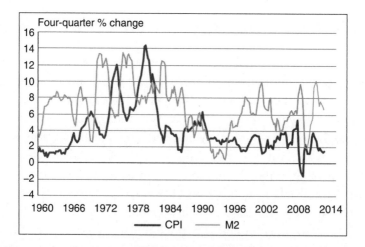

Figure 6.6 M2 Money Supply Growth and CPI Inflation
SOURCE: Bureau of Labor Statistics, Federal Reserve Board of Governors.

who took office in August of 1979, a time of rapidly accelerating inflation. In October of that year, the Fed's Federal Open Market Committee (FOMC) announced that, to better combat inflation, Fed policy would be based on targeting monetary aggregates, specifically banks' nonborrowed reserves, instead of the overnight federal funds rate—a key to overall interest rate levels.

Three decades later, when the economy was entering the Great Recession, the Fed, under Chairman Ben Bernanke, began targeting another financial aggregate—the size of the central bank's balance sheet. The expansion of the Fed's balance sheet via securities purchases has been known as quantitative easing (QE). To be sure, the Fed and many other observers have viewed QE as a tool for controlling interest rates. However, among economists and investors familiar with monetarism, there has been the fear that the huge volumes of bank reserves accompanying massive Fed asset purchases will eventually be followed by faster money supply growth and inflation.

A Quick Review of How the Money Supply Influences the Economy

When the Fed expands its balance sheet by purchasing assets, the sellers of those assets receive a payment from the Fed that essentially represents new money (aka fiat money) for the private banking system. Initially after this transaction is completed, private banks' deposit reserves held at Federal Reserve regional banks increase. With more deposits on the asset side of their balance sheet, private banks have the potential to expand loans by an amount equal to the new deposits (minus the incremental reserves that must be held at the Fed against private banks' higher deposit liabilities).

The recipients of those loans then have more private bank demand deposits. When these borrowers spend the proceeds of their loans, the recipients of these proceeds then have more income and deposits to place somewhere in the banking system. The banks receiving these deposits must hold a certain amount of required reserves at the Fed, diminishing their potential incremental lending power by the amount of those required reserves. As that potential lending power is converted to loans, more new deposits are created in the private banking system.

This chain-reaction process can continue until the banking system no longer has lendable reserves. Actual loan and deposit expansion is also affected by the public's demand for nondeposit cash, which reduces banks' deposits and their loanable funds. Another factor limiting bank loan and deposit expansion is the amount of reserves, above what is required by law, which banks choose to hold at the Fed. Statistically, the resulting ratio of the overall money supply to the monetary base—bank reserves plus currency in circulation—is called the *money multiplier.*

The deposits created in this process add to the nation's money supply. When these deposits are spent, the country's gross domestic product (GDP) increases. And as the incomes from producing that GDP are spent, GDP is further enhanced. The level of GDP versus the entire money supply is referred to as the *velocity of money.*

Criticisms of Monetarism

The erratic velocity of money has been the major reason that many economists are wary of using the money supply to forecast GDP. (See in Figure 6.7: The velocity of M2—currency in circulation, demand deposits, time deposits, and money market mutual funds.) Between the mid-1980s and mid-1990s, for example, a rising velocity of money meant that forecasters using historical relationships of the money supply to GDP would underestimate GDP growth. After the mid-1990s, monetary velocity was usually falling. Consequently, GDP would be overestimated if forecasts were based on those same historical relationships.

In defending monetarism with regard to the velocity issue, monetarists like Professor Friedman argued that the money supply affected nominal GDP with long and variable lags. If the lags were long and stable, a charted relationship between nominal GDP and lagged, earlier money supply growth would appear close. In other words, velocity—calculated as GDP divided by the lagged money supply—would not exhibit much variability. The variability in lags between monetary growth and nominal GDP growth meant that observed velocity, however calculated, would appear variable.

The debate between monetarism and its critics about long and variable lags offers some perspective on an issue that is always challenging to forecasters who seek to identify cause-and-effect relationships. Some critics contended that the

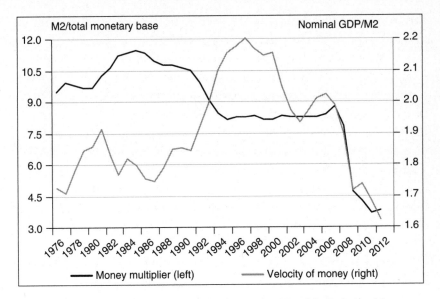

Figure 6.7 Critics of Monetarism Emphasize the Unstable Relationships between GDP Relative to the Money Supply (i.e., Velocity) and the Money Supply versus the Monetary Base (i.e., Money Multiplier)
SOURCE: Federal Reserve Board of Governors, Bureau of Economic Analysis.

concept of long and variable causal lags permitted almost any factor to be credited for eventually causing some future event. At the very least, they said, variable observed lags between hypothesized causes and their effects suggested that there were probably a number of contributing causes for a subsequent event. For their part, the monetarists conceded that factors other than the money supply played a role in subsequent GDP growth, but maintained that the money supply was the only causal variable that mattered much.

The Fed formally adopted the money supply as an important variable guiding its monetary policy in 1979. Fourteen years later, the Fed abandoned it. In July 1993, Federal Chairman Alan Greenspan testified to Congress that the Fed would no longer use monetary aggregates to guide FOMC interest rate policy. He stated that, "At one time, M2 was useful both to guide Federal Reserve policy and to communicate the thrust of monetary policy to others. . . . The so-called P-star model, developed in the late 1980s, embodied a long-run relationship between M2 and prices that could anchor policy over extended periods of time.

But that long-run relationship also seems to have broken down with the persistent rise in M2 velocity. . . ."[17]

Two decades later, however, economists are still trying to determine whether changes in the Fed's balance sheet and in the private banking system's reserves have had much subsequent influence on GDP. Just as the Great Inflation of the 1970s forced the Fed to shift its focus to the money supply, the financial crisis accompanying the Great Recession caused the Fed to shift its emphasis from interest rates to another financial aggregate—its balance sheet. The Fed responded aggressively to the dramatic deterioration of the national economy and its financial underpinnings by sharply reducing the Federal funds rate on overnight money—its traditional interest rate tool—from 5.25 percent the summer of 2007 to a range of 0 percent to 0.25 percent by the end of 2008. However, with the economy and the financial system still reeling, the Fed had to start offering another type of support.

In November of 2008, the Fed announced that it would commence large-scale purchases of mortgage-backed securities for its own portfolio. That was followed by a March 2009 announcement that the Fed would broaden its securities purchases program to include U.S. Treasury notes and bonds. This expansion of the Fed's balance sheet—known as quantitative easing (QE)—was what monetarists emphasized that the Fed had failed to do in the early 1930s, as the economy was sinking into the Great Depression and the Fed's balance sheet and the nation's money supply fell sharply. According to the monetarists, had the Fed aggressively expanded its balance sheet and provided liquidity to the banking system back then, the collapse in the money supply could have been averted. By allowing the money supply to plummet, argued the monetarists, the Fed permitted what could have been another temporary recession to become the Great Depression of the 1930s.

Seven decades later when the Fed initiated its QE balance sheet expansion program, the central bank's emphasis was on how its securities purchases could reduce longer-term interest rates rather than specifically boost the money supply. Fed economists had dismissed the money supply as a cause of the business cycle. However, they did believe that a higher Fed balance sheet achieved with securities purchases could provide critical support to the economy via lower interest rates and associated positive wealth effects. The latter would occur as sellers of securities to the Fed would purchase other financial assets, whose prices would start to recover.

Although QE was not undertaken for purposes of directly boosting the money supply, skeptics of QE's potential effectiveness repeated the same argument used against the monetarist school of thought. That argument was that monetary policy, whether it emphasized the money supply or interest rates, was akin to pushing on a string. In other often used words, you can lead a horse to water but you cannot make it drink. And as the economy only slowly recovered from the Great Recession, QE's critics adopted an "I told you so" attitude and frequently opined that the securities purchasing program should be terminated or at least dramatically cutback (i.e., "tapered"). However, *the failure of the economy to rapidly recover with QE does not mean that forecasters should ignore the monetarist viewpoint in considering the GDP outlook.*

There are several reasons not to dismiss monetarist arguments. In the first place, the fall in monetary velocity and in the money multiplier during QE (see Figure 6.7) hardly justifies concluding that central bank balance sheet expansion is ineffective. The over $3 trillion growth of the Fed's balance sheet between 2008 and mid-2014 represented an unprecedented injection of liquidity into the banking system. Thus, it was unrealistic to think that banks would be able to use the associated rise in deposits to make new loans immediately. But by 2011, the private banking system's loans began to recover.

Second, it is incorrect to judge QE's effectiveness by the initially slow rise of post–Great Recession GDP. QE was hardly the only element affecting growth. A tightening of overall governmental fiscal policy until 2014, along with many other factors, contributed as well. Numerous studies conducted with a variety of methodologies have concluded that economic growth would have been noticeably weaker had it not been for QE's constructive effects on interest rates, and on real estate and stock market wealth recoveries also.[18]

Third, if we accept the monetarists' claim that money supply and interest rates influence the economy with long and variable lags, then it is premature to judge QE's ultimate impact by examining only GDP growth between 2008 and 2014, the period of the QE policy. As of mid-2014 when the QE securities purchasing program was being phased out, private banks, as a result of earlier QE, still had around $3 trillion in cash held as excess reserves at the Fed. To be sure, banks cannot convert such cash into loans unless there is adequate demand. But having so much cash and cheap deposits in the banking system created incentives for banks to expand their loan activity by easing their lending standards. Lending standards, in turn, are a leading indicator of future economic activity as easier standards eventually generate more loan demand.

Supply-Siders: Still a Role to Play?

Any student of economic fashion will remember that between the reign of monetarism in the 1970s and the more recent fascination with Minskyites' models, the 1980s and 1990s saw the rise of supply-side economics. In the words of the economist Arthur Laffer—probably the most well-known advocate of supply-side economics: "Supply-side economics emphasizes economic growth achieved by tax and fiscal policy that creates incentives to produce goods and services. In particular, supply-side economics has focused primarily on lowering marginal tax rates with the purpose of increasing the after-tax return from work and investment, which result in increases in supply. The broader supply-side policy mix points to the importance of sound money; free-trade; less regulation; low, flat-rate taxes; and spending restraint, as the keys to real economic growth."[19]

Supply-side economics dates back to the classical economists who, over 250 years ago, wrote about prices, taxes, markets and incentives. Prior to the Great Depression, the economics profession's understanding of the economy was primarily shaped by a belief in markets as mechanisms best left untouched by government interference in the form of regulation and taxes. As we discussed in Chapter 3, the Great Depression caused economists to question their assumption that market forces alone would always lead to satisfactory market clearing conditions, and it led the profession to view government intervention in the regulatory and taxation spheres more favorably.

However, there still were influential thinkers who viewed taxation and regulation as potentially harmful for longer-term economic growth. There was Ayn Rand, for instance, who in 1957 published what has become one of the most important works of fiction influencing conservative economic thought about supply-side economics. It was titled *Atlas Shrugged*.[20] In this story, the economy's crucial business leadership class essentially went on strike in reaction to government regulation and taxation. At the time it was written, the top U.S. Federal marginal income tax rate was 91 percent in the everyday world of nonfiction.

Rand's influence was largely confined to a group of intellectuals. Supply-side economics became a more popularly understood concept in the 1970s thanks to an economist, Arthur Laffer, and a politician, Republican Congressman Jack Kemp representing Buffalo and upstate New York. Laffer became famous for representing in a curve the concept that once tax rates rose beyond a certain level, further rate increases would actually reduce tax revenues because of their disincentive effects on the economy's supply of labor, capital, and investment. Professor Laffer did not identify any specific tax rate level triggering such an adverse impact, but Congressman Kemp argued that in the 1970s such a high level of taxation had already been reached. Thus, he proposed a 30 percent across-the-board cut in Federal income tax rates, arguing that the government would not lose any revenue because of the positive incentive effects of lower marginal tax rates.

President Ronald Reagan also believed in this version of supply-side economics. The Economic Recovery Act of 1981 resulted in a 23 percent cut in Federal marginal income-tax rates and, ever since, the economics profession has been debating whether this policy ever worked as initially advertised. Democratic economists advising President Bill Clinton in the 1990s did not believe that tax rates were near the "disincentive inflexion point" of the Laffer curve, and in the Omnibus Budget Reconciliation Act of 1993 the top Federal marginal income tax rate was raised from 31 percent to 39.6 percent. The subsequent period of stronger than generally expected economic growth led many observers to believe that tax rate increases are not necessarily harmful. After the turn of the century, though, President George W. Bush viewed tax cuts as being helpful, and the top Federal marginal income tax rate was reduced from 39.6 percent to 35.0 percent. (See history of U.S. Federal income tax brackets in Table 6.1.)

Table 6.1 History of Income-Tax Rates Adjusted for Inflation (1913–2010)

Year	Number of Brackets	First Bracket Rate (%)	Top Bracket			Comment
			Rate (%)	Income ($)	Adj. 2011 ($)	
1913	7	1	7	500,000	11.3M	First permanent income tax
1917	21	2	67	2,000,000	35M	World War I financing
1925	23	1.5	25	100,000	1.28M	Postwar reductions
1932	55	4	63	1,000,000	16.4M	Depression era
1936	31	4	79	5,000,000	80.7M	
1941	32	10	81	5,000,000	76.3M	World War II
1942	24	19	88	200,000	2.75M	Revenue Act of 1942
1944	24	23	91	200,000	2.54M	Individual Income Tax Act of 1944
1946	24	20	91	200,000	2.30M	
1964	26	16	77	400,000	2.85M	Tax reduction during Vietnam war
1965	25	14	70	200,000	1.42M	
1981	16	14	70	212,000	532k	Reagan era tax cuts
1982	14	12	50	106,000	199k	Reagan era tax cuts
1987	5	11	38.5	90,000	178k	Reagan era tax cuts
1988	2	15	28	29,750	56k	Reagan era tax cuts
1991	3	15	31	82,150	135k	Omnibus Budget Reconciliation Act of 1990
1993	5	15	39.6	250,000	388k	Omnibus Budget Reconciliation Act of 1993
2003	6	10	35	311,950	380k	Bush tax cuts
2011	6	10	35	379,150	379k	
2013	7	10	39.6	400,000	388k	American Taxpayer Relief Act of 2012

NOTE: M = millions; k = thousands
SOURCE: Tax Foundation.

Although Republican politicians continue to advocate supply-side economic policies for the country's economic future, should forecasters take supply-side economics seriously in projecting U.S. GDP growth over a multiyear horizon? My experience is that many investors and business leaders are sympathetic to at least the logic of supply-side economics. Moreover, I have frequently observed that in the United States, for one, investors' and business leaders' expressed enthusiasm, or lack thereof, with regard to future economic growth prospects is conditioned by their beliefs about taxes and government regulation.

For forecasters, there are four reasons why supply-side economics is a topic they must address.

1. Supply-side economics relates to the labor force participation rate, capital spending, and productivity—important determinants of potential GDP growth.

2. Taxation and business regulation are a political football. With inevitable swings in political power, forecasters over the course of their careers will be periodically challenged to assess the economic implications of changes in taxes and regulation. As much slower growth of the working age population likely starts to spell more pervasive labor shortages in the next few years, supply-side tax cuts aimed at raising the labor force participation rate will almost surely be an issue in the 2016 Presidential election.

3. If enough investors and business decision makers view supply-side economic policies as important, then changing government regulatory and taxation policies can start to have results that are self-fulfilling prophesies.

4. Supply-side economics concepts are important for estimating government revenues. Many politicians and some economists argue that Federal budget deficit estimates should reflect supply-side feedbacks on the economy—"dynamic scoring." (For instance, in early 2013 the United States Senate adopted an amendment to the concurrent budget resolution for fiscal 2014 that would require the Congressional Budget Office and the Joint Committee on Taxation to derive estimates of the revenue effects of tax changes that include their macroeconomic feedbacks.)

Some Studies on Supply-Side Economics

Most economists, in principle at least, are sympathetic to the logic that tax rates can influence the labor supply and capital formation. However, there has been a good deal of skepticism about whether such effects are very large. Proponents of supply-side economics point to the economy's rapid growth in the 1980s following the Reagan tax cuts. Opponents of supply-side economics also like to point out that in the following decade there was much improved growth after top marginal tax rates were increased, which supposedly illustrates that any negative effects must be minor. Supply-siders respond that the years of rapid growth after the Clinton tax increase reflected the tech boom, which had little to do with President Clinton's fiscal policies. *My reading of the evidence is that tax rate effects on the labor supply are not very significant, although there is some research suggesting a more substantial impact on entrepreneurship.*

For example, consider some conclusions of studies on the behavioral responses to the sharp reduction in marginal tax rates that were part of the Tax Reform Act of 1986. Economists Robert Moffitt and Mark Wilhelm report finding "essentially no responsiveness of the hours of work of high-income men to the tax reduction."[21] But they do acknowledge other research suggesting that the married female labor force participation is sensitive, although only by a small amount, to tax rates. A relatively low response of the overall labor supply to tax rate changes makes sense. In order to maximize their after-tax incomes, firms and households must maximize pretax incomes, which they can control via their labor force participation. Rising tax rates lower after-tax real wages, but very few of us can afford to stop working.

What about marginal income-tax rate impacts on entrepreneurs' capital investment decisions? Economists Robert Carroll, Douglas Holtz-Eakin, Mark Rider, and Harvey S. Rosen studied the income tax returns of a sample of sole proprietors before and after the Tax Reform Act of 1986.[22] In comparing these two periods, they concluded that a 5 percentage point rise in marginal income tax rates would cause a 10 percent reduction in the fraction of entrepreneurs who make capital investment and their mean investment expenditures. Such a finding seems reasonable. Because small firms often are capital-constrained and often face limited access to outside financing, a cut in taxes raises their after-tax cash flows, thereby permitting more investment.

I am very cautious about using behavioral evidence from more than a half century ago to draw any conclusions about contemporary actions. However, such evidence can corroborate other more recent research. With that in mind, consider the conclusions of economists Christina and David Romer, who have studied the revenue effects of large swings in the Federal marginal income-tax rate in the period between World War I and World War II.[23] The top marginal income-tax rate fell from 77 percent at the end of World War I to 24 percent in 1929 before rising up to 79 percent in 1936. In those years, they report that the top 0.2 percent of the income distribution paid approximately 95 percent of the individual income tax. Thus, the interwar years, are a useful period for examining the effects of marginal tax rates on the behavior of the wealthy. The Romers conclude that higher marginal tax rates on the wealthy had just minor negative disincentive effects on work effort. They estimate that the elasticity of taxable income with respect to the tax rate was -0.2. That means that a 10 percent rise in the marginal income tax rate would lead to a smaller 2 percent fall in taxable income. Thus, overall tax revenues would rise by 8 percent. On the other hand, the Laffer curve theory argues that at relatively high marginal tax rates there would be more than a 10 percent decline in taxable income in response to a 10 percent rise in the marginal tax rate. However, the Romers also conclude that while they found "no evidence that cuts in marginal tax rates increased machinery investment or business construction," there was "evidence suggesting that they increased business formation."

Keynesians: Are They Just Too Old-Fashioned?

Supply-side economists often frame their creed as an alternative to the more traditional demand-side economics identified with the famed British economist John Maynard Keynes. My view is that *successful forecasters should blend both supply-side and demand-side considerations, with the relative mix dependent on the state of the current economy and the forecast horizon.* When unemployment is rising or still high, demand-side economics issues are key, although some supply-side concepts (e.g., incentives) remain relevant. At times of comparatively low unemployment and relatively high capacity utilization, supply-side issues take on more importance. For short-term forecast horizons, demand-side economics questions usually are key. However, for multiyear forecasting at most stages of the business cycle, supply-side economics becomes more important for determining how far the economy can go before it hits critical resource constraints.

Most forecasters organize their analysis on the framework built by Keynes and his disciples. When Milton Friedman—the founder of modern monetarism—was famously quoted as saying, "we're all Keynesians," what he meant, in part, was that he and his fellow economists used the common language system developed for the economics profession by Keynes and his followers.[24] At the same time, when Republican President Nixon surprised some conservatives by stating "I'm a Keynesian now," he was speaking about something different: the proactive public policies advocated by Keynesians. The Keynesian framework, in other words, has been broad enough to encompass a variety of ideological and public policy perspectives.

Organizing Consistent Demand-Side Components

The most basic Keynesian formulation is as follows. Gross domestic product (GDP)—which is equivalent to national incomes (often represented in textbooks by the letter "Y")—equals the sum of consumer spending (C), investment in housing, inventories, plant and equipment (I), government spending (G), and exports (X) minus imports (M). Consumer spending (C) depends on income (Y), the personal tax rate (t), the saving rate (s) and the import share of consumer spending (m).

The common algebraic rearrangement of terms in this equation yields C being equal to the sum of I + G + X divided by the sum of t, s, and m. (See Figure 6.8.) This expression has important implications for both forecasters and forecast users as they judge whether the components of a GDP forecast are credibly consistent.

For example, forecast consumption growth should be fairly close to the growth of the sum of housing and investment, government spending, and exports. Why? Because these three statistics are pivotal for the cyclical variability of overall wages and salaries that fuel consumer spending. In 2012, for instance, jobs in government, durable goods manufacturing, construction, and real estate generated almost 30 percent of wage and salary incomes. Thus, if forecast consumer spending is sharply higher

Gross domestic product (GDP)	= C + I + G + X − M
Consumer spending (C)	= (I + G + X)/(s + t + m)
Multiplier (see explanation in text)	= 1/(s + t + m)

GDP = Gross Domestic Product
C   = Consumer spending
I   = Investment in inventories, housing, plant and equipment
G   = Government spending
X   = Exports
M   = Imports
s   = Marginal propensity to save
t   = Marginal tax rate
m   = Marginal propensity to import

Figure 6.8   Key Formulas in Standard Keynesian GDP Model

than the forecast sum of government spending, fixed investment, inventory spending, and exports, how is this growth in consumer spending supposed to happen? If we look at the GDP components, how can household income grow quickly enough to support the forecast spending growth? For that to occur, there must be explicit recognition that either personal tax rates and/or the personal saving rate are declining.

Over the business cycle, the construction, real estate, and durables manufacturing industries are the most variable elements of wage and salary growth—a key swing factor for total consumer incomes and spending. For instance, in 2008 those three sectors represented just 14 percent of overall wages and salaries. However, in the following year as the Great Recession became more virulent, they accounted for 44 percent of the $282 billion decline in aggregate wage and salary incomes.

The Multiplier

Perhaps the key derivation from the standard Keynesian algebraic model is the multiplier. It represents how much GDP will cumulatively change when a key spending component, such as government spending or fixed investment, changes. For example, consider the total cumulative GDP change associated with a rise in government spending on goods and services. The initial GDP change is the change in government spending. As the recipients of government spending subsequently spend their additional income, there are spread effects on the incomes and spending of those who produce what is purchased. Thus, the cumulative GDP impact from the change in government spending is the initial change in government spending *plus* the sum of the related spread effects on subsequent domestic spending and incomes.

The derived multiplier from the standard Keynesian model is the number 1 divided by the sum of the marginal (incremental) propensities to save and import, plus the marginal tax rate. As the marginal propensities to save and import rise and tax rates increase, a given increase in government spending, for example, has less of a cumulative GDP impact. In the Keynesian framework, higher rates of saving, importing and taxation limit the spread effects on domestic output demand coming from the chain reaction of spending rounds following new spending stimulus to the economy.

The key components of the Keynesian multiplier are displayed in Figures 6.9 through 6.11. Net private savings, overall government tax receipts, and goods and services imports are depicted as a percentage of nominal GDP. In a recent year such as 2012, these three components were 43 1/2 percent of nominal GDP. This calculation applied to

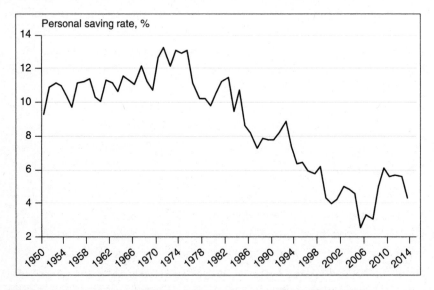

Figure 6.9   A Declining Personal Saving Rate Raises Multiplier Effects
SOURCE: Bureau of Economic Analysis.

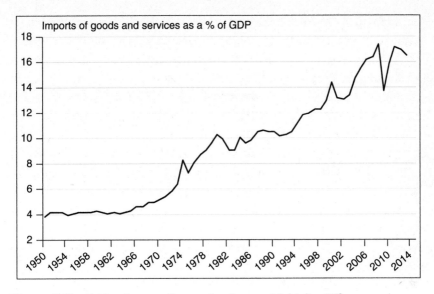

Figure 6.10   Rising Imports Penetration Lowers Multiplier Effects

SOURCE: Bureau of Economic Analysis.

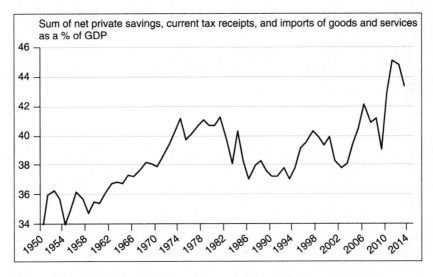

Figure 6.11   The Multiplier Depends on the Sum of Private Saving, Income Tax, and Import Ratios

SOURCE: Bureau of Economic Analysis.

the standard Keynesian multiplier framework results in a multiplier of around 2.3 (i.e., 1 divided by 0.435). Such a numerical multiplier means, for example, that a $1.00 rise in incremental government spending ultimately generates a $2.25 cumulative GDP gain.

This numerical example differs somewhat from what is presented in most introductory economics textbooks, where the Keynesian model is explained in terms of households' saving, import, and tax rates. Those considerations are all that one needs to calculate the consumption multiplier used to determine how much consumer spending rises for a given increase in, for example, government spending. By way of contrast, our explanation above of the total GDP multiplier utilizes net private saving, taxes and imports for both the household and business sectors. That is because spending generates income for both households and enterprises.

(Note: Standard textbook expositions illustrate the marginal propensities to save and import and the marginal tax rates. Our numerical example above is based on averages of household and business savings, imports, and taxes as a percent of GDP. In so far as marginal saving and import propensities and tax rates exceed average propensities and tax rates, our example somewhat overstates the numerical value of the GDP multiplier.)

Keynesian Controversies

The basic methodology outlined above is not what makes Keynesian economics controversial. Rather, from the perspective of a forecaster, there are potential problems with how his followers apply Keynes' theories.

Writing during the Great Depression, Keynes was explaining that recessions are not self-correcting in the absence of government intervention to stimulate demand. He argued that there would not always be enough investment to recycle saving into demand. His focus, appropriate to the time, was on economic weakness and vulnerability. However, *Keynesians can remain too pessimistic in more typical, less extreme cyclical settings, in which households and businesses often wish to borrow and spend savings.*

Keynesians can also overestimate the effects of fiscal policy actions on government spending and taxes that raise Federal budget deficits. Specifically, critics claim deficits are less stimulating than otherwise when the accompanying government borrowing raises interest rates and/or is viewed adversely by the business community. Some economists have also argued that the anticipation of future taxes, needed to repay added government debt, can reduce consumer spending.

Keynesian economists are identified with advocacy of anticipatory counter-cyclical monetary and fiscal policies that can be impractical to implement. Among Keynes' followers are econometricians enamored with the forecasting potential of their models. These economists have argued that policymakers can use those models to anticipate potential weakness and preempt it with interest rate and fiscal policies that, based on their models' projections, will produce positive outcomes. As a practical matter, there are limits to how well forecasters can anticipate potential weakness and how much offsetting stimulus is required.

Key Takeaways

1. Whether one agrees with the public policy prescriptions attributed to Keynes and his followers, Keynes' basic analytical framework is useful for assembling a GDP forecast with internal consistency among GDP components.
2. The observed weak linkages between bank reserves, the money supply, and GDP still do not justify forecasters completely abandoning some monetarist principles. Milton Friedman's dictum, that Fed asset purchases and money creation influence the economy with long and variable lags, reminds us that we could be observing positive economic consequences of the Fed's quantitative easing (QE) program well after the associated Fed securities purchases cease.
3. Supply-side economics will be important for intermediate-term growth and inflation forecasts that depend on potential GDP growth.
4. Minskyite flow of funds accounting models were useful in forecasting the Great Recession because of their emphasis on the economic consequences of periodic financial system fragility. The drawback of this approach, though, is that its focus on debt can lead to premature and excessive caution in forecasting.

Notes

1. "We Are All Keynesians Now," *Time*, December 31, 1965.

2. John A. Tatom, "We Are All Supply-Siders Now!" *Federal Reserve Bank of St. Louis Review* (May 1981): 18–30.

3. Robert Pollin, "We're All Minskyites Now," *Nation*, November 17, 2009, 5–7.

4. Dirk Bezemer, "Why Some Economists Could See the Crisis Coming," *Financial Times*, September 7, 2009.

5. Ibid.

6. Justin Lahard, "In Time of Tumult, Obscure Economist Gains Currency," *Wall Street Journal*, August 18, 2007.

7. C. J. Whalen, "The Credit Crunch—A Minsky Moment," *Studie Note di Economia*, Anno XIII, 2008–1, 3–21.

8. Dirk Bezemer, "'No One Saw This Coming': Understanding Financial Crisis Through Accounting Models," Munich Personal RePEc Archive No. 15892, June 24, 2009.

9. Ibid.

10. Hyman Minsky, *Stabilizing an Unstable Economy* (New Haven, CT: Yale University Press, 1986).

11. Lahard, "In Time of Tumult."

12. Charles C. Kindleberger, *Manias, Panics and Crashes: A History of Financial Crises* (New York: John Wiley & Sons, 1978).

13. Charles Whalen, "Post-Keynesian Institutionalism after the Great Recession," Levy Economics Institute of Bard College, Working Paper No. 724, May 2012.

14. Bezemer.

15. Bezemer, ibid.

16. Milton Friedman and Anna Schwartz, *A Monetary History of the United States* (Princeton, NJ: Princeton University Press, 1963).

17. Alan Greenspan, "Semi-Annual Monetary Policy Report to Congress," July 1993.

18. Jeffrey C. Fuhrer and Giovanni P. Olivei, "The Estimated Macroeconomic Effects of the Federal Reserve's Large-Scale Treasury Purchase Program," Public Policy Brief 11–2. Federal Reserve Bank of Boston, 2011.

19. Arthur Laffer, "Supply-Side Economics," The Laffer Center at the Pacific Research Institute, 2001.

20. Ayn Rand, *Atlas Shrugged* (New York: Random House, 1957).

21. Robert A. Moffitt and Mark Wilhelm, "Taxation and the Labor Supply Decisions of the Affluent," NBER Working Paper No. 6621, June 1998.

22. Joel Slemrod, *Does Atlas Shrug? The Economics of Taxing the Rich* (Boston: Harvard University Press).

23. Christina D. Romer and David H. Romer, "The Incentive Effects of Marginal Tax Rates: Evidence from the Interwar Era," University of California, Berkeley, September 2013.

24. "Letter: Friedman & Keynes," *Time*, February 4, 1996.

Chapter 7

The "New Normal": Time to Curb Your Enthusiasm?

I am suspicious of the idea of a new paradigm, to use that word, as an entirely new structure of the economy.

—Paul Volcker

What do we mean by the "new normal"? And how real is it? While a reading of postwar economic history indicates that economic recoveries eventually pick up speed after recessions (see Figure 7.1), numerous forecasters have projected a different outcome this time around. In the aftermath of the Great Recession, economists and other observers are predicting a steadily below average

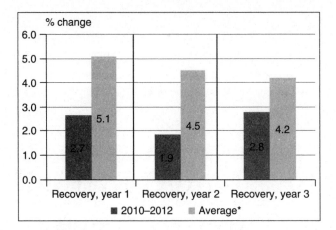

Figure 7.1   There Was Unusually Slow U.S. Real GDP Growth in the First
Three Years of Recovery from the Great Recession of 2008–2009
*Average during recessions from 1960 to 2001. 1980 was not included as it was an abnormal,
short-lived recovery.
SOURCE: Bureau of Economic Analysis.

growth recovery—a disturbing scenario that has become known as the
new normal.

The new normal coinage is often credited to investment strategists
at the Pacific Investment Management Company (PIMCO).[1] In
2009, they argued for a significant slowing in trend growth due to
"de-levering, de-globalization, and re-regulation." Since 2010, the
term has also become associated with the earlier mentioned Reinhart
and Rogoff book on the historical fallout from financial crises, such as
the one that triggered the Great Recession.[2]

*If the new normal school of thought turns out to be right, the implications
for business planning will be quite significant.*

The longer-term annualized growth of U.S. real gross domestic
product (GDP) was 3.4 percent per annum over the quarter century
before the start of the Great Recession in 2008. If that growth were
halved for an entire decade, the GDP level at the end of the decade would
be 18 percent less than if historical patterns had continued. North-
western University Economics Professor Robert Gordon—one of the
nation's most prominent macroeconomists—believes that long-term
U.S. growth could be "half or less of the 1.9 percent annual rate
experienced between 1860 and 2007."[3] If growth was just 1 percent per

annum, the end-of-decade GDP level would be 27 percent less than if the quarter-century trend before the Great Recession had repeated itself.

Must Forecasters Restrain Multiyear U.S. Growth Assumptions?

Choosing whether to adopt the unusually slow new normal U.S. growth assumptions entails consideration of many issues that interest forecasters.

For example, Professor Gordon's comparatively pessimistic new normal growth outlook reflects six headwinds: "demography, education, inequality, globalization, energy/environment, and the overhang of consumer and government debt."[4] Demographers agree that a further slowing of the working age population is in store. With weaker demand for less-skilled jobs, the U.S. education system has become steadily more challenged to successfully prepare an ever-larger fraction of students for skilled labor force participation. One public policy implication of growing income inequality could be more government-led income redistribution away from higher-income savers, whose savings help finance the capital goods needed to enhance productivity growth. Globalization of product and labor markets has resulted in a growing pool of cheap, accessible labor. The accompanying displacement of U.S. workers and slower wage growth dampens domestic purchasing power expansion. A negative growth implication of addressing energy/environmental concerns is the diversion of capital to maintain a livable environment instead of expanding the capital goods required for higher productivity growth. Finally, too much consumer debt can lead to consumption cutbacks as debt problems are addressed. At the government level, too much debt and the related debt-servicing burden also can eventually necessitate government spending cutbacks. I do not necessarily agree that all of these potential headwinds cited by Gordon will be sufficient to materially stunt the U.S. growth potential.

The new normal scenario is often expressed quantitatively with the "potential output growth" concept. The term describes how fast an economy can grow via expansion of labor, capital, and productivity—the gain in output per unit of input. In the years since the Great Recession, economists at the International Monetary Fund (IMF), the

Table 7.1 Evolving Estimates of Potential Output Growth (Percent Change)

	As of 2008	As of 2009	As of 2013
IMF[1]	2.1	0.9	1.8
OECD[2]	2.3	1.5	1.8
CBO[3]	2.4	1.9	1.7
CEA[4]	2.9	2.5	2.1

[1]IMF estimates are from October 2008, October 2009, and April 2013.
[2]OECD estimates are from December 2008, December 2009, and June 2013.
[3]CBO estimates are from September 2008, August 2009, and February 2013.
[4]CEA estimates are from January 2009, February 2010, and March 2013.
SOURCE: William Waschler Reifschneider and David Wilcox, "Aggregate Supply in the United States: Recent Developments and Implications for the Conduct of Monetary Policy, Finance and Economics," Discussion Series: Division of Research & Statistics and Monetary Affairs, Federal Reserve Board, Washington, D.C., 2013–77.

Organization for Economic Cooperation and Development (OECD), the Congressional Budget Office (CBO), and the President's Council of Economic Advisers (CEA) have been publishing lower potential growth estimates than they did in 2008, before the last recession had become so serious. (See Table 7.1.)

In considering whether—and by how much—business and financial forecasts should incorporate contemporary new normal assumptions, we should emphasize that the potential output representation of new normal growth is a supply-side concept. However, macroeconomic projections reflect both supply and demand.

Potential output growth represents how fast output can grow due to expansion of labor, capital, and productivity *after* they are fully employed. As of 2014, labor and capital were still underutilized, with above-average unemployment and below-average industrial capacity utilization. Until those resources are more fully employed, economic growth will at least partly reflect demand growth and not how rapidly the economy's potential supply-side can expand after existing labor and capital are fully utilized.

In subsequent chapters, we address the forecasting of household and business demand for goods and services. That demand determines how quickly existing resources can become more fully deployed. In this chapter, though, we focus on determinants of potential output—the supply-side of the new normal hypothesis. In doing so, we review some of the most important questions in contemporary forecasting. With regard to the labor supply, the issues to be discussed include population growth, immigration, the education system, and retirement. We also discuss labor productivity determinants, including capital spending and research and development (R&D).

Supply-Side Forecasting: Labor, Capital, and Productivity

The economy's longer-term potential output growth (i.e., the supply-side) depends on the growth of labor and capital, and the productivity of those inputs. Table 7.2 displays the ingredients for a potential output forecast and the Congressional Budget Office (CBO) projections through 2023. To set the stage for our forecasting discussion, the following definitions and introductory historical observations should be helpful.

When considering potential GDP prospects, note the growth differential between potential GDP output in the overall economy and output growth in the nonfarm business sector GDP. Potential business output grows somewhat faster than overall GDP potential output for two reasons. First, the public sector is included in calculating the overall GDP, and economists believe that productivity rises faster in the private sector than in the public sector. Second, in recent decades the public sector growth has slowed relative to private sector growth as fiscal restraints at various governmental levels have limited the expansion of public sector hiring. Looking ahead, these trends are apt to continue, and the CBO, for example, foresees nonfarm business sector potential output rising faster than overall GDP potential output by 0.4 percentage points per annum. *The distinction between overall GDP growth and nonfarm business output growth is important for investors in private sector securities.* One reason stock prices can do well despite slow overall GDP growth is that corporate earnings are more closely related to business output growth than to overall GDP growth.

Potential overall GDP output growth per annum has been trending down for more than 30 years. It has gone from almost 4 percent in the 1950 to 1973 period to just over 3 percent from the early 1980s to the

Table 7.2 Key Assumptions in CBO's Projection of Potential GDP (by Calendar Year, in Percent)

	Average Annual Growth						Projected Average Annual Growth		
	1950–1973	1974–1981	1982–1990	1991–2001	2002–2012	Total, 1950–2012	2013–2018	2019–2023	Total, 2013–2023
Overall Economy									
Potential GDP	3.9	3.3	3.1	3.1	2.2	3.3	2.2	2.3	2.2
Potential labor force	1.6	2.5	1.6	1.3	0.8	1.5	0.6	0.5	0.5
Potential labor productivity(a)	2.3	0.8	1.5	1.8	1.4	1.7	1.6	1.8	1.7
Nonfarm Business Sector									
Potential GDP	4.0	3.6	3.2	3.5	2.5	3.5	2.6	2.6	2.6
Potential hours worked	1.4	2.4	1.6	1.2	0.5	1.3	0.5	0.5	0.5
Capital services	3.8	4.3	4.1	4.7	2.3	3.8	3.3	3.3	3.3
Potential TFP	1.9	0.7	0.9	1.3	1.4	1.4	1.2	1.3	1.3
Potential TFP excluding adjustments	1.9	0.7	0.9	1.2	1.3	1.4	1.3	1.3	1.3
Adjustments to TFP (percentage points)(b)	0	0	0	0.1	0.2	*	**	0	**

Contributions to the Growth of Potential GDP (Percentage Points)

Potential hours worked	0.9	1.7	1.1	0.8	0.9	0.9	0.3	0.4	0.3
Capital input	1.2	1.3	1.2	1.4	0.7	1.1	1.0	1.0	1.0
Potential TFP excluding adjustments	1.9	0.7	0.9	1.3	1.4	1.4	1.2	1.3	1.3
Total contributions	4.0	3.6	3.6	3.5	2.5	3.5	2.6	2.6	2.6
Potential labor productivity(c)	2.6	1.2	1.6	2.3	2.0	2.1	2.1	2.1	2.1

GDP = gross domestic product; TFP = total factor productivity.

* = between zero and 0.05 percentage points.

** = between −0.05 percentage points and zero.

(a)The ratio of potential GDP to the potential labor force.

(b)The adjustments reflect CBO's estimates of the effect of the unusually rapid growth of TFP between 2001 and 2003 and the effect of the 2007–2009 recession on potential TFP.

(c)The estimated trend in the ratio of potential GDP to potential hours worked in the nonfarm business sector.

NOTES: Potential GDP is the maximum sustainable level of output in the economy.

SOURCE: Congressional Budget Office.

turn of the century. Since then, it has grown at an even slower rate—just above 2 percent per year. And as earlier discussed, many economists believe this trend to slower potential output growth will continue.

Part of the estimated slowdown reflects a reduction in the growth of the potential labor force. This growth has moderated as the expansion of the working age adult population—which had grown relatively quickly as postwar baby-boomers entered adulthood—has slowed. (Note: In calculating potential GDP growth, the labor input ingredient is total hours worked, which can deviate from labor force growth due to changes in the length of the workweek.) More recently, labor force growth also has been limited by a falling participation rate that we discuss later.

The slower potential output growth witnessed in the current century has also been due, in part, to a slower expansion in the stock of capital goods—"capital input" in Table 7.1. This growth has been approximately half of what it was during the tech boom in the 1990s. And one of the concerns about future potential output growth is the urgency—or lack thereof—with which businesses will want to undertake new expenditures on plant and equipment.

The growth of productivity—output per unit of input—is critical for how fast a country's potential output can expand. In evaluating productivity, distinguish between labor productivity—output per unit of labor input—and total factor productivity—output per unit of all inputs. This definitional difference explains why trend growth is greater for labor productivity than it is for total factor productivity. The 1990s tech boom often is credited for the productivity growth pickup in that decade. As we discuss later, productivity growth in the current economic recovery has been subpar to date—a key consideration in the new normal argument for slower overall trend output growth.

Population growth is critical for estimating how fast an economy can grow. Demand for goods, services, and space closely track the pace of population expansion. And an economy's ability to supply those demands through its own domestic resources is very dependent on the growth of the adult, working-age population. On both accounts, there are causes for concern in the next decade.

Are Demographics Destiny?

Annual U.S. population growth in the postwar period has been as high as 2.4 percent in 1947 but has been slowing and is expected to continue slowing even further. Although life expectancy has been rising, the birth rate has been falling. (See Figures 7.2 to 7.4.) Immigration can make some difference. However, barring very radical changes in U.S. immigration policy, immigration can at best make a modest contribution to overall population growth. (Net international migration per annum in the current century has ranged between 0.1 percent of the domestic population in 2000 to as high as 0.4 percent in 2001.) By 2020 the U.S. Census Bureau projects annual U.S. population growth ranging from 0.69 percent, with a low net international migration assumption, to 0.83 percent assuming a relatively high level of immigration.

While forecasters have little leeway in their population growth assumptions, they have a somewhat wider range of options in forecasting the growth of the labor force supply determinant of the economy's potential supply-side expansion. The Census Bureau estimates that U.S. adult population growth

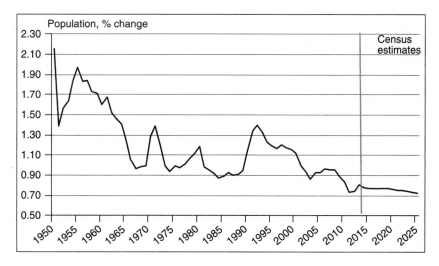

Figure 7.2 U.S. Population Growth Is Slowing
SOURCE: U.S. Census Bureau.

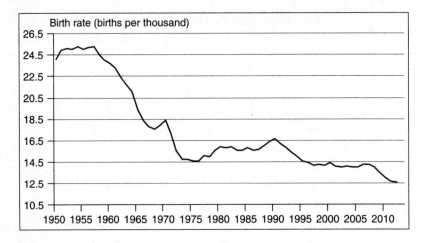

Figure 7.3   A Falling Birth Rate Lowers Longer-Term Labor Force Growth
SOURCE: U.S. Census Bureau.

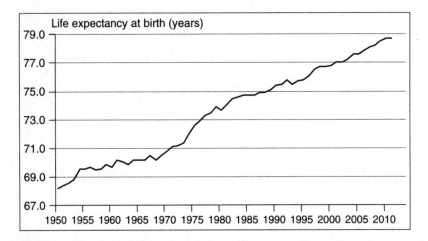

Figure 7.4   Rising Life Expectancy Means Future Aggregate Supply Will Grow Less Than Future Aggregate Demand
SOURCE: U.S. Census Bureau.

will slow to 0.76 percent in 2020 from 1.12 percent in 2012. However, growth of the civilian labor force will also reflect the "labor force participation rate"—the percentage of the adult population in the labor force.

The labor force participation rate is a supply-side wildcard that challenges forecasters.

Assuming a likely 0.8 percent per annum growth of the adult population over the next few years, the annual growth of the civilian labor force could differ noticeably due to the possible variation in the labor force participation rate. Each 0.1 percentage point change in the labor force participation rate alters labor force growth by the same amount. And in recent years the annual labor force participation rate has changed by as much as 0.3 percentage points in a year. To forecast the labor force participation rate, it is necessary to make assumptions about two of its key determinants—the age distribution of the adult population and age groups' behavioral changes in the desire/need to participate.

Labor force participation is lower for older age categories, where workers are more likely to be retired. Therefore, in a society with an aging adult population the labor force participation rate will decline. This is the case in the United States and many other developed nations. For forecasting purposes, the effects of an aging workforce on the aggregate labor force participation rate can be estimated as follows. Multiply the most recently reported labor force participation rates for individual age categories by the Census Bureau's forecasted evolving population shares. The changes in reweighted aggregate labor force participation rates for coming years then represent effects of population share changes on the overall labor force participation rate. Performing this exercise for the second half of the current decade (see Figure 7.5) indicates that *in each*

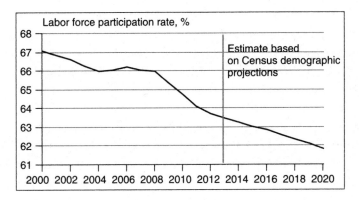

Figure 7.5   The Labor Force Participation Rate Is Projected to Continue Declining

SOURCE: Census Bureau, author's calculations.

of the next few years after 2014 an aging U.S. population will subtract between 0.2 and 0.3 percentage points from the aggregate labor force participation rate.

The next, and often more difficult, step in projecting the labor force participation rate is to estimate behavioral changes in the adult population's choices about working or not. Such alterations in behavior will reflect lifestyle changes, incentives, and job availability. Examples of relevant lifestyle changes are changing preferences with regard to raising children or self-fulfillment. These changes are hard to predict for sociologists and are beyond the expertise of most business and financial forecasters. That said, we can nonetheless make assumptions about whether trends in various age/sex labor force categories will continue, and we can use them in forecasting labor force participation. From the standpoint of forecast credibility, it is important to state, clearly, the assumptions being made.

Among the incentives affecting labor force participation, for example, are the availability and magnitudes of government assistance for the unemployed and the wages being offered for work. Some economists believe that more generous or prolonged unemployment insurance and disability benefits lower the labor force participation rate. However, when labor markets tighten enough for wages to pick up, various government payments for not working become relatively less attractive.

Trends in worker disability benefits provide an example of explicitly incorporating assumed behavioral changes into projected labor force participation. Since the early 1990s there has been a reasonably steady upward trend in the percentage of working-age persons receiving government disability benefits. (See Figure 7.6.) Specifically, that percentage has been rising by 0.1 percentage point per annum, which is equivalent to a 0.1 percentage point per annum decline in the labor force participation rate. Whether a forecaster should extrapolate that trend partly depends on whether persons receiving disability payments remain out of the labor force until retirement. That is an assumption supported by some recent research.[5]

Another challenge in forecasting the labor force participation rate is the difficulty of accounting for the potential reentry into the civilian labor force of persons who, at present, are not included in it. That can be a sizeable group. In calculating the U.S. civilian labor force, the Bureau of Labor Statistics includes persons either working or seeking employment.

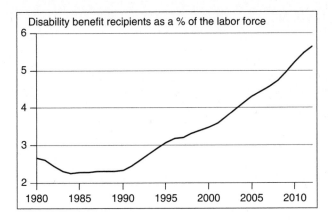

Figure 7.6   The Growing Number of People Receiving Disability Payments Is a Negative for the Labor Force Participation Rate
SOURCE: Bureau of Labor Statistics.

Excluded are discouraged workers who had been looking for work and could not find it. Also excluded are persons who have at some point in the past year sought work but who did not look for work in the most recent monthly labor market survey period for which the labor force is reported. In its official monthly labor market reports, the government labels these two excluded groups as "marginally attached," which the Bureau of Labor Statistics defines as being available to work but not in the labor force. The economy's potential growth and unemployment rate will partly reflect the willingness of persons not counted in the labor force to return.

We can assess the potential effect of such persons' reentry by examining the marginally attached workers as a percentage of the labor force. (See Figure 7.7.) In a healthy economy these workers represent just under 1 percent of the civilian labor force. When the economy is in recession or experiencing just sluggish growth, this percentage can rise above 1.5 percent. To project the labor force participation rate effect of such persons becoming job seekers, a forecaster can make reasonable assumptions about how much time it will take for this percentage to recede to a more normal level associated with a healthier economy and labor demand. For instance, after the first four years of recovery from the Great Recession, I have assumed that this percentage would fall from

Figure 7.7   Persons Marginally Attached to the Labor Force Represent
Potential Reentry
NOTE: Shaded areas represent recessions.
SOURCE: Bureau of Labor Statistics.

1.5 percent to 1 percent of the civilian labor force over a two-period time span. This particular assumption adds around 0.25 percent per annum to the labor force participation rate and the labor force growth rate.

The new normal bias toward slow growth in the labor supply may be too pessimistic, because rising wages can raise the labor force participation rate. Although an aging population reduces participation in the labor force, it also increases the aggregate demand for goods and services versus the labor supply. (For example, retirees may consume less than when they were working, but they are no longer supplying goods and services, thus raising the difference between what they purchase and their contribution to production.) In such a setting, where demand for goods and services rises relative to the labor supply, wage gains should accelerate. That, in turn, should keep the aggregate participation rate higher than it would otherwise be, were it based solely on the aging population.

Pivotal Productivity Projections

Estimating productivity gains is critical for potential growth projections, and also for the forecasts of other economic variables. Productivity helps determine real (inflation-adjusted) wages and employment—both keys to consumer spending. Unit labor costs—a major element of business profitability and the economy's inflation rate—also hinge on productivity.

When analyzing productivity, economists often refer either to labor productivity—annual output per hour worked—or multifactor productivity—output per unit of all inputs. Labor productivity typically grows faster than multifactor productivity, since output per unit of labor input is partly determined by the other inputs used in combination with labor. Over the quarter of a century period ending in 2012, labor productivity grew at a 2.1 percent annual rate versus a 0.9 percent annual rate of expansion of multifactor productivity.

Labor productivity—the probably more frequently cited concept—has exhibited four distinct growth trends in the postwar era. (See Figure 7.8.) After an annualized growth pace of 2.8 percent from 1948 to 1973, labor productivity in the nonfarm business sector grew at a just 1.5 percent rate over 1974 to 1995. However, it then reaccelerated during 1996 to 2004 to a 3.1 percent pace before slowing again to an only 1.5 percent growth rate during 2005 to 2013. (Note: Slower growing multifactor productivity showed similar trends. For instance, its annualized growth slowed from 1.35 percent during 1995 to 2007

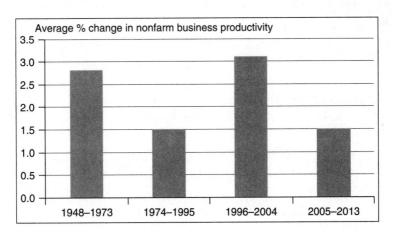

Figure 7.8 Labor Productivity Intermediate-Term Growth Trends Can Change Considerably

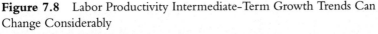

SOURCE: Bureau of Labor Statistics.

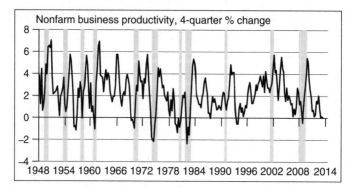

Figure 7.9   Short-Term Productivity Changes Are Cyclical
NOTE: Shaded areas represent recessions.
SOURCE: Bureau of Labor Statistics.

to 0.5 percent during 2007 to 2012.) *The considerable variation over time in productivity growth trends is a reminder to be wary of extrapolating from the more recent productivity developments.*

In forecasting productivity growth on a shorter-term, year–ahead horizon, the stage of the business cycle is an important consideration. (See Figure 7.9.) Labor productivity typically weakens in recessions only to snap back in the early stages of economic recoveries. Before more recent recessions, labor hoarding was the typical explanation of falling labor productivity in a recession. Employers did not cut their labor input as much as their output or sales were falling. This was partly because of uncertainty about future labor needs. Also, it makes sense to retain employees with specific skills that might be difficult to reacquire quickly in the subsequent business recovery.

In the Great Recession, however, labor productivity did not decline as it usually does in business downturns. Why were employers cutting back on their labor input as fast as their output and sales were declining? One possible explanation is that the Great Recession's unusual severity could have meant that employers were unusually pessimistic about their future labor requirements. Also, as unemployment soared, firms may have started to believe that it would be easier than normal to replace laid–off workers when demand eventually improved. When labor productivity temporarily snapped back immediately after the Great Recession, it was partly a reflection of employers remaining especially cautious about hiring.

However, *after initially snapping back following the Great Recession, labor productivity subsequently grew unusually slowly—prompting economists to begin speculating on whether the U.S. economy was starting to exhibit a more troubling, longer-term period of weak productivity growth.*

Forecasters are struggling with the question of whether the weak productivity growth, on balance, after the Great Recession is just temporary or is a longer-lasting trend that should be built into their potential growth, real wage, and unemployment outlooks. Both the pessimistic and optimistic viewpoints about future productivity include some reasonably credible arguments about the crosscurrents impacting recent and prospective productivity trends. After reviewing these differing perspectives, I explain why I lean toward a relatively more optimistic productivity outlook.

Pessimists argue that productivity growth was slowing even before the Great Recession of 2008 to 2009, which exacerbated an already worrisome trend. In 2006 and 2007, multifactor productivity in the nonfarm business sector suddenly slowed to an only 0.35 annualized growth pace following relatively healthy 2.1 percent growth in the first four years of recovery from the 2001 recession. After rising 2.6 percent in the first year after the Great Recession, multifactor productivity growth slowed again, to a pace of approximately 1 percent in the following two years.

One reason cited by pessimists for the initial slowdown in productivity growth prior to the Great Recession is the waning positive impact from the information technology (IT) revolution. It enhances productivity via faster computational capabilities, enabling workers and machines to be more productive. In addition, the communications revolution related to IT has better connected labor and capital resources so as to enhance creativity and efficiency.

Economists specializing in the effects of technology's historical growth have quantified the contribution of the IT boom to U.S. labor productivity increases. Some of the most widely cited research in this field has been conducted by Federal Reserve Board economists David Byrne, Daniel Sichel and Steven Oliner. Their updated 2013 analysis provides a useful framework for assessing future productivity trends, especially as they relate to the IT role.[6] (See Table 7.3.)

Labor productivity growth reflects contributions from capital deepening, the composition of the labor input and multifactor productivity. Capital deepening is the change in output due to the production of

Table 7.3 Contributions to Growth of Labor Productivity in the Nonfarm Business Sector[a]

	1974–1995 (1)	1995–2004 (2)	2004–2012 (3)	Change at 1995 (2) – (1)	Change at 2004 (3) – (2)
1. Growth of labor productivity[b]	1.56	3.06	1.56	1.50	–1.50
Contributions (percentage points per year)					
2. Capital deepening	0.74	1.22	0.74	0.48	–0.48
3. IT capital	0.41	0.78	0.36	0.37	–0.42
4. Computer hardware	0.18	0.38	0.12	.20	–0.26
5. Software	0.16	0.27	0.16	0.11	–0.11
6. Communication equipment	0.07	0.13	0.08	0.06	–0.05
7. Other capital	0.33	0.44	0.38	0.11	–0.06
8. Labor composition	0.26	0.22	0.34	–0.04	0.12
9. Multifactor productivity (MFP)	0.56	1.62	0.48	1.06	–1.14
10. Effect of adjustment costs	0.07	0.07	–0.02	.00	–0.09
11. Effect of utilization	–0.01	–0.06	0.16	–0.05	0.22
12. MFP after adjustments	.50	1.61	0.34	1.11	–1.27

13. IT-producing sectors	0.36	0.72	0.28	0.36	−0.44
14. Semiconductors	0.09	0.37	0.14	0.28	−0.23
15. Computer hardware	0.17	0.17	0.04	.00	−0.13
16. Software	0.06	.10	0.08	0.04	−0.02
17. Communication equipment	0.05	0.07	0.02	0.02	−0.05
18. Other nonfarm business	0.13	.90	0.06	0.77	−0.84
Memo					
19. Total IT contribution(c)	0.77	1.50	0.64	0.73	−0.86

(a) Detail may not sum to totals due to rounding.

(b) Measured as 100 times average annual log differences for the indicated years.

(c) Sum of lines 3 and 13.

SOURCE: Byrne, David M., Stephen D. Oliner, and Daniel E. Sichel, "Is the Information Technology Revolution Over?" Finance and Economics Discussion Series Divisions of Research & Statistics and Monetary Affairs Federal Reserve Board, Washington, D.C., 2013–36.

capital goods. The composition of the labor input reflects the deployment of labor among industries with different labor productivity levels. As earlier defined, multifactor productivity is the output from using all inputs. Productivity contributions via capital deepening and multifactor productivity enhancement can be disaggregated at the industry level into contributions from IT and other capital. IT capital contributors are computer hardware, software, and communication equipment.

Per the Fed economists' calculations, the annual growth of labor productivity just about doubled from 1.56 percent between 1974 and 1995 to 3.06 percent between 1995 and 2004. Approximately half of that 1.50 percentage point acceleration was due to the IT boom. The deepening of IT capital contributed 0.37 percentage points to a 1.22 percent rise in labor productivity, and contributed 0.36 percentage points to a 0.73 percentage point gain in multifactor productivity. After 2004 and through 2012, the growth of labor productivity slowed by 1.50 percentage points to 1.56 percent, with just over half of the slowdown attributable to smaller contributions from the IT sector. Looking ahead, what should forecasters assume about the critical IT contribution to growth and productivity?

A good example of the pessimistic case comes from the economist Robert Gordon.[7] In viewing U.S. economic development since 1750, he distinguishes three separate industrial revolutions. He relates the timing of these revolutions to fast and slow growth eras. The first revolution, from 1750 to 1830, was led by steam and railroads. The second revolution, from 1870 to 1900, resulted from developments in areas such as electricity, internal combustion engines, running water, indoor toilets, communications, entertainment, chemicals and petroleum. The third revolution, which began in 1960 and is still going, is powered by computers, the web, and mobile phones. Gordon argues that the second revolution was the most important of the three, spawning eight decades of comparatively fast productivity growth in the 1890 to 1972 period. However, after the productivity gains reaped from the second industrial revolution's spinoffs (e.g., airplanes, air conditioning, and interstate highways), productivity growth slowed again, as the 1974 to 1995 period in Figure 7.8 indicates. From his perspective, Gordon views the third revolution as ultimately generating only a short growth revival between 1996 and 2004.

Hardly all economists are as pessimistic as is Gordon about the prospects for technological change driving faster output and productivity growth. For example, consider the viewpoint of researchers affiliated with McKinsey & Company.[8] They conclude that: "Technological opportunities remain strong in advanced manufacturing, and the energy revolution will spur new investment, not only in energy extraction, but also in the transportation sector and in energy-intensive manufacturing. Education, health care, infrastructure (construction) and government are large sectors of the economy that have lagged behind in productivity growth historically. This is not because of a lack of opportunities for innovation and change but because of a lack of incentives for change and institutional rigidity."

They believe there could be further important technological advances in the factory sector from industrial robotics and automation, 3D printing and additive manufacturing, big data and related advanced analytics, and the Internet.

For the energy sector, they cite advances in drilling technologies. These allow much higher productivity in energy exploration. (Note: In gauging drilling activity and expenses, the traditional rig count measure of the number of operating rotary rigs has become outdated as individual drilling sites become much more productive.)

Also, the accompanying increase in domestic natural gas output via shale gas extraction innovations has meant increased availability and lower relative costs of natural gas produced in the United States. These developments encourage energy-intensive manufacturers to locate manufacturing facilities in the United States instead of abroad. And such facilities often are characterized by relatively high labor productivity, which can contribute to higher overall U.S. productivity. For instance, economists at the American Chemistry Council have estimated that a 25 percent increase in U.S. production of the natural gas derivative ethane could trigger enough new petrochemicals production facilities to raise U.S. jobs by 182,450 (0.1 percent) and national output by $83.4 billion (0.5 percent).[9]

Hysteresis?

The productivity of the labor force partly reflects its education and experience. Over time, the U.S. labor force has become older and more educated. That consideration by itself suggests higher productivity.

However, age and education do not necessarily add up to higher productivity as the economy's needs change.

The most relevant experience in a dynamic economy is the more recent experience of its workforce. If previously employed workers are unemployed for an unusually long time, their marketable skills could atrophy. Also, as new labor force entrants encounter difficulty finding a first job, they are denied skill development via necessary on-the-job training. The related *hysteresis* hypothesis has become quite publicized in the slow recovery from the Great Recession. Hysteresis is defined as lagging behind. The commonly cited hysteresis hypothesis is that the long-term unemployed increasingly lag in their acquisition and mainte-nance of employers' evolving required skills. Through 2013, the decline in the overall unemployment rate mainly reflected reduced joblessness for persons who had been unemployed for less than half a year. The job-less rate for those persons who have been seeking a job for more than a half-year remained stubbornly high before finally easing off in 2014.

A forecasting issue is whether the longer-term unemployed will eventually get a chance to work and develop experience or will instead become structurally unemployed: those whom employers may regard as unqualified. As of 2014, this question had yet to be answered. A sense of history and economic logic suggest to me, though, that forecasters should adopt the following assumption. Once the pool of more experienced workers becomes increasingly depleted, employers will need to undertake the necessary on-the-job training of less experienced workers. *As the competitive wages of increasingly more experienced workers rise at a faster pace, expansion-oriented firms will find it in their interests to incur the added expenses of hiring and training initially less productive workers with relatively less experience.*

Capex to the Rescue?

When unemployment continues to fall, capacity utilization eventually rises enough to trigger higher capital spending. (See Figures 7.10 and 7.11.) New capital goods embody state-of-the-art technological changes that allow workers and their firms to become more productive. In the slow recovery from the Great Recession, through 2013 there had yet to be the typical cyclical pickup in business equipment spending.

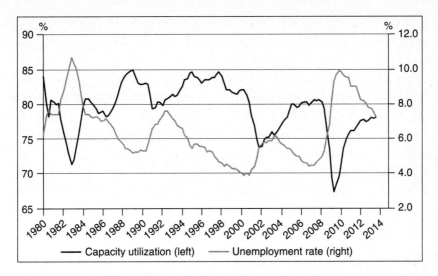

Figure 7.10 Falling Unemployment Is Accompanied by Higher Capacity Utilization
SOURCE: Bureau of Labor Statistics, Federal Reserve Board of Governors.

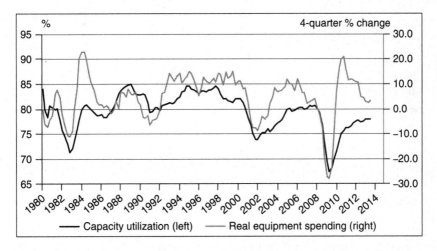

Figure 7.11 Higher Capacity Utilization Helps Trigger Capital Spending
SOURCE: Federal Reserve Board of Governors, Bureau of Labor Statistics.

Industrial capacity utilization had earlier been unusually depressed, was only slowly recovering, and had yet to reach the levels that triggered higher capital spending in earlier business recoveries.

Reflecting a weak capital spending recovery following the Great Recession, there was a marked slowing in the growth of capital services—a measure of the capital goods input. In the private nonfarm business sector during the tech boom in the second half of the 1990s, capital services were growing at a 6 percent annual rate—about double the longer-term growth trend. (See Table 7.4.) Relative to the growth of the labor input, capital services per hour worked rose at an unusually

Table 7.4 Compound Annual Growth Rates for Productivity, Outputs, and Inputs in the Private Nonfarm Business Sector[1] for Selected Periods, 1987–2012

	1987–2012	1987–1990	1990–1995	1995–2000	2000–2007	2007–2012	2011–2012
Productivity							
Multifactor productivity[2]	0.9	0.5	0.5	1.3	1.4	0.5	0.9
Output per hour of all persons	2.1	1.4	1.6	2.7	2.6	1.7	1.0
Output per unit of capital services	−0.6	−0.4	−0.4	−1.0	−0.5	−0.8	1.0
Output	2.8	3.2	2.9	5.0	2.7	0.5	2.9
Inputs							
Combined inputs[3]	1.9	2.7	2.4	3.6	1.3	0.0	2.0
Labor input[4]	1.1	2.3	2.0	2.5	0.4	−0.7	2.1
Hours	0.7	1.7	1.3	2.2	0.1	−1.2	1.9
Labor composition[5]	0.5	0.6	0.7	0.3	0.3	0.5	0.1
Capital services	3.4	3.6	3.3	6.0	3.2	1.3	1.8
Analytic ratio							
Capital services per hour of all persons	2.7	1.8	1.9	3.8	3.1	2.5	−0.1

[1]Excludes government enterprises.
[2]Output per combined units of labor input and capital services.
[3]The growth rate of each input is weighted by its share of current dollar costs.
[4]Hours at work by age, education, and gender group are weighted by each group's share of the total wage bill.
[5]Ratio of labor input to hours.
SOURCE: Bureau of Labor Statistics.

fast 3.8 percent annual rate, which was associated with an unusually rapid annualized productivity growth.

However, *until capacity utilization recovers to levels historically motivating a faster pace of capital expenditures growth, it is premature to write off capital spending as a positive contributor to faster labor productivity growth.* In Chapter 8 on business animal spirits, we discuss in some detail issues in forecasting capital spending.

Technological Change to the Rescue?

It also is premature to dismiss the possibility of a renewed faster pace of productivity growth via technological change and innovation. To be sure, it is quite challenging to predict the emergence and effects of new technologies. However, there are some signposts on which forecasters should be focused.

One important metric is research and development (R&D) spending. (See Figure 7.12.) Overall (private and public) R&D expenditures as a percentage of U.S. GDP fell in advance of the productivity growth slowdown that occurred from the mid-1970s through the mid-1990s. Prior to the productivity growth resurgence in the second half of the 1990s, the R&D percentage of GDP was rising. Subsequently, a decline in this metric preceded the productivity growth slowdown in the current economic recovery. More recently, a hopeful sign is that R&D spending

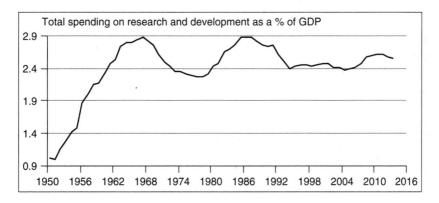

Figure 7.12   Higher R&D Spending as a Percent of GDP Is a Positive Sign for a Faster Future Pace of Technological Change
SOURCE: Bureau of Economic Analysis.

Table 7.5   Private R&D Spenders

	2012	
	Level, $ Billions	Share, %
Research and development	269.1	
Business	248.7	**92.4**
Manufacturing	202.2	**75.1**
Pharmaceutical and medicine manufacturing	63.1	23.4
Chemical manufacturing, ex pharmaceutical/medicine	12.6	4.7
Semiconductor and other electronic component mfg	28.8	10.7
Other computer/electronic product manufacturing	31.4	11.7
Motor vehicles, bodies and trailers, and parts mfg	14.4	5.4
Aerospace products and parts manufacturing	7.4	2.7
Other manufacturing	44.4	16.5
Nonmanufacturing	46.5	**17.3**
Scientific research and development services	9.1	3.4
All other nonmanufacturing	37.4	13.9
Nonprofit institutions serving households	20.4	**7.6**
Universities and colleges	3.0	1.1
Other nonprofit institutions	17.4	6.5

SOURCE: Bureau of Economic Analysis.

as a percentage of GDP has recovered somewhat, albeit remaining below levels preceding the tech boom in the 1990s.

Knowing where R&D spending is focused (see Table 7.5) is critical for assessing its possible future productivity payoffs. Bryne, Oliner, and Sichel, in their productivity research, emphasize that semiconductor innovation "is continuing at a rapid pace, raising the possibility of a second wave in the IT revolution." As a result, they foresee "a reasonable prospect that the pace of labor productivity could rise to its long-run average of 2.25 percent or even above."[10]

Key Takeaways

1. The U.S. economy's longer-term growth potential is one of the most important and pivotal issues facing forecasters.

2. Once the economy recovers to near full resource utilization, potential GDP growth depends on labor force expansion and labor productivity growth.

3. The pessimistic new normal hypothesis about slower than normal intermediate-term U.S. growth reflects not-so-controversial assumptions about likely slow labor force growth but more controversial assumptions about future productivity.

4. An aging population dictates only slow labor force growth, although how slow depends on variability of the labor force participation rate.

5. The downward labor force participation rate effects of an aging population can be countered at certain stages of the business cycle by reentry of discouraged workers.

6. The historical range of annual productivity growth is a reminder that new normal pessimism may be overly pessimistic.

7. The slow labor force growth emphasized by new normal theorists suggests eventual wage pressures and labor shortages, which could trigger faster capital spending, technological change, and innovation to spur more than assumed labor productivity and potential GDP growth.

Notes

1. William H. Gross, "On the 'Course' to a New Normal," PIMCO Investment Outlook, September 2009.

2. Carmen Reinhart and Kenneth Rogoff, *This Time Is Different: Eight Centuries of Financial Follies* (Princeton, NJ: Princeton University Press, 2010).

3. Robert J. Gordon, "Is U.S. Economic Growth Over? Faltering Innovation Confronts the Six Headwinds," National Bureau of Economic Research Working Paper No. 18315, August 2012.

4. Ibid.

5. David Autor and Mark Duggan, "The Growth in the Social Security Disability Rolls: A Fiscal Crisis Unfolding," *Journal of Economic Perspectives* 20, no. 3 (2006): 71–96.

6. David Byrne, Stephen Oliner, and Daniel Sichel, "Is the Information Technology Revolution Over?" Federal Reserve Board Finance and Economics Discussion Series, 2013–36.

7. Gordon, ibid.

8. Martin Baily, James Manyika, and Shalabh Gupta, "U.S. Productivity Growth: An Optimistic Perspective," *International Productivity Monitor* 25 (Spring 2013).

9. American Chemistry Council, "Shale Gas New Petrochemicals Investment: Benefits for the Economy, Jobs and U.S. Manufacturing," March 2011.

10. David Byrne, Stephen Oliner, and Daniel Sichel, ibid.

Chapter 8

Animal Spirits

The Intangibles behind Business Spending

Nothing ever succeeds which exuberant spirits have not helped to produce.

—Friedrich Wilhelm Nietzsche, *The Twilight of the Idols*, 1888

Firms' spending on labor, capital, and inventories is critical for the economy's well-being. Correctly forecasting such business expenditures can be key to a forecaster's well-being, too. But doing so is a hard task. Certain determinants of future business spending, such as profits, sales, wages, capital goods prices, and capacity utilization can be measured. But it is often the psychological intangibles that are the pivotal drivers of behavior. Economists use the term *animal spirits* as a catchall label for these intangibles. John Maynard Keynes pioneered the concept for modern macroeconomic theory in his

1936 book, *The General Theory of Employment, Interest and Money*. Here's his characterization of the term *animal spirits*:

> Even apart from the instability due to speculation, there is instability due to the characteristic of human nature that a large proportion of our positive activities depend on spontaneous optimism rather than mathematical expectations, whether moral or hedonistic or economic. Most, probably, of our decisions to do something positive, the full consequences of which will be drawn out over many days to come, can only be taken as the result of animal spirits—a spontaneous urge to action rather than inaction, and not as the outcome of a weighted average of quantitative benefits multiplied by quantitative probabilities.[1]

The role of animal spirits in Keynesian macroeconomic analysis and forecasting is pivotal. Maintaining incomes at levels associated with full employment requires that the associated savings be rechanneled into investment. However, what if firms are no longer confident enough to undertake investment at the required level? There are excess savings, which means that not all of the incomes are being utilized for consumption and investment spending. The associated drop in demand triggers lower employment and incomes, until incomes finally fall far enough so that the lower accompanying savings are balanced by depressed investment.

But if there are excess savings, interest rates should decline. Could that rejuvenate investment to levels that would absorb the savings associated with incomes at full employment levels? Keynes said no. Investment was far more sensitive to fluctuating animal spirits than to interest rates. In other words, you can lead a horse to water but you cannot make it drink. If firms were pessimistic, the economy could not right itself through lower rates. This situation was labeled the *Keynesian inconsistency*. There was no level of private investment consistent with absorbing the savings generated at full employment income levels. In those circumstances, the only way to stimulate the economy was through public spending that exceeded taxes—government deficit financing.

Critics of Keynesian economics also utilized the animal spirits concept. However, they used it to refute the Keynesian fiscal policy prescriptions for addressing unemployment. These critics argued that

Federal deficit financing and other government intervention to fight recessions further depress the confidence of a business community skeptical about the wisdom of such policies. Where they agreed with Keynesians, though, was on the pivotal role of business confidence in driving the business cycle.

The theory is intuitively appealing. However, can animal spirits be measured and forecast? Even if animal spirits cannot be forecast, can they at least be used as a leading indicator if we can measure them? In this chapter we first address the measurement issue. Then we explore how business confidence influences firms' capital spending, hiring, and inventory decisions.

Animal Spirits on Main Street and Wall Street

Forecasters can quantify animal spirits with various published business confidence gauges. Three of the most popular indicators are (1) the Conference Board CEO Confidence measure, (2) the Business Roundtable CEO Economic Outlook index, and (3) the National Federation of Independent Business (NFIB) Small Business Optimism Index. We look at each of them. The first two represent sentiment in the corporate world, and the NFIB gauges the mood of the small business sector.

A comprehensive view of business sentiment requires examining both small business (Main Street) and corporate America (Wall Street), according roughly equal weight to each. The U.S. Small Business Administration (SBA) estimates that the 23 million small U.S. businesses account for 54 percent of all U.S. sales, 55 percent of all jobs, and 66 percent of all net new jobs.[2]

(Figure 8.1 shows two of the gauges and illustrates differences in sentiment between Main Street and Wall Street.)

Conference Board (CB) CEO Confidence Index (Wall Street)

Since 1977, the Conference Board (CB) has conducted quarterly interviews with 100 CEOs of large corporations. The CB CEO Confidence measure is based on answers to three opinion questions: current economic conditions versus those six months earlier, expectations for the economy six months ahead, and expectations for their own industry six

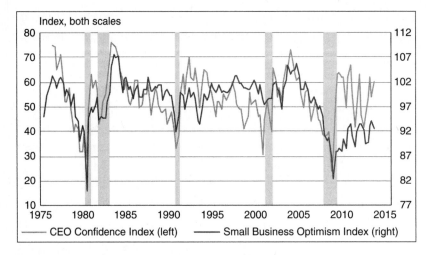

Figure 8.1 Animal Spirits: Main Street and Wall Street

NOTE: Shaded areas denote recessions.

SOURCE: Conference Board, National Federation of Independent Business.

months in the future. Individual replies to each question are assigned values of 100 for "substantially better," 75 for "moderately better," 50 for "the same," 25 for "moderately worse" and 0 for "substantially worse." The individual scores for each question then are averaged, with the score for each question potentially ranging from 0 to 100. The average scores for each of the three questions are then averaged to calculate the CEO Confidence measure, with an aggregate score over 50 reflecting more positive than negative responses.

Business Roundtable (BR) CEO Economic Outlook Index (Wall Street)

Quarterly CEO surveys are also conducted by the Business Roundtable (BR). (See Figure 8.2.) Approximately 200 CEOs are polled about their company's sales, capital spending, and employment expectations for the following six months. Response rates vary, with the fourth quarter of 2013 response rate, for example, at 57 percent (120) of the polled BR membership. In this survey the overall responses to each question are compiled into a diffusion index, which the BR defines as the percent of respondents expecting an increase minus the percent of respondents expecting a decrease. The diffusion indexes range between −50 and +150, readings more than 50 indicating expansion. Finally, the diffusion indexes for each question are averaged to create the overall outlook index.

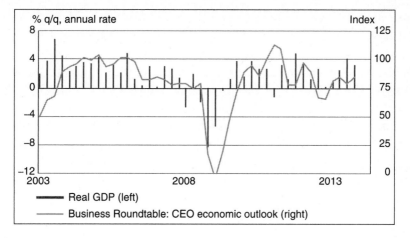

Figure 8.2 CEO Economic Outlook Index versus GDP Growth
SOURCE: Business Roundtable, Bureau of Economic Analysis.

National Federation of Independent Business (NFIB) Small Business Optimism Index (Main Street)

The National Federation of Independent Business (NFIB) began conducting quarterly surveys of its membership in 1973 and moved to monthly surveys in 1986. The response size varies. In 2012, for example, the average number of respondents in the monthly surveys was 726 with a range of 648 to 819. The Small Business Optimism index reflects responses by surveyed NFIB members to 10 questions on employment, capital outlays and inventory plans, expectations for economic improvement, real sales and credit conditions, current inventories and job openings, earnings trends, and whether it is a good time to expand. Net percentages of responses (e.g., "higher" minus "lower") to each question are seasonally adjusted. Finally these individual responses to each of the 10 questions are aggregated into a single index. Unlike the CEO sentiment gauges, with the NFIB index there is no single level delineating expansion or contraction.

Are the Business Optimism Measures Politically Biased?

The perceptions and expectations responses in the business optimism indexes are inevitably shaped, in part, by the respondents' public policy views. If businesses believe, therefore, that government tax and regulatory policies are harming the economy, won't their responses be biased downward? After all, the respondents in the Business Roundtable and NFIB surveys are also members of lobbying organizations that seek more business-friendly tax and regulatory policies. If these policies are considered to be less favorable under a Democratic administration and Congress than a Republican one, could the surveys understate underlying business conditions and expectations when the Democrats are in power?

In recent years, accusations of bias have been directed at the NFIB, which has been a highly visible critic of the Obama Administration's taxation and regulatory policies. Indeed, the NFIB was a party to the lawsuit challenging the constitutionality of President Obama's signature health care policies. The Affordable Care Act that passed in 2010 mandated that firms with 50 or more full-time employees have to provide health insurance for their employees or pay a fine. The NFIB vigorously lobbied against the legislation, claiming that the employer mandate would be a special hardship for small firms that would be forced to shed jobs. Their lobbying efforts were partly successful, because, unlike some earlier versions of the bill, the final legislation excluded firms with fewer than 50 full-time employees. And according to the NFIB, approximately 90 percent of its small business owner members run firms that have fewer than 50 employees. Nevertheless, the NFIB continued attacking the health care legislation even after its lobbying efforts on behalf of its membership were largely successful. The NFIB website's persistent criticism of the Obama Administration's health care and regulatory policies has at least the potential for a negative impact on the sentiments of those NFIB survey respondents who frequent that site.

My view, however, is that only some of the questions in the NFIB, CB, and BR surveys are possibly biased downward due to the political preferences of those organizations. Specifically, it seems that responses to questions about a respondent's own business and own industry should be conditioned by what respondents are seeing in their everyday business life. However, respondents' perceptions and expectations for the overall economy could be less well informed and, perhaps, relatively more influenced by political biases.

All three of the BR survey questions are about respondents' own companies. One of the three questions in the CB survey is explicitly about respondents' own industries. And almost all of the 10 questions in the NFIB survey relate specifically to respondents' own firms. Thus, in so far as responses about one's own firm are conditioned more by informed knowledge than political preferences, the political bias in these surveys is likely limited. Even if business confidence gauges are not particularly politically biased, though, the question of their usefulness as economic indicators remains.

What Does Business Confidence Tell Us?

As discussed in earlier chapters, this task can be more difficult than it seems. Insofar as confidence reflects the current environment, indexes of business confidence should represent relatively informed opinions about the economy's condition at the time the surveys are conducted. After all, persons running small businesses or corporations are on the front line. They are apt to sense a change in business conditions ahead of the official government reports published a month or three after the fact. Moreover, corporate business survey participants head organizations that are probably surveyed regularly by government statistical agencies.

The reality is that *business confidence indexes do a decent but far from perfect job as coincident indicators*. Visual correlations suggest that the directions of the BR, CB, and NFIB business sentiment gauges often appear to stack up well versus the directions of quarterly real GDP growth rates. (See Figures 8.2 to 8.4.) How well? The one-on-one simple correlations between quarterly real GDP growth and the CB and NFIB are

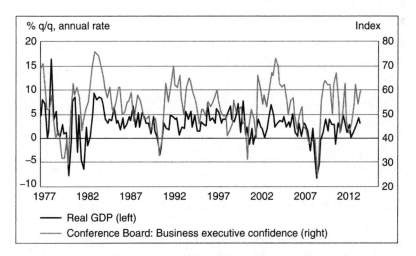

Figure 8.3   Real GDP Growth versus CB CEO Confidence Index
Source: Conference Board, Bureau of Economic Analysis.

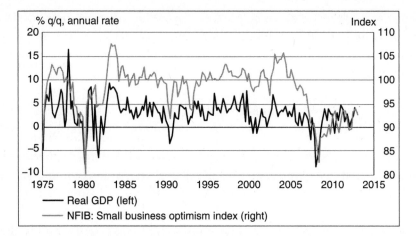

Figure 8.4   Real GDP Growth versus NFIB Small Business Optimism Index
SOURCE: National Federation of Independent Business, Bureau of Economic Analysis.

50 percent and 56 percent, respectively, over the 1977 to 2013 time span. Because these correlations are relatively close to each other, it makes sense to grant them equal weights in a composite index of the two. (See Figure 8.5.) When the composite is matched with real GDP growth, the correlation rises modestly to 59 percent. (Note: Such a correlation is equivalent to a seemingly moderate 0.35 R-square statistic indicating

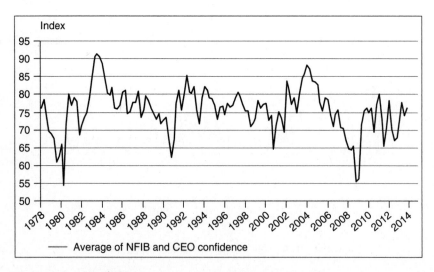

Figure 8.5   CB-NFIB Composite Business Sentiment Index
SOURCE: Author's calculation.

the fraction of the real GDP variation explained by the composite of the two business sentiment indexes. However, considering the wide variation in quarterly real GDP growth, the accompanying 0.35 R-square is respectable.)

Can We Base Forecasts on Confidence Indexes?

Although a statistical indicator may exhibit only decent correlation with a concurrent event, such as real GDP growth, it might be inherently better at predicting future events. But this is not the case when we assess the ability of business confidence indicators to forecast real GDP growth in subsequent quarters. Over the 1977 to 2013 time period, the correlation of the CB CEO business confidence index with real GDP growth falls from 52 percent in the concurrent period to 46 percent versus such growth in the following quarter and to 34 percent versus growth in the two-quarter ahead period. For the NFIB optimism index, these particular correlations go from 57 percent to 29 percent and then 28 percent.

A "first cousin" of the business sentiment indexes is the Institute for Supply Management's (ISM) composite index of purchasing agents' observations about their firms' orders, production, inventories, employment, and delivery lead times. I use the term *cousin* rather than *sibling* because the ISM survey reports observations as opposed to sentiment and expectations. According to calculations reported by the NFIB, correlations with concurrent quarterly real GDP growth are 60 percent for the ISM and 61 percent for the NFIB Optimism Index.[3] (Note: The correlation between real GDP growth and the NFIB index is slightly different from the earlier discussed correlations that were performed over a somewhat longer time span.)

In all fairness to these two confidence measures, their components were not selected based on correlations with future growth. Rather, these indexes were designed to gauge confidence. Moreover, correlations, which represent an average relationship, are not always the best way to judge an indicator's usefulness in forecasting. To forecast some variables, an indicator's performance in relation to critical turning or inflexion points is more important.

Can business confidence measures forecast subsequent business expenditures on labor, inventories, and capital? In theory, animal spirits clearly are critical for business spending. However, from a practical perspective, to what extent should forecasters rely on the related gauges? Might it be more effective to forecast business outlays using confidence determinants such as sales, profits, and capacity utilization?

We should also consider that the amount of confidence required to stimulate specific spending categories depends on multiple considerations. When can purchased inputs start to enhance production? For instance, there are multiyear lead times between the ordering of civilian aircraft and the delivery of those planes. For how long will the input produce results? A decision to step up finished goods inventories entails purchases that should help produce rather immediate results (e.g., higher sales). How easy will it be to discard inputs if they are no longer needed? For instance, it is easier to cut jobs than to resell capital goods. *The degree of confidence needed to trigger specific business outlays rises with longer delivery lead times, the difficulty of discarding inputs, and the length of payback periods.*

With these ideas in mind, we first examine the relationship between overall business confidence and nationwide spending on business inventory. It is the easiest expenditure to adjust in reaction to an incorrect sales forecast. Then we address how business confidence and hiring plans correlate with actual subsequent hiring. Versus inventory spending, hiring mistakes probably take more time to correct. Finally we investigate how business confidence and plans stack up against capital spending. Compared to both hiring and inventory purchases, capital spending decisions have longer-lasting and harder-to-reverse consequences.

Business Confidence and Inventory Building

To assess the role of business confidence in inventory spending, and to forecast inventory spending, the first step is to distinguish voluntary from involuntary inventory building. Voluntary inventory spending is associated with optimistic sales expectations for purchased finished goods inventories, or expectations of higher prices and/or shortages of materials and supplies inputs. Involuntary inventory accumulation is when inventories pile up—primarily because of disappointing sales. To distinguish voluntary from involuntary inventory building, the following guidelines should prove helpful for forecasters.

Judging Inventories

The growth rate of inflation-adjusted inventories should be judged versus the growth rate of inflation-adjusted final sales of goods. Given the volatility of monthly data, use of quarterly data is preferable. (Correlations of such real inventory growth versus gauges of business confidence and sales expectations are displayed in Table 8.1.) In assessing inventory versus sales growth, a couple of pointers are particularly germane.

Inventories are expressed as a four-quarter percentage change as opposed to an annualized change in real dollar terms. My experience is that a percentage growth rate of inventories is far easier for clients to understand than the more familiar annualized dollar change. It is in the published GDP tables and appears in most financial press descriptions of inventory behavior. (To calculate the percentage growth rate, compute an annualized growth rate of the published quarterly stock of outstanding real inventories.)

Inventory growth is about goods and should be compared to final sales of *goods*. A common mistake is to judge inventories versus the often-cited final sales of all goods, services, and structures produced in the United States.

Table 8.1   Real Nonfarm Inventory Growth Correlations with Firms' Confidence and Expected Sales

Forecast Horizon For Real Inventory Growth	Confidence Gauges			Expected Sales Indexes		
	BR[1]	NFIB[2]	Mfg. ISM[2]	BR[1]	NFIB[2]	Non-Mfg. ISM[3]
Current quarter	.77	.46	.56	.72	.47	.76
One quarter ahead	.82	.50	.75	.79	.59	.80
Two quarters ahead	.71	.44	.68	.67	.53	.69

[1]2004–2013.
[2]1980–2013.
[3]1998–2013.
SOURCE: Business Roundtable (BR), Institute for Supply Management (ISM), National Federation of Independent Business (NFIB), Bureau of Economic Analysis, author's calculations.

Another way to judge whether inventories are too high is by comparing the growth of inventory spending with business sales expectations. (See Figures 8.6 to 8.8.) An inventory buildup without a concurrent, or recent, rise in either sales growth or indexes of sales expectations may warn of a coming cutback in inventory investment. When comparing sales expectations indexes to quarterly annualized real nonfarm

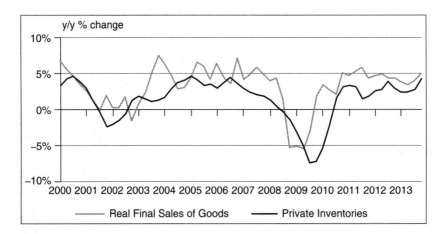

Figure 8.6   Growth of Real Inventories versus Final Sales of Goods Growth
SOURCE: Bureau of Economic Analysis.

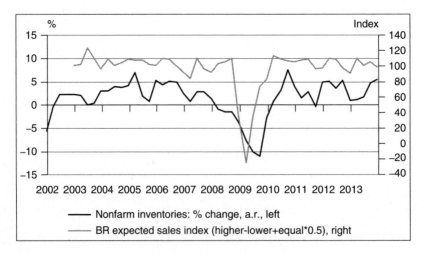

Figure 8.7   Real Inventory Growth versus Large Firms' Sales Expectations Index
SOURCE: Bureau of Economic Analysis, Business Roundtable.

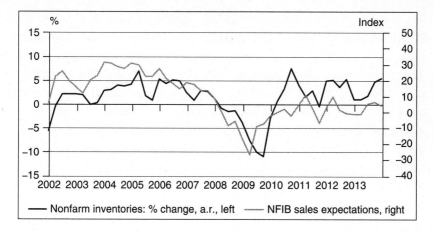

Figure 8.8 Inventory Growth versus Small Business' Sales Expectations Index
SOURCE: Bureau of Economic Analysis, National Federation of Independent Business.

inventory growth, the closest correlation is between quarterly annualized inventory growth for the current quarter and sales expectations from
the previous quarter. The same conclusion also applies to the relationship between inventory growth and various business confidence gauges.
(See Table 8.1.)

A complementary approach for judging inventory adequacy is to
study inventory/sales ratios. (See example in Figure 8.9.) They remind

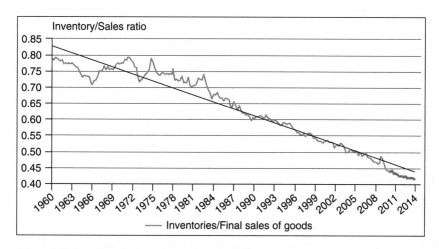

Figure 8.9 Real Inventory/Sales Ratio
SOURCE: Bureau of Economic Analysis.

forecasters not to overreact to sudden annualized inventory investment accelerations. Inventory investment as reported in the quarterly GDP statistics is expressed as a change at a seasonally adjusted annualized rate. That represents multiplying a quarterly change by four to show what would happen *if* that quarterly change was repeated for three more quarters. Thus, a reported sudden upswing in quarterly annualized inventory investment can overstate whether inventories are building too fast, since the more rapid buildup has been happening for a single quarter. The inventory/sales ratio gets around that problem because inventories are stated as an absolute level as opposed to a change at an annual rate.

However, a problem with interpreting the inventory/sales ratio is that it has steadily trended downward over time. This is because of ever-improving inventory management.

One option for overcoming this problem is to study deviations from trend. A second alternative is to examine manufacturing purchasing agents' perceptions of whether their customers' inventories are too high or too low. (See example from the manufacturing ISM survey in Figure 8.10.) When the net percentage indicates customers' inventories

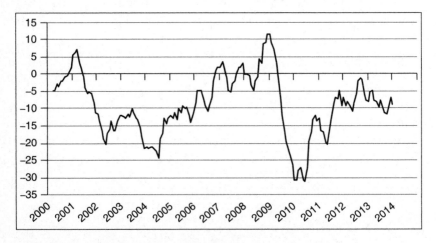

Figure 8.10   Manufacturing Purchasing Agents' Perceptions of Customers' Inventories

Manufacturing ISM, net %, nsa (% of purchasing agents saying customers' inventories are too high minus % of purchasing agents saying customers' inventories are too low), 3-month moving average
SOURCE: Institute for Supply Management.

are too high, inventory investment starts declining. This type of negative correlation is strongest with a three-quarter lag of inventory perceptions in the manufacturing ISM survey. The negative correlation was −.50 over the 1997–2013 period. In the nonmanufacturing survey, there was a somewhat shorter two-quarter lag but with a relatively low −.37 correlation during the 1998–2013 years.

Another perspective on the desirability of inventories comes from small business respondents assessments of their own inventory conditions in the monthly NFIB survey. Over the 1980–2013 time span, there was a negative 0.50 correlation between real nonfarm inventory growth and the net percent of respondents reporting that their inventories were too high.

How Do Animal Spirits Relate to Job Creation?

Although inventory building is comparatively easy to correct, hiring entails a somewhat longer horizon. It may not be as easy to reverse quickly as is inventory buying and accumulation. Thus, versus inventory accumulation, nonseasonal hiring requires confidence in a future further than next quarter's sales.

Job formation reflects the balance of layoffs and hiring. Layoffs are a component of the Conference Board's leading economic indicator (LEI) index. Layoffs' role as a leading indicator coming out of a recession reflects stabilization of early falling headcounts. That requires less confidence than is needed to renew hiring. Looking only at turning points, though, hiring plans appear more coincident with layoffs than with actual jobs. (See Figure 8.11. Note: In interpreting the plotted Manpower hiring plans survey, many economists believe it to be a coincident, rather than a leading, indicator of payroll growth.)

In the half decade following the Great Recession, job formation was unusually slow, owing in part to a less than complete recovery in business confidence. As of mid-2014, small business confidence was still well below its prerecession highs, and CEO confidence was under its prerecession peaks as well. (See Figure 8.12.)

The fundamental role that employer confidence plays in hiring decisions is reasonably intuitive. From a forecasting perspective, though, are

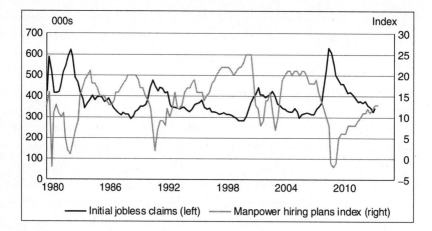

Figure 8.11   Hiring and Firing Usually Go in Opposite Directions
SOURCE: Bureau of Labor Statistics, Manpower.

business confidence statistics a useful leading indicator? Consider what happened before and after the Great Recession in 2008–2009.

Let's first examine the world of corporate America as portrayed by the Conference Board (CB) CEO confidence index. (See Figure 8.12 for its comparison with payroll growth at larger companies—those with 500 or more employees. Note: This handy data series from Automatic

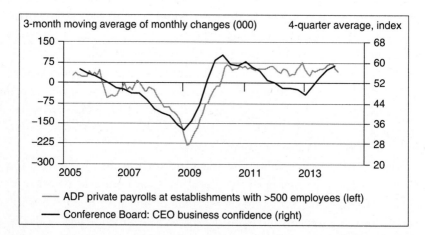

Figure 8.12   Corporate Confidence versus Large Firms' Job Formation
SOURCE: Business Roundtable, Automatic Data Processing.

Data Processing [ADP] only begins in 2005.) As larger firms' payroll changes began to turn negative in the middle of the last decade, the CB CEO Confidence Index also was heading south. However, it started to improve in 2009 before the job losses at large firms began to narrow. Early in the current decade, though, the CB CEO Confidence Index began to wane somewhat, but without a commensurate diminution in job formation at large firms. In summary, *the Conference Board's corporate economic confidence index has had a mixed record as a reliable leading indicator of job formation at large employers in recent years.*

Small businesses (defined here as those with fewer than 50 employees) are often viewed as pivotal for job creation. But does that mean that confidence on Main Street is a leading indicator of small business hiring? Figure 8.13 illustrates the relationship between the National Federation of Independent Business's (NFIB) Small Business Optimism Index and average monthly payroll changes in companies with fewer than 50 employees.

In recent years, the NFIB index has not correlated well with job formation at establishments having fewer than 50 employees. Before the Great Recession, the NFIB index had been declining for over two years. During the Recession itself, the index actually climbed upward a few months before the easing of job cuts at small firms. However, *a forecaster using the index's*

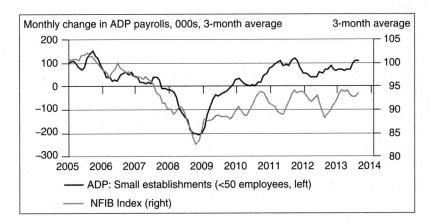

Figure 8.13 Small Firms' Jobs and Confidence

SOURCE: Automatic Data Processing, National Federation of Independent Business.

prerecession relationship with small firms' jobs to forecast the employment impli-cations of postrecession index readings would have understated small business job formation. As earlier discussed, a case can be made that during the years of the Obama Presidency, the NFIB survey respondents may have allowed their political preferences to bias downward their views about the health of their own businesses.

Business sentiment and plans gauges being more like coincident than leading indicators of job formation does offer some insight into identi-fying the underlying causes of sentiment shifts. Instead of driving the business cycle, animal spirits may be a reflection of coincident indi-cators. In other words, *business confidence may reflect, rather than affect, economic conditions, which may be driven by factors other than business senti-ment.* That said, animal spirits can still be seen as an important element in the transmission mechanism between underlying cyclical determinants and the behavior of coincident indicators such as jobs. (Mathematical economists might say that jobs and confidence are jointly determined variables in a system of simultaneous equations. In these models, the ulti-mate drivers are exogenous variables such as monetary and fiscal policies and foreign growth.)

If Animal Spirits Are Not Necessarily Driving Job Formation, What Else Could Be?

Credit conditions are a good example of a factor affecting the observed timing relationships between business confidence and hiring. Credit conditions at banks can enable smaller firms, which are often dependent on bank lending, to expand. The willingness of lenders to provide credit to small businesses varies during the business cycle, and at times small business expansion becomes credit-constrained. Figure 8.14 illustrates the relationship between average monthly payroll changes at employers with fewer than 50 employees and the net percentage of commercial banks that are tightening loan standards for businesses with less than $50 million in annual sales. (Note: A negative reading for this bank statis-tic means there are more bank lenders reporting easier lending standards than there are bank lenders reporting tighter standards.)

Banks had been steadily easing their small business lending stan-dards through the middle of the decade prior to the Great Recession. During the latter part of 2007, however, a positive net percentage of

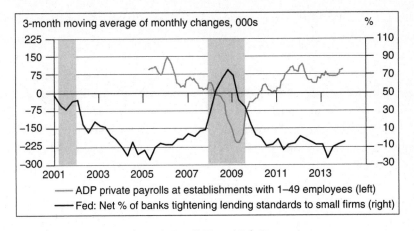

Figure 8.14 Easier Credit Aids Small Firms' Job Formation
NOTE: Shaded area denote recessions.
SOURCE: Automatic Data Processing, Federal Reserve Board of Governors.

banks began to tighten those standards. Payroll growth at small businesses started to slow in the 2006 to 2007 period and turned negative in 2008, as the net percentage of banks tightening their lending standards increased sharply. Approximately half a year after banks began, once again, to relax their small business lending standards, the pace of headcount reduction measures at small businesses decreased. And in 2011, as lending standards continued to ease, small business net job formation finally became positive.

Confidence and Capital Spending: Do They Move in Tandem?

Capital goods spending entails an even longer business commitment than hiring. The payoff periods are multiyear and it is hard to reverse such spending once it has occurred. Thus, a greater degree of confidence is required to motivate capital spending on long-lived business equipment than is needed to trigger inventory spending and hiring.

Capex Characteristics

Before discussing the role of animal spirits in analyzing and forecasting capital goods spending, it is first necessary to review the key characteristics of U.S. business equipment expenditures. As discussed in

Chapter 2, the initial step in forecasting any variable is to understand its composition. In the case of capital goods spending, we first examine what is purchased, and by whom.

The composition of U.S. capital goods spending changes over time. (See Figure 8.15.) In 1970, information processing equipment was 21 percent of overall current dollar business equipment spending. At the peak of the tech boom in 2000, that share had almost doubled to 38 percent, before receding to 31 percent in 2012. The rising tech share was accompanied by a decline in industrial equipment spending over this time period from 30 percent in 1970 to 21 percent in 2012. Shares of transportation and other equipment each account for almost one-fourth of capital goods spending, a percentage that has remained relatively consistent over time. (See Table 8.2 for a more detailed breakdown of recent shares.)

Understanding and forecasting capital goods spending is enhanced by considering the often-overlooked shares of industry in overall business equipment spending. (See Table 8.3.) Such Census Bureau data are overlooked partly because they are not available on a timely basis, with annual data reported only two years after the fact. However, such data are an important guide to which industries merit extra focus in the capital goods outlook.

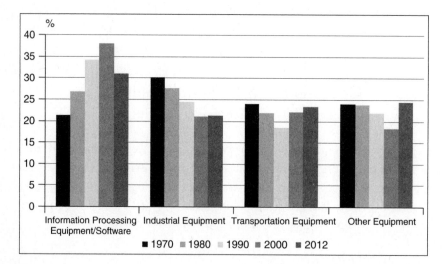

Figure 8.15   Trends in the Percentage Composition of U.S. Capital Goods Spending
SOURCE: Bureau of Economic Analysis.

Table 8.2   Shares of Current Dollar Business Equipment Spending (2012)

Info Processing Equipment	**31.3%**
Computers and peripheral equipment	11.2
Communication equipment	10.6
Medical equipment and instruments	8.1
Nonmedical instruments	0.8
Photocopy and related equipment	2.8
Office and accounting equipment	—
Industrial Equipment	**21.5**
Fabricated metal products	2.0
Engines and turbines	0.9
Metalworking machinery	3.4
Special industry machinery, n.e.c.	4.0
General industrial machinery including materials handling	7.9
Electric transmission/distribution/apparatus	3.5
Transportation Equipment	**23.6**
Trucks, buses, and truck trailers	11.5
Light trucks incl utility vehicles	6.9
Other trucks/buses/truck trailers	4.5
Autos and equipment	6.3
Aircraft equipment	3.8
Ships and boats	0.7
Railroad equipment	1.4
Other Equipment	**24.6**
Furniture and fixtures	3.7
Agricultural machinery	2.5
Construction machinery	6.2
Mining and oilfield machinery	2.7
Service industry machinery	3.4
Electrical equipment, n.e.c.	0.5
Other miscellaneous equipment	5.6

SOURCE: Bureau of Economic Analysis

The first characteristic to note is that the manufacturing, mining, and utilities sectors account for only around a third of equipment spending. However, these industries are the ones represented in the widely followed Federal Reserve data on industrial capacity utilization. That data is often used in discussing the outlook for overall capital spending.

The services, trade, and transportation sectors represent almost two-thirds of overall equipment spending. Right at the top of the

Table 8.3   Who Spends on U.S. Business Equipment?

Industry	Mill $ 2012	Share of Total (%)
Total expenditures: Equipment	801,905	
Finance and insurance	112,407	14.0
Mfg Durable goods industries*	93,265	11.6
Information	82,351	10.3
Real estate and rental and leasing	73,595	9.2
Mfg Nondurable goods industries*	67,517	8.4
Utilities*	54,036	6.7
Transportation and warehousing	49,330	6.2
Mining*	45,998	5.7
Retail trade	44,937	5.6
Health care and social assistance	42,817	5.3
Wholesale trade	31,891	4.0
Professional, scientific, and technical services	24,202	3.0
Construction	21,064	2.6
Administrative and support and waste management	15,215	1.9
Accommodation and food services	14,648	1.8
Other services (except public administration)	7,711	1.0
Educational services	5,908	0.7
Arts, entertainment, and recreation	5,241	0.7
Management of companies and enterprises	4,359	0.5
Forestry, fishing, and agricultural services	2,653	0.3
Structure and equipment expenditures serving multiple industry categories	2,760	0.3

*Components of industrial capacity utilization data.
SOURCE: Bureau of Economic Analysis.

capital spenders' list are the financial services and information sectors, which together represent almost one-fourth of overall business equipment spending.

Capex Cyclicality

Capital goods spending exhibits some very distinct cyclical properties. (See Figure 8.16.) Examination of these characteristics is critical both for forecasting business equipment spending and for its relationship to business confidence.

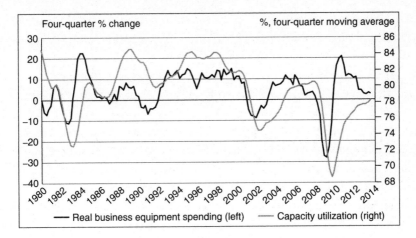

Figure 8.16   Real Business Equipment Spending versus Capacity Utilization
SOURCE: U.S. Census Bureau, Federal Reserve Board.

Business confidence and capacity utilization are two of the most often cited determinants of capital goods demand. However, despite low industrial capacity utilization and still relatively depressed business confidence, soon after the two most serious postwar recessions—the 1981–1982 downturn and the Great Recession—business equipment spending mounted a sharp, albeit temporary, recovery. This teaches us about another capital spending driver—pent-up, delayed demand. In a recession, some high-priority capital spending projects are postponed until firms are more certain that the recession has ended. But historically, the postrecession pop in capital spending has been short-lived, lasting only until high-priority purchases are completed.

Afterward, business equipment spending growth slows again until industrial capacity utilization rises to just over 80 percent. (See Figure 8.16.) However, *identifying the precise industrial capacity utilization threshold for fast demand growth in capital goods is complicated by the fact that the sectors covered in industrial capacity utilization data—manufacturing, mining, and utilities—account for only about 34 percent of business equipment spending.*

Do Interest Rates Play a Big Role in Capital Spending?

Whenever interest rates rise, reduced spending on capital goods is one often-cited potential consequence. When interest rates decline, it is frequently asserted that capital goods spending should rise. However, the evidence for rates playing much of a role in capital spending decisions is only mixed.

A recent analysis by two economists working at the Federal Reserve Board (Steve Sharpe and Gustavo Suarez) concludes that, "investment is much more loosely linked to interest rates than most traditional economic models would suggest."[4] They note that estimates, based on analyzing time series data of capital spending sensitivity to changing user costs of capital, are frequently "surprisingly small, particularly in the short run. What is more, attempts to separately estimate effects of the three components of user cost—interest rates, capital goods prices, and taxes—tend to find no negative effect from the interest rate component."[5]

Why have economists had trouble identifying interest rate effects on capital spending? One reason is that, in the case of capital spending, it is statistically difficult to disentangle cause and effect. Capital spending affects credit demand and interest rates, but rates also influence capital expenditures. Thus, when examining historical time series data, one often observes interest rates and capital spending moving up and down in tandem. To get around the problems with time series analysis, economists study cross-section data that permit comparing investment by firms facing different interest rates. Such studies suggest the rate effects on capital spending are larger than is implied in time series analyses.

Studying Chief Financial Officers' (CFOs) responses to questions about their firms' investment behavior vis-à-vis interest rates is the approach utilized by Sharpe and Suarez. They evaluated a web-based survey of more than 500 CFOs in nonfinancial industries in September 2012, when it was widely perceived that a moderate economic recovery was underway. The participants were in both large and small industries. However, only 22 percent of the CFOs at publicly owned companies responded, suggesting that the sample was somewhat biased away from exceptionally large firms.

Two specific questions in the survey were posed as follows: "Assuming demand and cost conditions faced by your firm and industry remain the same, please answer the following: By how much would your borrowing costs have to decrease to cause you to initiate, accelerate, or increase investment projects in the next year? By how much would

Table 8.4 Effects of Interest Rate Changes on Investment Prospects

Rate Change	Percent of Respondents Who Would Alter Their Investments*
−50 bp	3%
−100 bp	5%
−200 bp	8%
−300 bp	5%
> −300 bp	11%
+ 50 bp	6%
+ 100 bp	10%
+ 200 bp	15%
+ 300 bp	11%
> + 300 bp	20%

*No investment response was reported by 68% of the respondents for rate decreases and by 38% of respondents for rate increases.
SOURCE: Duke University/*CFO Magazine* Global Business Outlook Survey, September 2012.

your borrowing costs have to increase to cause you to delay or stop investment projects?"

Note in Table 8.4 that it took relatively large rate changes to make much difference in business investment. It would take rate declines of at least 200 basis points to raise investments for just 16 percent of respondents. However, rate rises of at least 200 basis points would trim investments for 31 percent of respondents. Sharpe and Suarez conclude that comparatively large rate changes are required to make a difference for investments because hurdle rates are around 15 percent. Also, it is worth noting that rate sensitivity is greater for firms citing working capital management as a top concern, firms with current plans to borrow, and firms with just moderate revenue expectations. (See Table 8.5.)

I believe the results of this survey, conducted in September 2012, might understate the sensitivity to rate declines, and overstate the sensitivity to rate rises, in more normal times. When the survey was fielded, incoming economic data suggested that U.S. growth was slowing enough for the Fed to announce a new quantitative easing (QE) securities purchase program aimed at preventing unacceptably weak growth. The survey asked respondents to assume demand and cost considerations were not changing when rates changed. Had those questions been asked in a

Table 8.5   Borrowing Cost Increase Required to Induce Delay or Cutback (Percent of Firms Responding)

Subsample of Firms (Number)	(1) Very Sensitive (50 or 100 Basis Points)	(2) Somewhat Sensitive (200 or 300 Basis Points)	(3) Not Sensitive (>300 Basis Points or No Change)
Working capital management is: A top concern (138)	24	25	51
Working capital management is: Not a concern (379)	12	28	60
To finance capital expenditures, a firm has: Plans to borrow (249)	19	31	50
To finance capital expenditures, a firm has: No plans to borrow (268)	12	23	60
Expected 12-month revenue growth is: Less than 1 percent (91)	15	35	50
Expected 12-month revenue growth is: 1 percent to 5 percent (89)	13	29	57
Expected 12-month revenue growth is: More than 5 percent (14)	6	20	74

SOURCE: Duke CFO Magazine Global Business Outlook Survey, September 2012; Steve Sharpe and Gustavo Suarez, "Do CFOs Think Investment is Sensitive to Interest Rates?" The Federal Reserve Board, September 26, 2013.

stronger economic climate, there could have been more investment activity spurred by rate declines but less investment timidity in the face of higher rates.

Are Capital Spending Plans a Useful Leading or Coincident Indicator of Investment?

It is worthwhile for forecasters to know if business capital spending plans are a decent leading indicator of equipment spending. Even if such plans prove not very useful as a leading indicator, they still might serve as a timely coincident indicator of equipment spending data. That indicator status can be helpful if the plan information is published on a timelier basis than the sometimes hard-to-forecast business equipment spending data.

Larger corporations account for the bulk of capital spending. According to the NFIB, the median capital spending by respondents in the business optimism survey is only around $2,000 over a six-month horizon or $4,000 per year. For the approximately 6 million small business employers in the United States, such a median expenditure would roughly sum to around $24 billion per annum—a tiny sliver of the almost $2 trillion in 2013 capital expenditures.

The quarterly Business Roundtable CEO Economic Outlook survey includes a question on capital spending plans six months in the future. (See Figure 8.17.) It behaves more like a coincident than a leading indicator. That can still be helpful for forecasters needing to know at least where capital spending stands before the information is published in subsequent government economic data.

The monthly NFIB Small Business Optimism survey also solicits responses on six-month ahead capital spending plans. (See Figure 8.18.) It, too, has performed mostly as a coincident indicator. However, in the current business expansion it has understated national business equipment spending growth. In part, this is because the post-Great Recession small business credit crunch abated only gradually. Also, as discussed earlier, in recent years there may been somewhat of a downside political bias in this survey.

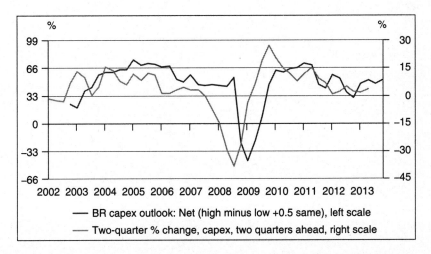

Figure 8.17 Corporate Capital Spending Plans versus Equipment Spending
SOURCE: Business Roundtable, Bureau of Economic Analysis.

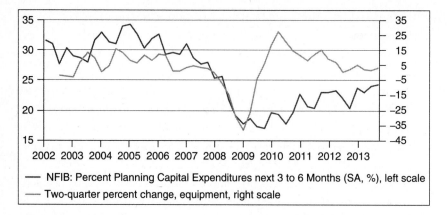

Figure 8.18   Small Firms' Planned Capital Spending versus Equipment Spending
SOURCE: National Federation of Independent Business, Bureau of Economic Analysis.

Animal Spirits and Capital Spending

Although near-term capital spending plans are more of a coincident than a leading indicator, measures of business sentiment are useful in predicting capex. For example, an annual composite index of small and large business confidence—animal spirits—created at the UBS investment bank research department is a decent forward indicator of year-ahead growth in real (inflation-adjusted) capital goods expenditures. (See in

Table 8.6   Business Equipment Forecasting Model

$$\%\Delta \,[\![Capex]\!]\_t = \alpha + \beta \times \% \,\Delta[\![CapU]\!]\_t + [\![\gamma \times UBS\_index]\!]\_(t-1)$$
$$+ \,\delta \times AR(1) + \varepsilon\_t$$

Sample: 1988–2011 Annual Data

Variable	Coefficient	Std. Error	*t*-Statistic
Intercept	−33.219 (α)	13.335	−2.491
% Δ [CapU] (*t*)	1.538 (β)	0.198	7.759
*Spirits*_(−1)	0.374 (γ)	0.125	3.003
AR(1)	0.653 (δ)	0.140	4.665

Notes:
%Δ: Percent change in cal avg real private nonresidential investment in equipment.
%Δ(t): Percent change of FED capacity utilization in concurrent period.
_(−1): 1-year lag of UBS Animal Spirits Index.
AR(1): Autoregressive component.
SOURCE: UBS.

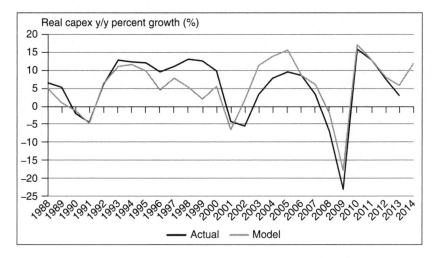

Figure 8.19 Actual versus Predicted Capital Spending Growth
Source: UBS

Table 8.6 a capex forecasting model utilizing the change in capacity utilization and the lagged value of an animal spirits composite index of corporate and small business sentiment. Actual versus predicted values are illustrated in Figure 8.19.)

Key Takeaways

1. Economists with divergent theoretical frameworks and political preferences generally agree on the critical business cycle role played by firms' animal spirits—business confidence.
2. Business confidence indexes published by the Conference Board (CB) and the Business Roundtable (BR) help quantify animal spirits for corporate America (Wall Street). Confidence of small business (Main Street) can be gauged with National Federation of Independent Business (NFIB) survey data.
3. Business confidence indexes at times can be politically biased.
4. From an analytical perspective, firms' confidence is important for business spending on inventories, labor, and capital.

5. From a forecasting perspective, business confidence gauges are a leading indicator of business spending on inventories and capital goods, but more of a coincident indicator of job formation.

6. Key causal fundamentals for future inventory spending are expected sales and assessments of whether existing inventories are too high or too low. Capital spending is very sensitive to capacity utilization but not interest rates.

7. Examination of published data on which industries do the most capital spending is an often overlooked but useful information source. For instance, the Fed's industrial capacity utilization gauge represents sectors accounting for only around a third of business equipment spending.

Notes

1. John M. Keynes, *The General Theory of Employment, Interest and Money* (London: Macmillan, 1936), 161–162.

2. U.S. Small Business Administration, "Small Business Trends," www.sba.gov/content/small-business-trends.

3. Michael J. Chow, "Small Business Indicators of Macro-Economic Performance: An Update," National Federation of Independent Business Research Foundation, 2012.

4. Steve Sharpe and Gustavo Suarez, "Do CFOs Think Investment Is Sensitive to Interest Rates?" *The Economists' Notebook*, Federal Reserve Board of Governors, September 26, 2013.

5. Ibid.

Chapter 9

Forecasting Fickle Consumers

When men are employed, they are best contented; for on the days they worked they are good-natured and cheerful, and, with the consciousness of having done a good day's work, they spent the evening jollily; but on our idle days they were mutinous and quarrelsome.

—Benjamin Franklin, *Autobiography*, 1793, Chapter X

C onsumer spending is perhaps the most important of all business forecasts. The consumption of goods and services accounts for approximately two-thirds of gross domestic product (GDP), and it is typically the first topic that my investor clients wish to discuss. A national consumer spending projection is a key starting point for most marketing studies and, during my career, expected consumer spending has generally been the issue separating optimists from pessimists.

I am usually optimistic about consumer spending. I agree with pessimists that the American consumer should be saving more for rainy days and retirement. However, when forecasting *I always distinguish how I believe households and firms should behave versus what they are likely to actually do*. Moreover, I often disagree with pessimists about potential purchasing power and the American standard of living. For instance, although some observers fret about the domestic jobs lost to outsourcing, I focus more on what the accompanying cheap imports mean for purchasing power.

In this chapter, the challenge of making accurate consumer spending forecasts is approached from both the income and savings perspectives. After reviewing the rich variety of publicly available, but sometimes overlooked, consumer spending data, we turn our attention to income formation. That requires an understanding of jobs, wages, transfer payments, investment incomes, and small business profitability. The purchasing power of these incomes will depend on price inflation—a topic that is introduced in the next chapter. Then we tackle the always-topical saving rate issue, analyzing key national determinants such as public confidence, wealth, and demographics. Finally, we look at some recent consumer spending subjects, including student debt and household formation.

Making and Spending Money

How do Americans spend their money? And how can we go about determining the answer?

As discussed in Chapter 2, the first step in forecasting is to understand the particular dependent variable to be modeled and then predicted. For U.S. consumer spending, the most comprehensive data set lies in the personal consumption expenditures published monthly by the Bureau of Economic Analysis (BEA). This richly detailed information is presented in both current dollar and real (inflation-adjusted) terms. (See aggregate personal consumption expenditures growth in Figure 9.1.) For more detailed data on spending by income segment, the Bureau of Labor

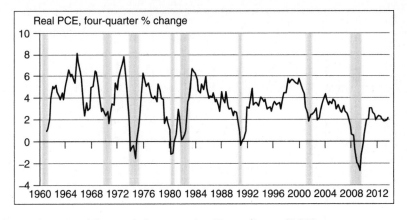

Figure 9.1 Real Personal Consumption Expenditures (PCE)
NOTE: Shaded areas are recessions.
SOURCE: Bureau of Economic Analysis, National Bureau of Economic Research.

Statistics' annual Survey of Consumer Expenditures is useful, albeit not particularly timely. (See Table 9.1.) The more immediate alternative is the Census Bureau's monthly retail sales data, which are usually reported two to three weeks before the more comprehensive personal consumption spending figures are released.

How Do Americans Make Their Money?

According to monthly statistics published by the BEA, almost three-fifths of Americans' personal income comes from wages, salaries, and benefits. An additional one-sixth is accounted for by transfer payments—government benefits (e.g., mainly Social Security payments) and pension disbursements. Interest, dividends, and rent add about another one-seventh. (See shares of these and other income categories in Figure 9.2.) The BEA also reports after-tax disposable income, which is usually around 85 percent of gross personal income.

In order to construct forecasts for personal income and real (inflation-adjusted) personal disposable (after-tax) income, I have found the following methodology quite helpful.

Table 9.1 Consumer Spending Allocation (2012)

Quintiles of Income before Taxes: Expenditure % Allocation for Each Income Class	All Units	Lowest 20% of Income	Second 20% of Income	Third 20% of income	Fourth 20% of Income	Fifth 20% of Income
Average annual consumption expenditures	100	100	100	100	100	100
Shelter	19.2	24.6	21.6	19.9	18.3	17.6
Pensions and Social Security	10.2	1.8	4.5	7.9	10.5	14.7
Food at home	7.6	10.9	9.2	8.4	7.7	6.0
Utilities, fuels, and public services	7.1	9.8	9.1	8.3	7.0	5.4
Health care	6.9	7.6	8.5	7.8	7.0	5.8
Vehicle purchases (net outlay)	6.2	4.5	4.9	6.5	7.5	6.2
Gasoline and motor oil	5.4	5.5	6.2	6.4	5.8	4.3
Food away from home	5.2	4.9	4.7	5.0	5.4	5.4
Entertainment	5.1	4.5	4.9	4.8	4.9	5.5
Cash contributions	3.7	3.2	3.4	3.0	3.6	4.3
Apparel and services	3.4	3.4	3.5	3.1	3.5	3.4
Household furnishings and equipment	3.1	2.4	3.2	3.0	2.9	3.4
Education	2.3	2.8	1.3	1.2	1.7	3.4
Alcoholic beverages	0.9	0.7	0.8	0.8	0.9	0.9
Life and other personal insurance	0.7	0.4	0.4	0.5	0.7	0.9

SOURCE: Bureau of Labor Statistics.

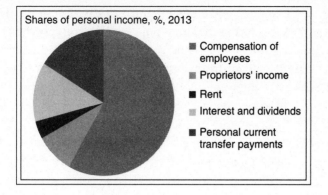

Figure 9.2   Functional Distribution of Income
SOURCE: Bureau of Economic Analysis.

Let's begin by summarizing a reasonably simple but efficient eight-step recipe:

1. Personal income is estimated based on its historical average relationship with its critical wage and salary component.
2. The estimated wage and salary income component reflects job and wage forecasts.
3. Payroll jobs are forecast via their relationship with past credit conditions.
4. Wages are forecast based on their historical relationship to the unemployment rate.
5. The employment component of the unemployment rate calculation is estimated based on its historical relationship with payroll jobs.
6. The labor force component of the unemployment rate is based on Census projections of adult population growth and assumptions about the labor force participation rate.
7. The average overall personal tax rate is used to calculate after-tax disposable personal income.
8. The price inflation used to convert nominal, current dollar personal income into real (inflation-adjusted) income is estimated based on its recent relationships with labor costs.

In understanding this recipe's rationale, it is important to remember that labor compensation is the largest component—almost three-fifths—of personal income. The other major components (e.g., transfer payments, investments, and rent incomes) can be forecast individually, although my experience is that they can be hard to pin down. Moreover, the potential error in an overall personal income forecast may cumulate with the miscalculations from each component's forecast, unless these inaccuracies have a high negative correlation with each other. With this in mind, how have I made the personal income forecasting exercise less arduous?

The answer is that *I let the personal income growth forecast be a function of its historical relationship to the estimated wage and salary component growth estimate*. Specifically, over the 1960 to 2013 period, the average annual relationship between the growth of current dollar personal income (PI) and its wage and salary (W&S) component was:

Percent change (PI) = 1.23 percent + 0.88 (percent change W&S)

For instance, if (W&S) growth is 3.0%, PI growth would be:

$$1.23 + 2.64\% = 3.87\%$$

I chose this methodology partly because PI growth was reasonably well correlated (e.g., 89 percent R-square) with W&S growth. Note: This finding may reflect the fact that some nonlabor income components (e.g., proprietor's incomes, dividends, and rents) respond to the business cycle in a fashion similar to wage and salary incomes.

To forecast the labor component of personal income, one must make projections for both employment and wages.

With the business cycle importantly determined by the credit cycle, I find it useful to forecast this year's job growth with regression models that reflect earlier credit conditions. Private payroll job growth depends, in part, on earlier changes in bank and bond market lending standards. These bank lending standards can be quantified through the Federal Reserve's quarterly Senior Loan Office Opinion Survey. (See example in Figure 9.3.) Bond market credit conditions can be proxied by changing quality yield spreads between yields on lower rated corporate bonds and yields on risk-free Treasury securities of a similar maturity.

Wage rate growth usually picks up only after the civilian unemployment rate falls to the 5 to 6 percent level. History suggests that the eventual wage acceleration from its postrecession low should be between 1 and 1.5 percent, approximately. (See Figure 9.4.) Thus, when unemployment drops into

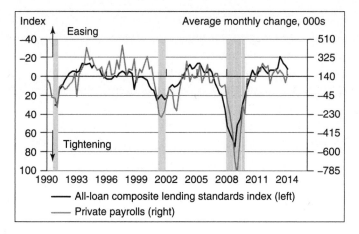

Figure 9.3 Jobs and Bank Lending Standards

*Composite index of bankers' assessment of lending standards for individual loan categories.
NOTE: Shaded areas are recessions.
SOURCE: Bureau of Labor Statistics, UBS.

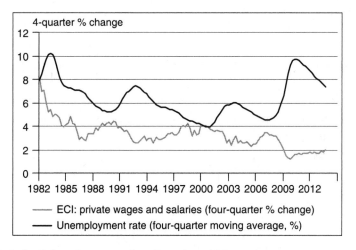

Figure 9.4 Labor Compensation Growth and Unemployment
SOURCE: Bureau of Labor Statistics.

the 5 to 6 percent range, add 1 to 1.5 percent to whatever hourly compensation growth was observed prior to the fall. Conversely, when the unemployment rate starts to rise steadily above 6 percent, subtract 1.5 to 2 percent from the growth of hourly compensation observed before the rise.

To forecast the unemployment rate, I use the payroll growth rate forecast discussed earlier to estimate the growth in the number of persons either self-employed or working on a payroll. This overall household employment concept is compared to the size of the civilian labor force to estimate the unemployment rate. Over the 1960 to 2013 period, here was the average relationship between annual overall employment (E) growth and the growth of nonfarm payrolls (P):

$$\text{Percent change E} = 0.21\% + 0.73\%(\text{change P})$$

For instance, if (P) growth is 2%, E growth would be:

$$0.21\% + 0.73(2\%) = 1.67\%$$

To project the unemployment rate also requires an estimate of the labor force growth. To do so, multiply the growth of the adult population by the assumed change, if any, in the labor force participation rate. (See further discussion in Chapter 7.)

To get from growth in estimated pretax personal income to growth in after-tax disposable personal income, the forecaster must *adjust for taxes*. The shortcut here is to multiply the forecast personal income level by 1 minus the recent ratio of total personal taxes paid to personal income. (The latter can be accessed from the personal income link on the Bureau of Labor Statistics website: www.bea.gov.) When Federal tax policies change during the forecast period, the Congressional Budget Office (CBO) publishes a dollar amount, which can then be used to adjust the tax ratio.

Estimating real (inflation-adjusted) after-tax disposable personal income entails an inflation forecast—a topic discussed in Chapter 10. For the time being, here is a convenient rule of thumb for forecasting annual inflation of the chain price index for personal consumption expenditures (a.k.a. PCE chain price index). It is used to convert nominal income into real income and reflects the cost of the market basket consumed in the previous period. Annual inflation of the PCE chain price index for personal consumption expenditures in the first 14 years of the twenty-first century averaged around half a percentage point less than the annual growth of earlier discussed hourly wages.

Will We Ever Start to Save More Money?

Real income formation is generally the most important determinant of consumer spending. That said, how much we *save* always seems to be the first topic my clients raise when talking about the American consumer. U.S. households save a much smaller percentage of their incomes than do families in the other developed economies on this planet. And in this country the personal saving rate—personal saving as a percent of disposable personal income—has been declining over time. (See Figure 9.5.) Therefore, a common question is: "When will we Americans start saving like we used to—like everyone else in other countries?"

The frequency of this query reflects concerns about the implications of a lower personal saving rate. For equities investors considering consumer-oriented investments, the worry is that consumer spending growth would be tepid if households started saving more money. Fixed-income investors are concerned about a too-low personal saving rate, but for a different reason: a lower saving rate is viewed as keeping interest rates higher than they would otherwise be in those stages of the business cycle when overall credit demand is relatively strong.

My observation, however, is that *concerns about a possible sharp jump in the personal saving rate often are false alarms that lead to incorrect investment*

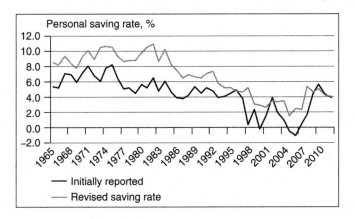

Figure 9.5   Initially Reported and Revised Saving Rate
SOURCE: Bureau of Labor Statistics.

decisions. Investors awaiting a higher personal saving rate before placing their bets usually have been frustrated, as the personal saving rate has remained comparatively low versus its levels from the mid-1970s through the early 1980s. And to make matters even more exasperating, *initially reported personal saving rates have at times been revised upward.* (See Figure 9.5.) To be sure, the revisions since the early 1980s have not been enough to raise saving rates to their previous levels. The upward revisions, though, suggest that earlier fears about especially low personal saving rates were overblown. They have also become a problem for forecasters utilizing the earlier discussed Keynesian multiplier, which is partly determined by the personal savings rate. If the savings rate is revised up, the multiplier will be somewhat less than was estimated earlier.

Even if it was not subject to such large revisions, the personal saving rate would still be a problematic statistic. As presented in the National Income and Product Accounts (NIPA), the personal saving numerator of the reported personal saving rate is not directly measured. Instead, it is a residual between measured incomes and measured personal consumption. Consequently, errors in accurately measuring personal savings can reflect mistakes in estimating both income and consumption. Both may be revised substantially as the BEA collects more complete information over time.

As an alternative to the NIPA personal saving rate measure, the Federal Reserve's quarterly Flow of Funds (FOF) report includes a

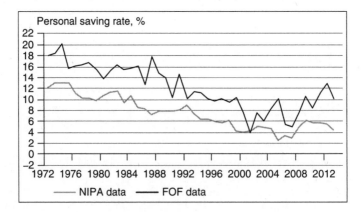

Figure 9.6 Two Personal Saving Measures
SOURCE: Bureau of Economic Analysis, Federal Reserve Board of Governors.

personal saving estimate based on adding households' net accumulation of financial assets. Its relative volatility on a quarterly basis, though, makes it a particularly difficult measure to assess. (See Figure 9.6.) Moreover, it, too, can occasionally be subject to large changes if there are revisions to its disposable personal income denominator, which is the same NIPA income measure used in calculating the NIPA personal saving rate. Still, economists often view the FOF personal saving rate as being, if averaged over a number of quarters, a more accurate picture of true personal saving behavior. Since it is usually above the NIPA version of the personal saving rate, the FOF measure is sometimes cited as evidence that the NIPA version of the personal saving rate is understating the true personal serving rate. Nevertheless, even by FOF measurements, the personal saving rate is not what it used to be.

Why Don't Americans Save More?

Why do Americans save less of their incomes than in the past? And why is the U.S. personal saving rate less than that of other developed countries? To address these two questions, I always distinguish what consumers should do from their actual behavior.

Financial advisers and economists generally agree that Americans do not save enough for so-called rainy days and retirement. This conclusion is often derived by estimating how much money families and individuals may need for emergencies and retirement and then working backward. So, for given ages, planned retirement dates and assumed rates of investment return, how much of one's current income must be saved to achieve one's goals? The answer is usually a good deal more than the nickel on the dollar that American families, on average, have been saving in recent decades.

Indeed, when asked what percentage of their usual incomes should be saved for precautionary purposes, polled U.S. households in 2010 cited an average of 10.8 percent—around double the amount that, according to NIPA data, is actually saved.[1] Moreover, people are plenty worried that they are not saving enough. Consider their responses to the following question: "How worried are you about not having enough money for retirement?" Either "not at all" or "not too" were answered by 30 percent of respondents. A higher 42 percent responded that they were "very worried" and another 27 percent answered that they were "somewhat worried."[2] Nevertheless, despite advice from professionals and notwithstanding their own perceptions of their saving behavior, today's Americans are saving less than in the past. Why?

When economists seek to understand the public's saving behavior, they usually study wealth, debt, interest rates, and demographics—four key areas of input. Positive wealth effects on consumption have long been identified as a key determinant of the personal saving rate. Debt becomes an increasingly studied factor in savings rates when households' financial leverage mounts. Macroeconomic theorists have always given interest rates an important role when modeling savings behavior. And with an aging population, demographic impacts on saving are receiving more attention.

More Wealth = Less Saving

Wealth consists of all financial and nonfinancial assets on households' balance sheets. However, stocks and residences are the two categories, other than incomes, normally considered pivotal drivers of consumer spending. Studying the United States through the middle of the first decade of the twenty-first century—*before* the subsequent crash in stocks and home prices—Case, Quigley, and Shiller report that a 10 percent change in either stock market or housing wealth will impact consumer spending by 0.4 percent.[3] (Note: That is equivalent to a similar percentage point change in the personal saving rate.)

Why are stock market effects on consumption only around a nickel on the dollar?

The typical answer is that stock market wealth is not broadly distributed. It mostly accrues to wealthier individuals and families with comparatively high saving rates. Consider data from the Fed's Survey of Consumer Finances.[4] In 2010 only around 15 percent of U.S. households *directly* held stock. However, around half of families in the top 10 percent of the income distribution directly held stock, with that statistic falling to around one-fourth for the preceding decile. Looking at *direct and indirect* stock holdings, the picture is somewhat different. (Indirect stock holdings are those in pooled investment trusts, retirement accounts, or other managed accounts.) In 2010, half of American households fell into that category. That said, the distribution of stock market wealth and savings is skewed toward higher-income families. For instance, in 2010 only 52 percent of all families saved during the year. And the median portfolio value for all families with direct and/or indirect stock holdings was $29,000. In contrast, the 2010 median value of holdings for the 91 percent of families in the top income decile who also had direct or indirect holdings of stock was $267,500. And 81 percent of the families in the top income decile saved. Thus, the distribution of stock ownership is skewed to relatively high-income families who are very likely to be savers.

Residential real estate wealth effects on consumption are apt to be less than were estimated prior to the home price collapse that began in the 2007 to 2008 period. Until then, home equity extraction via borrowing (e.g., home equity loans and second mortgages) was becoming an increasingly utilized method of converting rising real estate worth into consumer spending. Over the 15 years through 2006, the S&P/Case Shiller U.S. home resale price index rose by around 250 percent. With the accompanying surge in households' home equity, lenders became increasingly willing to lend on homes' heightened value as collateral. This willingness to lend was facilitated by the development of asset-backed securities collateralized by mortgages and home equity loans. However, with the collapse in home prices and the related values of these securities, home equity extraction via borrowing was severely restrained. Even after home prices started to recover in 2013, banks and investors remained leery of venturing again into this type of lending.

That said, there is still some positive real estate wealth effect on consumer spending via improved consumer confidence and the renewed perception that "the house is doing my saving for me." Homeowners are important contributors to overall consumer spending. As of 2012, approximately 64 percent of households owned their homes, and they accounted for around 75 percent of consumer expenditures.[5]

Too Much Debt?

Although increased wealth for the country can support forecasts of less saving and more consumption, I find that many forecasters focus more on how rising debt burdens might reduce consumption when borrowers have to repay their loans. Borrowing money can allow consumption to grow faster than incomes. But what happens when borrowers subsequently have to repay their debt? To service it, will they cut back on *their* consumption so that spending grows less than incomes and the saving rate consequently rises? My view is that *usually, although not always, too much time is wasted on unnecessary worries about possibly deleterious impacts of household debt.*

My reasoning, I believe, is relatively straightforward. *Debt represents an intertemporal transfer of purchasing power as opposed to a net change in aggregate purchasing power.* In other words, for every borrower there is a lender. Lenders are transferring purchasing power from their current incomes so as to enable borrowers to spend more than they earn. When that debt is subsequently repaid, borrowers consume less than their incomes. However, the repayments of principal and interest allow lenders' incomes and spending to rise. To be sure, repayments to foreign lenders reduce domestic purchasing power. However, as the foreign creditors either consume or lend, the accompanying funds are recirculated in the global economy. I think these points are almost too obvious to state. But I also believe that forecasters and investors often overlook such reasoning.

When, then, does household debt ever become a problem? The answer is simple. If borrowers cannot repay their debts, lenders' incomes and willingness to lend are adversely impacted. And as discussed in earlier chapters, sharply rising delinquencies and defaults can lead to a recession if individual lenders and lending intermediaries become less able and willing to recycle savings into investment in a timely manner.

Judging whether debt burdens have become high enough to spell serious repayment problems has always been a source of controversy among forecasters. Through the early twenty-first-century, aggregate debt-to-income ratios rose steadily. (See Figure 9.7.) Whenever these ratios reached a new high, some forecasters began predicting an imminent recession. But as each new debt-income high was exceeded by the next, no imminent recessions occurred. One reason was that, over time, a growing percentage of households were undertaking debt. By 2010, the fraction of households with any debt had risen to 75 percent from

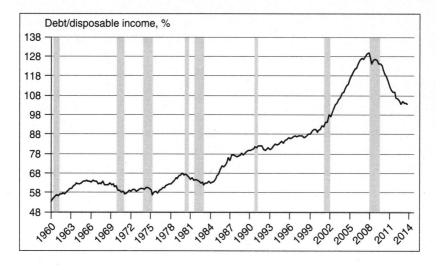

Figure 9.7 Ratio of Debt to Disposable Personal Income
NOTE: Shaded areas represent recessions
SOURCE: Bureau of Economic Analysis, Federal Reserve Board of Governors.

70 percent in 1983.[6] Thus, it was necessary to judge whether in the aggregate household sector there was more debt per debtor or just a greater percentage of households utilizing debt.

Another factor meriting consideration was the secular decline in interest rates that started in the 1980s, which by itself lowered repayment burdens for a given amount of debt. Thus, when making historical comparisons of debt burdens, it is also necessary to examine repayment-income percentages. (See Figure 9.8.) Before the past two recessions, they topped previous cyclical peaks—a useful prerecession warning. As of mid-2014, the debt repayment-income percentage was relatively low, partly because of the shift to renting. In this setting, repayment burdens should be judged in the context of overall financial obligations, including rent as a percentage of disposable personal income. (See Figure 9.8.)

In the middle of the second decade of the 21st century, *student debt* is seen by some forecasters as a limiting factor in consumer spending. This is still another legacy of the Great Recession. A combination of weak labor demand and the ready availability of government-guaranteed student loans boosted college enrollment to record levels.

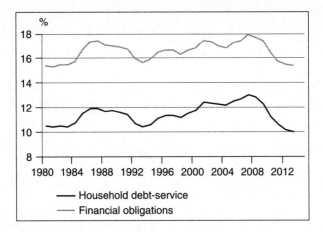

Figure 9.8   Debt Repayments and Overall Financial Obligations as a Percentage of Disposable Personal Income
SOURCE: Bureau of Economic Analysis, Federal Reserve Board of Governors.

As a consequence, though, there was an unusually large rise in student debt. Over the 10 years through 2013, outstanding student debt rose fourfold, to more than a trillion dollars, according to data compiled by the Federal Reserve Bank of New York.[7] During this time, the fraction of 25-year old young adults with any student debt jumped from 25 percent in 2003 to 43 percent in 2012. In addition, the average student loan balance nearly doubled, to just more than $20,000 per student in 2013. *In response to the student loan debt surge, should forecasters trim projected consumption and raise the expected saving rate as these loans are repaid? Not necessarily* is my answer. Why?

The overall debt burden of the household sector has not become heavier even with the buildup of student loans. (See Figures 9.7 and 9.8.) This is primarily because *student loans have been a substitute for other types of debt.* With falling home prices between 2008 and 2013, for example, many parents were unable to finance their children's higher education through either a mortgage refinancing or home equity loans. Thus, their college-bound children turned to student loans instead. (Note: The degree to which parents feel an obligation to service their children's student loans, if necessary, is unknown.) For the student borrowers themselves, more student debt meant that they borrowed less via other types of loans. Data from the Federal Reserve Bank of

New York indicate that between 2008 and 2012 per capita student loan debt for student borrowers rose by \$9,677, but their per capita nonstudent debt declined by \$15,364.

Another reason for my answer is that repayments and defaults for student loans have less negative consumer spending impact than repayments and defaults for most other types of loans. This is because the great bulk of student loans are guaranteed and held by the federal government. According to the Consumer Financial Protection Bureau, such federal student loans in May 2013 were approximately \$1 trillion, while privately originated student loans were around an estimated \$150 billion.[8] In effect, the federal government is in the student loan business and eager to recycle repayments into new student loans. In contrast, private lenders are not always as inclined to recycle repayments into new loans. Also, when privately held loans default there can be adverse chain reactions within the private lending system. When a loan is held or guaranteed by the federal sector and the borrower defaults, taxpayers could be on the hook. However, a more realistic assumption is that if the federal government loses money on student loans it will just run a larger overall deficit and borrow more rather than raising taxes. (Note: These comments should not be construed as an endorsement of a nationalized banking system. I think such a system would be less innovative and probably more prone to making bad loans than a largely private banking system.)

Saving and the Overall Balance Sheet

In order to assess the effects of asset and liability crosscurrents on the personal saving rate and personal consumption expenditures, economists study households' net worth—assets minus liabilities. Versus the personal saving rate, there is an inverse relationship between household net worth (NW) and the NIPA personal saving rate. (See Figure 9.9.) Note that NW is scaled versus a current dollar disposable personal income (DPI) denominator. The R-square relationship between NW/DPI and the personal saving rate was a respectable 0.73 from 1978 through 2013. Moreover, the visual correlation between these two variables has been convincing to numerous observers. Also, Figure 9.9 often has been included in the Federal Reserve System's Semi-Annual

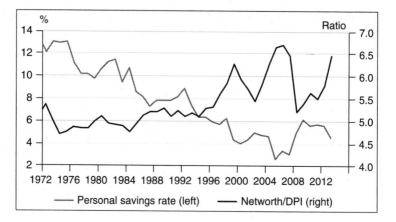

Figure 9.9   Saving Rate versus (Net Worth/Disposable Personal Income)
SOURCE: Bureau of Economic Analysis, Federal Reserve Board of Governors.

Monetary Policy Report to Congress. Relationships that are displayed regularly in high profile Fed reports tend to get economists' attention. Therefore, within the macroeconomic forecasting community, NW/DPI has been viewed as a so-called dominant variable determining the personal saving rate.

This perception was enhanced during the prerecession real estate boom. By 2005 NW/DPI had reached a new high of 6.7 and the personal saving rate had fallen to 1.6 percent, a postwar low. Then along came the Great Recession and the accompanying crash in home and stock prices. By 2008 NW/DPI had fallen to 5.2—its lowest level in 14 years. In contrast, the personal saving rate rose to 5.4 percent—its highest in 15 years. Since the 2005 to 2008 swings appeared consistent with the NW/DPI explanation of the personal saving rate, many forecasters chose to use that relationship to forecast the saving rate in the subsequent years of a slow economic recovery.

This methodology, however, proved less than ideal. During the 2009 to 2012 period, a model using only NW/DPI consistently *overstated* the personal saving rate. According to the author's calculations, such a model overstated the saving rate in all of those four years by an average of 1.65 percentage points. The errors ranged between 1 percent in 2011 to 2.5 percentage points in 2009. (Note: These regression calculations were estimated with the information available before the major 2013

NIPA data revision and definitional changes affected historical statistics on savings rates.)

Lesson for forecasters of consumer behavior. As the 2009 to 2012 personal saving rate was running below its normal relationship with the household balance sheet, forecasters had two choices. Some decided to emphasize that the saving rate was still too low and according to their models, was estimated to rise and be accompanied by very weak consumer spending. However, the other more appealing alternative was to try to understand why the conventional NW/DPI model was not performing well and with that knowledge improve the model's performance.

Interest Rates Were a Missing Link

My opinion is that the NW/DPI savings models overestimated the personal saving rate in the four years after the Great Recession because there was not enough attention being paid to interest rates. The Fed's quantitative easing (QE) interest rate policies were depressing interest rates to an unusually low level. And savings are positively related to interest rates for a couple of reasons.

First, *relatively high interest rates provide an incentive to defer consumption and save*. When rates are comparatively low, there is more incentive to borrow, with some households having a negative saving rate as consumption exceeds their incomes.

Second, *interest income is skewed to relatively more affluent families with comparatively higher personal saving rates*. In 2012, taxpayers with six-figure adjusted gross incomes represented just over 14 percent of all taxpayers, but their interest incomes were 72 percent of all reported interest income. And the 2.4 percent of income tax returns with adjusted reported gross incomes of $250,000 and more garnered 28 percent of all interest income reported to the Internal Revenue Service. When rates are high, at least part of the higher accompanying interest incomes are more likely to be saved. In other words, higher interest rates entail a redistribution of income from relatively low-saving borrowers to comparatively high-saving savers.

Third, *interest rates are positively related to inflation, which motivates higher savings as inflation expectations rise*. My opinion is that higher expected inflation necessitates more saving for retirement and other future contingencies. To be sure, lower expected inflation can temporarily raise the personal saving rate of those households postponing some forms of consumption (e.g., usually durable goods and homes) until prices are lower. However, at the same time low rates are enabling other households to borrow more and save less.

In the first four years of recovery from the Great Recession, saving rate models employing both NW/DPI and interest rates were more accurate than models based only on NW/DPI. According to the author's regression analysis, from 2009 through 2012 saving models utilizing both NW/DPI and the three-month Treasury bill yield (to represent interest rates) had a mean average error of +0.58 percentage points. That was considerably less than a mean average error of −1.65 percentage points for models with only NW/DPI as the independent variable.

Do More Confident Consumers Save Less and Spend More?

What else other than NW/DPI and interest rates helps to explain savings? Although a saving rate model with interest rates and NW/DPI outperforms a model based only on NW/DPI, there is still room for further improvement. After all, an 85 percent R-squared statistic over the 1978 to 2013 period for the saving rate model with two independent variables suggests that some explanatory variables are still missing. One obvious candidate is consumer confidence. Because savings are motivated partly by perceived contingencies, it stands to reason that more confident consumers would save less than otherwise at any given level of NW/DPI and interest rates.

Forecasters have a variety of alternatives for measuring consumer confidence. Two of the most popular monthly indexes, with a history long enough to enable back testing, are the Conference Board (CB) Consumer Confidence Index and the Reuters/University of Michigan (R/UM) Index of Consumer Sentiment. The weekly Bloomberg Consumer Comfort Index and the monthly *Investor Business Daily*/TIPP consumer confidence index have been developed more recently and are also widely followed.

Studies of the forecasting properties of the R/UM and CB consumer confidence gauges suggest that both measures have some, albeit limited, usefulness in forecasting consumer spending. For instance, Sydney G. Ludvigson from the New York University Economics Department has reported that over the 1968 to 2002 period, "Lagged values of both the Conference Board and Michigan overall index explain about 15 percent of the one-quarter ahead variation in total personal consumption expenditure growth."[9] She also reports that *the expectations components of both indexes do a somewhat better job of forecasting than the overall indexes.* In explaining the quarter-ahead growth of consumer spending, the CB expectations component explains 20 percent and the R/UM expectations component explains 19 percent.

A Multivariate Approach to Explaining Savings

It clearly requires more than one variable to adequately explain and forecast the personal saving rate. An example of such a model is presented in Table 9.2. In this model, the personal saving rate moves inversely with NW/DPI and consumer confidence, and positively with interest rates.

Table 9.2 Multivariate Model of Personal Saving Rate*

	Savings Rate (%)
Constant	18.89
	(10.70)
3-month Treasury bill (%)	0.39
	(7.69)
Net worth/Disposable income (ratio)	−2.11
	−(6.30)
Univ of Michigan index of consumer sentiment (index)	−0.03
	−(4.19)
R-square	0.91
Sample period	1978–2013

*T-statistics are shown in parentheses under regression coefficients.
SOURCE: Reuters/University of Michigan, Federal Reserve Board of Governors, Bureau of Economic Analysis, author's calculations.

Does Income Distribution Make a Difference for Saving and Consumer Spending?

So far our discussion of consumer spending and saving has focused on income, wealth, and consumer confidence. But we should also consider how those pies are divided. It's becoming a more important forecasting issue as economic inequality in the United States continues to grow. The government may not be able to do much to materially alter the distribution of wealth and income. However, attempts to address the situation by changing spending and tax policies can raise questions about the incremental effects of policy changes at the margin. For instance, will it make a difference if a tax cut favors the affluent or the middle class? Does public spending on defense have the same consumer spending impact as changing various entitlements for the poor?

Economists disagree about whether the distribution of income really makes much difference for *overall* spending and GDP. It is true, though, that savings rise with incomes. According to the Fed's Survey of Consumer Finances, only about a third of the families in the lowest income quintile saved in 2010, compared with four-fifths of those in the top 10th of income earners. But just because the wealthy have a higher personal saving rate does not mean that their incomes circulate less than those earned by others. Affluent families' savings are lent to and invested with other parties, who will spend these funds on consumer or business items. As discussed in Chapter 6, Keynes taught that savings would not always be channeled into lending and investment. That said, he did not necessarily mean that an imbalance between savings and borrowing and investment would persist throughout the business cycle. Nevertheless, with different groups behaving differently, who receives income affects consumer spending, though not necessarily GDP.

As seen in Table 9.1, the affluent and the not-so affluent spend their money differently. Thus, where money from a tax cut, for instance, is concentrated can affect consumer spending categories in very different ways. Consider the shares of spending represented by various income-earning classes (see Table 9.3). In 2012, families with $150,000 or more in pretax income represented approximately 7.4 percent of all consumer units. Yet they accounted for 18.5 percent of consumer spending, 21.1 percent of entertainment spending, 21.6 percent of

Table 9.3 Income Classes' Share of Specific Spending Categories

Before Tax Annual Incomes: Income Class % Shares of Consumption Category, 2012	Less Than $70,000	$70,000 to $79,999	$80,000 to $99,999	$100,000 to $119,999	$120,000 to $149,999	$150,000 or More
Consumer units	66.9	5.6	8.8	5.8	5.6	7.4
Annual consumption expenditures	45.1	6.5	11.6	8.8	9.7	18.5
Food at home	53.3	7.0	10.9	7.8	8.5	12.8
Food away from home	42.9	6.9	12.3	9.3	11.0	18.1
Alcoholic beverages	41.4	7.2	12.9	9.4	11.1	18.6
Shelter	49.5	5.9	11.0	8.1	8.9	16.6
Utilities, fuels, and public services	55.4	6.3	10.7	7.6	7.9	12.1
Household furnishings and equipment	41.7	6.5	11.6	8.2	10.8	21.6
Apparel and services	44.4	7.1	12.2	8.3	10.2	18.3
Vehicle purchases (net outlay)	41.1	7.4	14.5	11.0	9.0	17.0
Gasoline and motor oil	51.5	7.0	12.3	8.7	8.8	11.8
Health care	51.5	6.5	11.3	8.6	8.6	13.7
Entertainment	42.5	6.7	10.8	8.7	10.4	21.1
Education	31.0	4.8	9.0	9.2	11.4	34.7
Cash contributions	40.2	5.5	11.0	8.1	9.3	25.9
Life and other personal insurance	32.2	5.8	12.2	8.7	10.4	30.6
Pensions and social security	26.8	6.5	12.9	10.7	13.1	30.0

SOURCE: Survey of Consumer Expenditures, Bureau of Labor Statistics.

household furniture and equipment expenditures, and 35.4 percent of education outlays.

Beyond the issue of how individual consumer units spend their incomes, it is important for forecasters to understand where the overall economy might be headed if the distribution of income and wealth continues to skew to higher incomes. Under these conditions, consumer spending will likely grow less than it would if incomes were more evenly distributed. Investment spending and lending, however, are apt grow more quickly should current trends continue. Whether overall economic growth will be more or less if income is increasingly distributed to high earners will depend largely on investment opportunities and their contribution to productivity.

Finally, the forecaster also must determine what will happen to income distribution as we move into the middle of the second decade of the 21st century. In my view, the rather lopsided skew we have seen over the past few years reflects the unusual persistence of a relatively high unemployment rate, which has helped to squeeze real wages. However, *as unemployment continues to fall, eventually leading to tighter labor markets and faster real wage growth, the functional distribution of income should start to shift away from capital and toward labor—a development that will somewhat lessen the role of the affluent in the overall income picture.*

Pent-Up Demand and Household Formation

When consumer spending is less than expected, should forecasters trim their household outlay projections or assume that spending has been just temporarily postponed?

When economists believe that a type of expenditure is being delayed, they characterize the situation as a buildup in pent-up demand. This description often refers to postponable types of purchases, such as buying homes, autos, and household durable goods. In the first years after the Great Recession, with less than normal recoveries in home buying and household durables spending, the pent-up demand question became especially pertinent. Forecasters' have two major challenges in addressing pent-up demand issues:

1. Determining what is normal.
2. Determining how quickly spending will return to it.

Venting pent-up demand is a key cyclical issue for the automobile industry, among others. In the initial years following the Great Recession, the average age of autos reached a relatively high level. (See Figure 9.10.) To be sure, the average age had been increasing for a number of years. However, the rate of increase accelerated after 2007, partly because households postponed purchasing new autos. Consequently, an upside possibility for an auto sales forecast has been an at least partial return to somewhat faster consumer turnover of new cars (i.e., reduced average age).

One of my approaches to the pent-up demand issue is to evaluate household formation, the annual change in the number of occupied residences (both rented and owned). It is one of the most important expressions of pent-up demand. Sales of homes, household durable goods, and autos all depend, at least in part, on how many households are being formed. (See Figure 9.11.) And household formation poses a major challenge for forecasters, because decisions to form households can be either accelerated or delayed by at least a few years.

Household formation usually moves in line with the growth of the adult population. (See Figure 9.12.) When household formation deviates from adult population growth, there are typically two explanations. First, there can be changes in the share of the adult population represented by the 25 to 34 age group—the segment most likely to be forming households for the first time. Second, there can be changes in the ability and willingness to form households within the various age

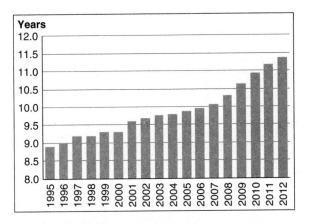

Figure 9.10   Average Age of U.S. Automobiles
SOURCE: J. W. Polk.

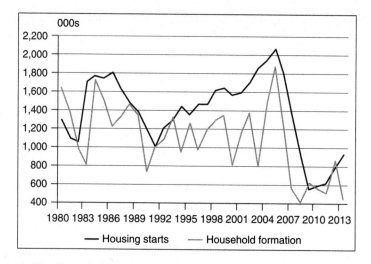

Figure 9.11   Household Formation and Housing Starts
SOURCE: Bureau of the Census.

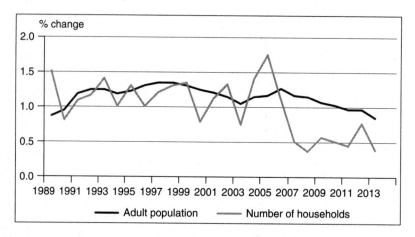

Figure 9.12   Household Formation and Adult Population Growth
SOURCE: Bureau of the Census.

categories, with behavior in the 25 to 34 year age range especially critical for overall household formation.

When household formation is above the growth of the adult population after being below it, pent-up space demand is being vented. On the other hand, *when household formation is consistently below the growth of the adult population, pent-up space demand is accumulating.* To estimate pent-up and vented space demand, it is necessary to *estimate the difference between the actual and potential level of households.*

The potential level of households is the number of households *usually* associated with the adult population's size and age composition. To estimate the difference between the level of potential and actual households in recent years, I have used the following procedure:

Potential households: Using annual data through 2007, I regress the level of households on the size of the adult population and the fraction in the 25 to 34 year age range. The resulting in-sample estimated response coefficients represent the historically average relationships between the number of households and the demographic characteristics of the adult population in the pre–Great Recession period. The model estimated through 2007 is then simulated for subsequent years, to determine what the number of households would have been *if* these pre–Great Recession relationships had continued. That projected household level is the *potential level*: it represents what would have been, had no changes in household formation behavioral patterns occurred since the Great Recession.

Pent-up demand: The growing positive difference between the potential and actual number of households in the post–Great Recession years represents the accumulation of pent-up demand for space. As such, this difference can then be used as a proxy for pent-up demand for both housing and durable goods. Figure 9.13 illustrates the derived pent-up demand variable that can be used to forecast home sales, housing starts, and durable goods sales. We obtain the variable by subtracting the actual household level from potential level, then expressing this number as a percentage of the estimated potential households. (Note: This measure of actual versus potential households is analogous to the familiar measures of actual versus potential real GDP.)

We can add this pent-up demand variable to equations used to forecast housing starts and various types of durable goods expenditures. When the pent-up demand variable falls (rises), consumption will be more (less) than normally associated with determinants such as incomes and unemployment.

Over the next few years, a key to consumer forecasting will be understanding why actual household formation was so weak versus its potential in the early years of recovery from the Great Recession. Is this development an illustration of the earlier discussed new normal economy, or will household formation return to historical levels?

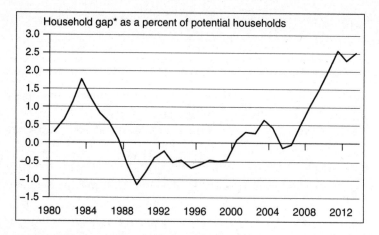

Figure 9.13 Estimated Pent-Up Demand Measure
*Estimated potential households minus actual households.
SOURCE: Bureau of the Census, author's calculations.

Demographers estimate that current population and immigration trends should be consistent with household formation of around 1.2 million households per year.[10] However, over the four years after 2009, average annual household formation was only around 600,000 per annum. This development was reflected in a sharp increase in the percentage of households that were shared (i.e., households where

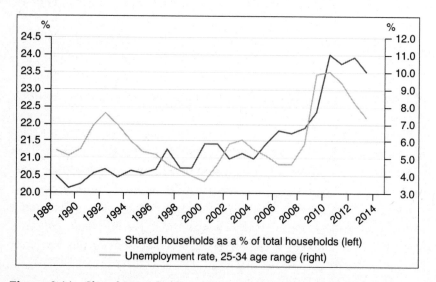

Figure 9.14 Shared Households and Young Adult Unemployment
SOURCE: Bureau of the Census.

single or married adults are living with other nonstudent adults). This development was accompanied by a relatively high unemployment rate for the 25 to 34 year age group, a group that is a key to forming new households. (See Figure 9.14.) As that unemployment rate declines further, I think there should be a reduction in shared households and a related return to more normal levels of household formation.

Key Takeaways

1. Labor compensation variations are key to the cyclicality of incomes.
2. The credit cycle is pivotal for job formation.
3. Wage rates depend importantly on the unemployment rate.
4. Concerns over too little saving and too much debt often are false alarms.
5. The personal saving rate is mostly determined by the ratio of net worth to disposable personal income, but interest rates and consumer confidence also can be important.
6. Recycling household debt repayments into new loans usually limits potentially adverse economic implications of higher aggregate personal debt burdens.
7. The deviation of potential versus actual household formation is a useful proxy for overall pent-up demand.
8. Weak household formation after the Great Recession reflected likely temporarily higher doubling up, which should decline with unemployment reductions for younger adults in the 25- to 34-year age range.

Notes

1. Jesse Bricker, Arthur B. Kennickell, Kevin B. Moore, and John Sabelhaus, "Changes in U.S. Family Finances from 2007 to 2010: Evidence from the Survey of Consumer Finances," *Federal Reserve Bulletin* 98, no. 2 (February 2012): 16.
2. Kaiser Health Tracking Poll, June 2013.

3. Karl E. Case, John M. Quigley and Robert J. Shiller, "Comparing Wealth Effects: The Stock Market Vs. The Housing Market," Cowles Foundation Paper 1181, Yale University, 2006.

4. Bricker, Kennickell, Moore, and Sabelhaus, "Changes in U.S. Family Finances."

5. "2012 Consumer Expenditure Survey," Bureau of Labor Statistics, Washington, D.C.

6. "Survey of Consumer Finances, 1983 and 2010," Federal Reserve Board of Governors, Washington, D.C.

7. "Household Debt and Credit Report," various issues, Federal Reserve Bank of New York.

8. Rohit Chopra, "Student Debt Swells, Federal Loans Now Top a Trillion," Consumer Financial Protection Bureau, July 17, 2013.

9. Sydney C. Ludvigson, "Consumer Confidence and Consumer Spending," *Journal of Economic Perspectives* 18, no. 2 (Spring 2004): 29–50.

10. Joint Center for Housing, "State of the Nation's Housing 2013," Harvard University, June 26, 2013.

Chapter 10

What Will It Cost
to Live in the Future?

Inflation is repudiation.

—Calvin Coolidge, Speech, Chicago, January 11, 1922

C onsumer spending projections may be crucial for business, but
for households, the single most important forecast is the cost
of living. The amount by which daily expenses might rise
is the key consideration when planning for future contingencies and
retirement. Defining an adequate level of personal saving, and selecting
appropriate categories of investments, hinge on expectations of future
inflation. A belief in accelerated longer-term inflation, for example, is
apt to trigger higher current savings to fund a more expensive future
cost of living. On the other hand, anticipated lower near-term prices
can postpone consumption.

Firms' success or failure will often turn on the behavior of business costs versus pricing power. For securities analysts and investors, forward guidance on pricing can play an important role in their valuation of a company's public securities. When firms have the ability to control prices, for instance, they may set those prices to discourage competitors from entering their territory.

From a politician's perspective, too much inflation can be more harmful to reelection prospects than excessive unemployment. Even during major recessions, only 10 percent of the labor force is unemployed. However, the well-being of all constituents depends, at least partly, on inflation's containment.

For monetary policymakers, inflation has to be just right. Too much can create speculative imbalances that may generate recessionary conditions. On the other hand, too little inflation may turn into price deflation, as expected lower prices become a self-fulfilling prophecy on the part of buyers awaiting price reductions.

Moreover, interest rates set in the fixed-income markets depend to a large degree on actual and expected inflation. In recent years the Federal Reserve's Federal Open Market Committee (FOMC) has sought to keep such rates relatively low through huge purchases of Treasuries and mortgage-backed securities (i.e., QE). Investors, however, are still concerned that these purchases, and the accompanying jump in financial system liquidity, might ultimately stoke inflation and raise interest rates materially.

Clearly, then, much of what happens in the economy and financial markets rides on inflation prospects—a challenging forecast for many prognosticators. In this chapter, we first review the key inflation measures that firms and investors must predict. Then we discuss some important forecasting concepts and contemporary issues.

Whose Prices Are You Forecasting?

Typically, the forecasts estimating overall business and consumer pricing are most in demand. The quarterly overall gross domestic product (GDP) chain price index is important to estimate when building forecasts of current dollar (nominal) GDP. For consumers, as previously mentioned, the most important concern is the overall monthly cost of living, as measured by the consumer price index (CPI) and the personal consumption expenditures (PCE) chain price index. For the business world, the most critical estimates of domestic firms' pricing power come from the monthly producer price index (PPI) and the quarterly nonfarm business price index. Before discussing forecasting concepts for these various price measures, we shall begin with the first step in forecasting—understanding the characteristics and history of the particular variable in question.

Humans Cannot Live on Just Core Goods and Services

When delving into specific inflation measures, it is useful to first address one of the most frequently asked questions about almost any inflation variable: "Why is there so much focus on core (nonfood, nonenergy) inflation when everyone both eats and depends on energy for transportation and temperature control?"

I answer as follows: *Whether one is interested in total or just core inflation reflects the specific purpose of an inflation analysis.* If the goal is to forecast overall household purchasing power and business costs, the emphasis should be on a gauge of overall inflation. For interest rate forecasting, it is important to consider total as well as core inflation, as investors in fixed-income securities want an interest rate to at least cover future overall rises in the cost of living. But in setting short-term interest rates and influencing long-term rates, the Federal Reserve System focuses on core inflation. It does so in the belief that core inflation is a true indication of underlying trends, whereas price changes in the more volatile food and energy segments can reflect erratic short-run swings in supply conditions.

From a forecaster's perspective, when core and total (a.k.a. headline) consumer price inflation deviate, it is necessary to judge which of them best foreshadows inflation trends. Mehra and Reilly[1] report that during the 20 years ending in the first quarter of 1979, when headline inflation rose more than core inflation, the gap between them was "eliminated mainly as a result of headline inflation not reverting and core inflation moving toward headline inflation." However, in the 1979 through 2007 period, this gap was "eliminated as a result of headline inflation reverting more strongly toward core inflation than core inflation moving toward headline inflation. This suggests *core inflation should be better than headline inflation in assessing the permanent component of inflation.*" (Italics added for emphasis.)

A corollary finding is that in the pre-1979 period core inflation was "persistently higher in response to surprise increases in food and energy inflation." However, that was not the case in the 1985 through 2007 period. Mehra and Reilly argue that price setting depends importantly on expected inflation, which in turn is much affected by views on monetary policy. If the Fed is viewed as accommodating temporary rises in food and energy inflation, wage and price setters are more likely to raise their expectations of future cost and price inflation. During the post-1979 years, when the Fed was led by the more inflation conscious Paul Volcker and then Alan Greenspan, the Fed was less likely to accommodate spurts in food and energy prices, in the view of wage and price setters. (In Chapter 11, we discuss how the real [inflation-adjusted] overnight Federal funds rate and Fed communications interact with the public's inflation expectations.)

Let's examine the four key characteristics of some specific indexes:

1. GDP chain price index
   - This index gauges the domestic cost of producing the nation's gross domestic product. Why is it is a chain price index? It measures the cost of producing the same market basket of goods and services as produced in the previous period but not in earlier periods. A chain price index is in contrast to a fixed-weight price index, which measures the cost of producing the same market basket over time.
   - The GDP price index measures only the prices of domestic output, whereas the CPI and PCE consumer price gauges measure prices of all that is consumed, including imports. Thus, the CPI is a more direct measure of households' cost of living, whereas the GDP price index measures what it costs to produce domestic output.
   - The GDP price index is a composite of the individual CPI and PPI price indexes for hundreds of individual goods and services produced domestically. For categories of public sector production

not included in the CPI and PPI, the Bureau of Economic Analysis (BEA) has developed additional price indexes.

- *The GDP price index plays a very different role in the government's calculation of real (inflation-adjusted) GDP than it does in private forecasters' estimating procedures.* (See Figure 10.1.) Government statisticians at the BEA estimate real GDP components mainly by dividing nominal (current dollar) data by GDP component price indexes. However, private forecasters typically forecast real GDP and the GDP chain price index separately. Why the difference? The government statisticians are acting as accountants, whereas forecasters are analyzing the behavioral considerations that determine unit spending and inflation.

  Note that since the Great Recession, this index has been in the 1 to 2 percent range—the same range seen in the early 1960s, before inflation accelerated dramatically. Since the early 1980s, the downtrend in this index has featured lower cyclical peaks and lower cyclical troughs.

2. Nonfarm business implicit price deflator

- This index represents prices of domestically produced private sector output, excluding the farm sector.

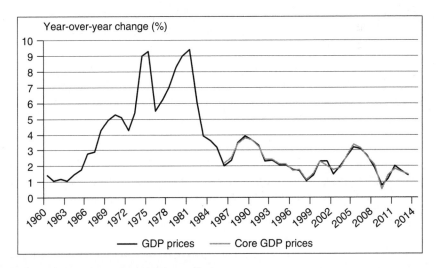

Figure 10.1 GDP Price Index Inflation
SOURCE: Bureau of Economic Analysis.

- It is used in computing the real output numerator of the nonfarm business labor productivity statistic.
- Current dollar value added in the nonfarm business sector is deflated (i.e., divided by) this index to compute real output.
- For most of the past 20 years it has usually been in a 1 percent to 2 percent range.

3. Producer price index (PPI)

- This index has traditionally represented prices received by domestic producers of crude and intermediate goods inputs and finished goods (a.k.a. Stage of Processing, SOP).
- Beginning in 2014 the Bureau of Labor Statistics (BLS) expanded the coverage to include publicly and privately provided services and structures prices. The new data is labeled as the Final Demand-Intermediate Demand (a.k.a. FD-ID) index system.
- The broader data are available only beginning in 2012.
- The finished goods PPI is analyzed as a reflection of pricing power exercised by domestic goods manufacturers. It differs from the CPI for goods as it excludes prices paid by end consumers.
- Over the past two decades the core (nonfood, nonenergy) finished goods inflation only rarely has exceeded the 2 percent per annum level that the Federal Reserve has identified as the most desirable overall U.S. inflation rate. (See Figure 10.2.)
- However, in 2002 and 2003 when the economy was just slowly exiting from the mild 2001 recession, the core PPI for finished goods just about stopped rising. In response, numerous Federal Reserve Board monetary policymakers expressed concern about potentially insufficient pricing power to motivate business expansion.

4. Consumer price indexes: CPI and PCE

The CPI is the price statistic with which the public is most familiar. Reflecting data compiled by shoppers for the Bureau of Labor Statistics (BLS), it is designed to measure the costs of all items purchased directly by consumers. It also is one of the oldest pricing indexes available in the U.S—annual data from the BLS go back to 1913. Currently, the monthly CPI report includes data for hundreds of separate items. These data are combined into an aggregate index that measures the cost of an unchanged market basket of goods and services. Statisticians call this a "fixed-weight price index."

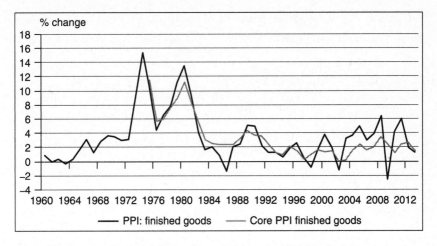

Figure 10.2 Finished Goods Producer Price Index (PPI) Inflation
SOURCE: Bureau of Labor Statistics.

Although the CPI may be the most familiar consumer price index, the personal consumption expenditures (PCE) chain price index is the more important one for financial markets and economists. It is preferred by the Fed and is the index used by the Bureau of Economic Analysis (BEA) to convert current dollar data into the real (inflation-adjusted) consumer spending estimates used to calculate the real national GDP.

Why do the Fed and most economists prefer the PCE? The major reason is that it is a chain weighted price index. Such an index measures the cost of consuming the previous period's market basket in the current period. Unlike the fixed-weight price index described earlier, the chain price index allows for changing consumption patterns in response to relative price changes for items in the basket of goods of services. *The allowance for substitution effects in the PCE is sometimes labeled as the formula effect.*

Another big difference between the CPI and PCE consumer price indexes is that the CPI measures out-of-pocket costs of what consumers directly purchase, while the PCE measures the costs of all that is consumed. The related difference in inflation between the two measures, labeled the *scope effect*, reflects third-party payments by various government agencies and insurance companies.

As a result, health care plays a much larger role in the PCE than in the CPI. In the CPI, though, housing expenditures play a

Table 10.1 Component Weights of Key Core CPI and Core PCE Price Indexes

Weights, within Core, %, 2013	Core CPI	Core PCE
Core CPI/PCE prices	100	100
Notable Core Components		
Shelter\housing	41.6	17.7
Owners' equivalent rent	31.0	12.9
Rent of primary residence	9.1	4.5
Lodging away from home	1.0	0.2
Medical care services	7.6	19.2
Medical care goods	2.2	3.9
Airline fares	1.0	0.5
New vehicles	4.6	2.5
Used vehicles	2.2	1.1
Apparel	4.5	3.6
Tobacco and smoking	0.9	1.1
Household furnishings	5.5	2.9

SOURCE: Bureau of Labor Statistics, Bureau of Economic Analysis.

larger role than they play in the PCE index. The differential in CPI inflation versus PCE inflation due to different weights is labeled the *weight effect*. (See comparison of core PCE weights as of 2013 in Table 10.1.) There are other differences between the two price indexes, which are reconciled on a monthly basis by the Bureau of Economic Analysis. The difference in the reported inflation rates of the PCE and CPI are sometimes called *the wedge*. (See the inflation rate differences between the core PCE and the CPI price index in Figure 10.3.)

Sound Judgment Trumps Complexity in Forecasting Inflation

Forecast makers and users should not be intimidated by the immense volume of research concerned with forecasting inflation. Economists Jon Faust and Jonathan Wright recently reviewed numerous forecasting methods, both simple and sophisticated, and concluded: "We find that judgmental forecasts (private sector surveys and the Greenbook) are remarkably hard to beat."[2] (Note: The Greenbook is the set of Fed

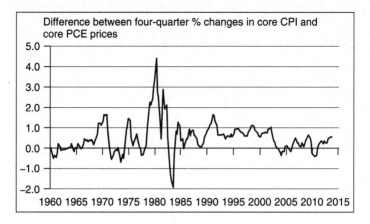

Figure 10.3 "Wedge" between Core CPI and PCE Growth
SOURCE: Bureau of Labor Statistics, Bureau of Economic Analysis.

internal forecasts made by the staff of the Federal Reserve Board.) In what follows, we review a variety of inflation forecasting approaches. Our objective is not necessarily to reproduce advanced analytical models for forecasting purposes. Instead, our goal is to use the knowledge gained from these studies to enhance judgment about important contemporary forecasting issues.

The volatility of observed inflation makes it a difficult variable for a forecaster. This volatility stems mainly from the considerable variation in energy and food price inflation. The rest of inflation—core inflation—is much more stable. (See Figure 10.4.) And, as it represented 76.8 percent of the CPI in early 2014, core inflation is the component that matters most. Moreover, considering that Fed policy is more focused on core than on overall inflation, a good score on the core forecast counts more in the eyes of the financial markets than the core's weight in overall inflation. That said, the food and energy questions still matter importantly.

Short Run Energy and Food Price Swings Are Often Caused by Supply Imbalances

The substantial *short run* variation in food and energy inflation usually reflects supply swings rather than large demand changes. Normally, the short run price sensitivity of food and energy demand is low, so

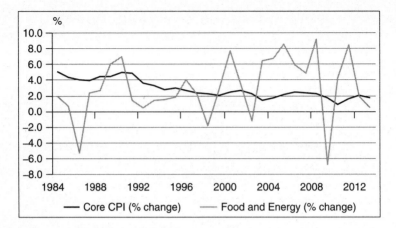

Figure 10.4   Core and Food and Energy Inflation
SOURCE: Bureau of Labor Statistics.

comparatively small changes in supply can have significant price impacts. Variation in food prices often reflects weather-related crop conditions. Short-run energy price volatility is due primarily to geopolitically related supply changes. Because temporary alterations in food and energy supplies are so difficult to predict, inflation forecasters can use food and energy price forecasts from organizations that specialize in them, and then translate those forecasts into the specific components of food and energy price indexes.

I find the annual overall retail food price forecasts by the U.S. Department of Agriculture are worth consulting, although inflation for the at-home component of the CPI is far less volatile. (See Figure 10.5.) This is mainly because labor and other expenses are a larger fraction of retail grocers' costs than raw food costs. For energy price forecasts, the regular updates from the U.S. Department of Energy on crude oil and natural gas prices can be helpful. However, as is the case with retail food prices, retail energy price inflation is far less volatile than the retailer's associated acquisition cost of goods sold. (See Figures 10.6 and 10.7.)

Evaluating Longer-Run Food and Energy Price Forecasts Is Important

Microeconomic analysis can play a helpful role in assessing longer-term food and energy price trends. My experience is that analysts with specific

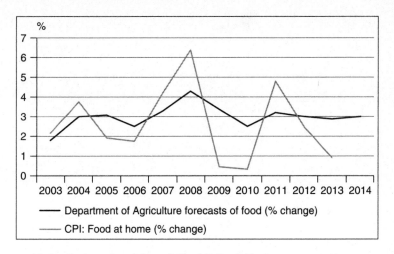

Figure 10.5 Projected and Actual Food Price Inflation
SOURCE: Bureau of Labor Statistics, Department of Agriculture.

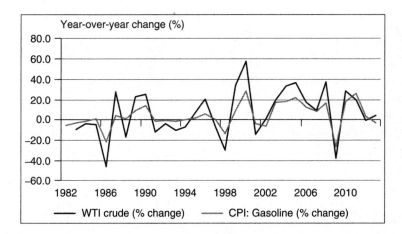

Figure 10.6 Crude Oil and Gasoline Price Inflation
SOURCE: Department of Energy, Bureau of Labor Statistics.

expertise in either raw food or energy supply conditions can sometimes extrapolate multiyear trends without placing enough emphasis on the potential longer-run price sensitivity of demand and supply. For instance, within the food sector there can be a good deal of substitution among various dietary alternatives. For energy items, very significant substitution effects can occur, especially in the business sector.

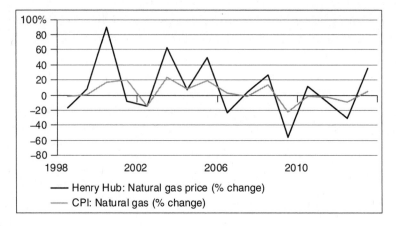

Figure 10.7 Natural Gas Prices
SOURCE: Department of Energy, Bureau of Labor Statistics.

Consumption Substitution Between Core and Noncore Goods and Services Affects the Inflation Rate

The impact of food and energy price inflation on the overall inflation rate also can be influenced by substitution effects between energy and nonenergy goods and services. Since food and energy consumption are relatively price insensitive in the short run, rises in such prices mean that current dollar expenditures will increase. The accompanying budget squeeze can limit spending, demand, and prices for core goods and services.

Monetarists Believe That Food and Energy Prices Have Only Limited Impact on Overall Inflation

In a related vein, monetarists have argued that monetary developments are the primary factor governing purchasing power. In the words of Milton Friedman—the founder of modern monetarism: "Inflation is always and everywhere a monetary phenomenon in the sense that it is and can be produced only by a more rapid increase in the quantity of money than in output."[3] One implication is that shifting food and energy prices will not influence overall price inflation as long as the central bank does not permit extra monetary accommodation to help the economy absorb higher energy costs.

Should We Forecast Inflation by Money Supply or Phillips Curve?

When choosing among approaches to forecasting inflation, there are two main alternatives. There are the monetarists, with their emphasis on the money supply, and the Keynesians, who focus on the Phillips curve trade-off between inflation and unemployment.

Though most forecasters choose the Phillips curve, let's begin by examining the monetarist perspective. Although most economists at the Fed and many forecasters in the private sector have abandoned monetarism as old fashioned and unrealistic, the creed still has its fans among the professional investors with whom I interact. And when the Fed was pumping the money supply through its quantitative easing (QE) policies, I was often asked if this actual and potential money creation would eventually become inflationary—a classic monetarist concern.

The monetarist view, as promulgated by Professor Friedman, is that a rise in the stock of money *per unit of output* is inherently inflationary. There are at least two issues that a forecaster should consider before deciding whether to accept this premise. First, does an increase in the money supply lead to an increase in demand for goods and services? As discussed in Chapter 6, the variability in monetary velocity suggests there is only a loose link between an expanding money supply and spending. Second, consider that even if demand were reasonably coordinated with monetary growth, increased demand does not necessarily need to be inflationary if output can be expanded. *If* the economy is utilizing all available resources (i.e., so-called full employment), further demand expansion should raise inflation. But whether the economy is, in fact, operating at full employment is a big "if." That said, the possibility of higher than acceptable inflation in the second half of the current decade should still be a concern for the longer-term bond markets. Considering the uncertainty about the level of the Non Accelerating Inflation Rate of Unemployment (NAIRU), the wariness is warranted.

Hitting Professor Phillips' Curve

While the monetarists posit a relationship between the money supply and price inflation, Keynesians have focused on unemployment as the key determinant of wage and price inflation. This inverse relationship came to be known as the Phillips Curve in recognition of the New Zealand economist A. W. Phillips. In a 1958 study of United Kingdom data from 1861 to 1957, he illustrated an inverse relationship between unemployment and wage-rate changes.[4]

A half-century later, most economists were using what came to be known as an *expectations-augmented Phillips Curve*. In this model, inflation depended on both the unemployment rate and inflation expectations. Why include inflation expectations? Their inclusion was a response to earlier critiques that there was no simple, permanent trade-off relationship between unemployment and price inflation. Other things being the same (i.e., ceteris paribus), a fall in unemployment could be associated with accelerated wage inflation pressures on prices. When unemployment moves, however, there can be related changes in other variables that also affect inflation. Specifically, Phillips curve critics argued that inflation expectations on the part of consumers, employers and employees also helped to determine inflation at any given level of unemployment.

For instance, consider a situation where unemployment declines and wages and prices initially respond by rising at a somewhat faster pace. That initial acceleration in wages and prices can raise inflation expectations beyond what they were at higher unemployment levels. With higher inflation expectations, workers will want to protect themselves with additional wage gains. Employers, sensing higher inflation ahead, will factor the expected rise in the costs of labor and other production inputs into their pricing. Consumers, anticipating faster price rises, will accelerate demand to avoid paying higher prices later on. And that pickup in demand can also work to raise prices, making higher inflation expectations a self-fulfilling prophecy. Thus, an initial rise in inflation can set into motion forces that, at the same unemployment rate, accelerate inflation further. In other words, the Phillips curve shifts.

Such criticism of the simple Phillips curve became more pronounced during the period of rising inflation in the 1970s. But 40 years later, following the Great Recession, there has instead been much more concern about disinflation—a slower inflation rate—as a possible gateway to destabilizing price deflation. (Destabilization occurs as lower prices discourage producers while encouraging consumers to postpone demand in anticipation of further price drops.) However, *in a low inflation environment, the initial criticism of a simple bivariate Phillips curve relationship between unemployment and inflation remains as valid as when it was voiced initially.*

For example, consider the consequences of reduced inflation expectations when there has been a low inflation rate at a relatively high unemployment rate level. As employers become more pessimistic about their already limited pricing power, they reduce wage gains so as to attain tighter cost control. Those reduced wage increases harm consumer incomes. In addition, consumer spending and demand can be further constrained if consumers' inflation expectations diminish and consumers decide to postpone purchases in anticipation of even cheaper prices in the future. As a result, *there can be an even lower rate of inflation at a given unemployment rate if inflation expectations are declining.* Thus, when core price inflation was slowing in 2013, the Federal Reserve System in its post-FOMC meeting public statements felt it necessary to emphasize that, "inflation expectations remain well anchored."

How does a forecaster measure inflation expectations?

When incorporating inflation expectations into an augmented Phillips curve model, a forecaster has two choices. One is to model the determinants of inflation expectations. This can be done in a couple of ways. The *adaptive expectations approach* is to assume that consumers extrapolate more recent information on prices. The *rational expectations approach* is to model variables (e.g., money supply) that are believed to determine inflation expectations. The other approach to representing inflation expectations is to utilize survey data. Two frequently used measures of inflation expectations come from the Survey of Professional Forecasters and the Reuters/University of Michigan consumer sentiment survey. (See Figure 10.8. Note: Former Federal Reserve Board Governor Frederic S. Mishkin has suggested that the latter measure may systematically overstate actual PCE inflation by around 0.75 percent.[5])

Let's look at some issues associated with the Phillips curve, and let's consider the various Phillips curves relevant to forecasters.

- The Phillips curve slope and "sacrifice/tradeoff"

  The degree to which inflation changes as unemployment does is reflected in the estimated response coefficient for the historical statistical relationship between inflation and unemployment.

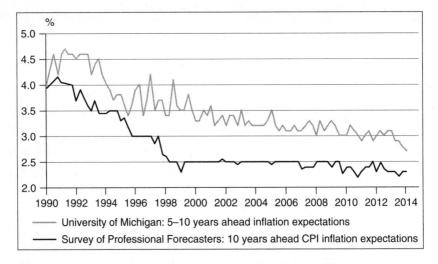

Figure 10.8   Consumers' and Forecasters' Expected CPI Inflation
SOURCES: Survey of Professional Forecasters, Thomson Reuters/University of Michigan.

This response coefficient is the slope of the Phillips curve. The slope is interpreted as showing the tradeoff between lower unemployment and higher price inflation. That trade-off is sometimes expressed as the sacrifice ratio. It is defined as how many years must the unemployment rate be 1.0 percentage point above NAIRU in order to reduce the inflation rate by 1.0 percentage point.

Some researchers estimate that the trade-off between inflation and unemployment lessened in recent decades. For example, Mishkin has estimated that the sacrifice ratio in the middle of the last decade may have been 40 percent larger than it was two decades earlier. In other words, the Phillips curve is argued to have flattened. The practical implication for inflation forecasts is as follows: *Compared to earlier decades, unemployment may now have less impact on inflation.* Therefore, when estimating the relationship between the two, forecasters should place more emphasis on models estimated only over recent decades as opposed to those covering longer time spans.

Why has inflation become less sensitive to unemployment? Mishkin attributes this to the public's becoming more confident that the Fed will take proactive steps to counter potentially higher inflation or higher unemployment. Such a perception helps to stabilize the public's inflation expectations—the earlier discussed important determinant of actual wage and price setting. Thus, when unemployment falls to a level that might become inflationary, price and wages setters may assume that the Fed will be successful in taking preemptive actions to soften the economy and dampen employment enough to head off threatened wage and price pressures. And when actual and/or expected unemployment rises, the Fed will step in to counter this trend before it has time to reduce inflation unacceptably. Support for this hypothesis is that inflation expectations have changed much less in recent than in past business cycles.

- Nonlinear and "piecewise" Phillips curves

Is the relationship between unemployment (U) and inflation linear (i.e., a straight line) or nonlinear (i.e., a curve)? I have always viewed the relationship as nonlinear (e.g., a 3 percent U rate affects inflation by more than double the effect of a doubled 6 percent U rate). In regression estimates of the Phillips curve, this nonlinearity can be represented by using the inverse of the unemployment rate (i.e., $1/U$).

Another alternative to a linear relationship is to estimate what are known as piecewise Phillips curves. The idea here is that extreme unemployment rates—those that are either very high or very low—have a greater impact on inflation than more moderate ones. The statistical solution, as explained by Federal Reserve Bank of New York economists Richard Peach, Robert Rich, and Anna Cororaton is as follows: First, identify so-called threshold unemployment rates—the extremes that produce more pronounced inflation effects than those between the two thresholds. Then, estimate separate Phillips curves for each of these three different unemployment rate ranges. This methodology suggests that *inflation becomes more sensitive to unemployment when the unemployment rate is approximately 1.5 percentage points above or below NAIRU.*[6]

- Disaggregated Phillips curves

Another route to better estimating the Phillips curve is to estimate separate curves for both the goods and the services components of core inflation. The rationale is that they are determined by different factors. Peach, Rich, and Linder report that unemployment rates affect services, but not goods, in a statistically significant manner. Also, inflation in service prices is correlated with longer-term inflation expectations, whereas goods inflation is related more to short-term outlooks. They find that *core PCE inflation forecasts from separately estimated Phillips curves for goods and services inflation are more accurate than those from a single Phillips curve model.*[7]

- "Sticky" versus "nonsticky" prices in modeling the inflation expectations variable in Phillips curve models

  Michael Bryant and Brent Meyer—two economists who have worked at the Federal Reserve Banks of Atlanta and Cleveland—have published research suggesting that more accurate Phillips curves models might be achieved by refining how the inflation expectations component of Phillips curve models is estimated. That component can be represented either by survey measures of inflation expectations or with measures of historical inflation rates. They argue that inflation expectations are more closely related to the past behavior of "sticky" prices—those that do not change often—than to flexible prices that change frequently.[8] (See Figure 10.9.) And they report that *Phillips curve models that use sticky prices for the inflation expectations component can be more accurate than models utilizing overall price behavior as the inflation expectations component.*

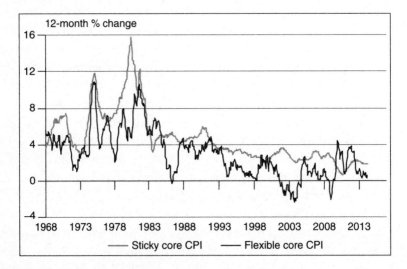

Figure 10.9   Inflation of Flexible and Sticky Core Prices
SOURCE: Federal Reserve Bank of Atlanta.

- *Shocking Phillips curves*

    To better estimate inflation, the standard Phillips curve mod-
els can be augmented by variables such as food, oil, and nonoil
import prices and productivity shifts. When inflation is impacted by
foreign-related developments, such as big swings in oil and import
prices, economists label these factors as "shocks." Inflation forecasting models using unemployment, inflation expectations and shock
factors are sometimes called *triangle Phillips curves*.[9]

- What unemployment rate matters most for inflation?

    When estimating the effects of unemployment on inflation, the
forecaster can choose among a variety of unemployment rates. Every
month the BLS reports a multitude of them. There are six separate
unemployment rates for the overall economy, labeled U1 to U6, with
successively more comprehensive definitions of labor market slack.
Most inflation researchers have traditionally settled on the U3 measure, which is commonly cited as the official unemployment rate. In
recent years, however, some inflation analysts and forecasters have
found it useful to distinguish between people jobless for less than
six months and those unemployed for longer periods. By the spring
of 2014, the jobless rate for persons unemployed less than 27 weeks
had shrunk to around 4 percent, which was near the lows observed
at the peak of the previous two business expansions when wage and
price inflation were accelerating. However, the unemployment rate
for people out of work for 27 weeks or more was just over 2 percent,
which was above the levels posted at the end of most past recessions,
when the economy was in a trough. (See Figure 10.10.)

    If the long-term unemployed are less qualified than the shorter-
term unemployed, an estimated Phillips curve inflation model
should find a relatively stronger relationship between wage inflation
and short-term unemployment. Economists at the Federal Reserve
Bank of New York have tested that hypothesis.[10] They compared the
out-of-sample forecasting performance of a wage inflation Phillips
Curve model using the standard deviation of the unemployment
rate from NAIRU with the performance of a Phillips Curve model
utilizing the short-run (less than 27 weeks) unemployment rate.
They report that the latter model is about 10 percent more accurate.

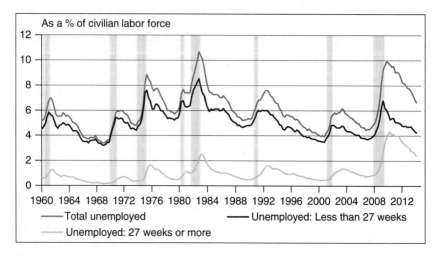

Figure 10.10   Long-Term and Short-Term Unemployment Rates
NOTE: Shaded areas are recessions.
SOURCE: Bureau of Labor Statistics.

Using a Phillips Curve price inflation model, Gordon reports a larger inflation impact from short-term unemployment than from long-term unemployment, and notes similar findings for Europe.[11] However, using metropolitan data, Michael Kiley—an economist at the Federal Reserve Board of Governors—reports that both unemployment measures have similar inflation impacts.[12]

- Shifty Phillips curve and NAIRU

    Identification of the unemployment rate below which inflation begins to accelerate (a.k.a. NAIRU) is one of the most important and controversial challenges in the field of economic forecasting. Projecting when and at what level of unemployment inflation will accelerate is key to forecasting Fed monetary policy, bond yields, price-earnings ratios, and the longevity of an economic expansion.

    The Congressional Budget Office (CBO) estimate of NAIRU is the benchmark most forecasters use to judge remaining labor market slack. (See Figure 10.11.) However, just because the CBO's 5.2 percent NAIRU is commonly cited in research hardly indicates agreement among economists about the "true" NAIRU. Most of the Federal Reserve's Federal Open Market Committee (FOMC) members in recent years have believed that the unemployment rate at which core PCE inflation will not accelerate above the

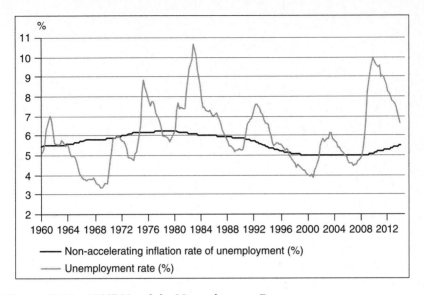

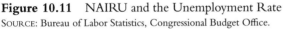

Figure 10.11 NAIRU and the Unemployment Rate
SOURCE: Bureau of Labor Statistics, Congressional Budget Office.

Fed's 2% objective is between 5.25 percent and 5.75 percent. That estimate is consistent with the experience in the past two decades. (See Figure 10.12.) Robert Gordon—a prominent Phillips curve scholar—has recently suggested that NAIRU may instead be around 6.5 percent.[13]

Whether NAIRU will prove to be higher than in recent business recoveries will reflect whether a larger portion of unemployment is structural (i.e., mismatch between the demand and supply of labor). The Fed's view has been that with strong or at least sustained moderate GDP growth, employers will eventually start hiring more of the longer-term unemployed even if they were not first choices earlier in the recovery (before short-term unemployment became relatively low). My view is that, going forward, *structural unemployment might be permanently higher, and we may see a higher NAIRU than in recent business cycles.*

The major reason is that it has become harder to find jobs for poorly educated workers. Such jobs increasingly have been either automated or performed by unskilled workers outside of the U.S. *It is debatable as to whether the public education system is doing a better or worse job in educating the entry-level workforce. However, there is general agreement that the challenges for*

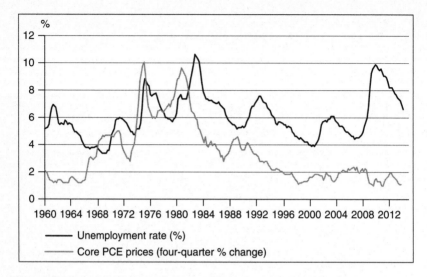

Figure 10.12 Core PCE Inflation and the Unemployment Rate
SOURCE: Bureau of Labor Statistics, Bureau of Economic Analysis.

the education system have become greater as job opportunities for poorly educated workers have shrunk.

A less important but still relevant reason for higher structural unemployment is that the workforce has become less mobile, which makes it more difficult for labor supplies to adjust to shifting labor demands in different locations. This is partly because of an aging workforce. Also, as of mid-2014 approximately one-sixth of homeowners still had negative equity in their homes—a factor lessening mobility, because these homeowners, if they sell and move to a new job, will have to have to come up with cash to make up the difference between home sale proceeds and a higher remaining home mortgage.

A Statistical Lesson from Reviewing Phillips Curve Research

One-on-one (bivariate) statistical relationships rarely reveal if any theory, including the Phillips curve, is working consistently over time. Simply looking at a time series graph comparing wage or core price inflation with the unemployment rate superficially suggests that the Phillips curve theory is either wrong or that the hypothesized inflation and unemployment relationship has changed over the years. To isolate the effect of unemployment on inflation, researchers have used multivariate models and controlled for other inflation drivers. Among these are inflation expectations, oil and nonoil import price shocks, unusual swings in productivity, and price controls. (Note: This last factor must be addressed using a dummy variable when developing models that include data for the first half of the 1970s, when price controls temporarily delayed inflation.)

Even if it's hard to see the Phillips curve relationship with the naked eye, the related research helps explain recent and future inflation.

For instance, why did core PCE inflation actually rise with the unemployment rate in the 1970s? This was partly because of higher oil prices and rising inflation expectations engendered, in part, by perceptions of monetary policy. Two decades later in the second half of the 1990s why did core inflation remain tame despite a relatively low unemployment rate? Part of the answer was unusually strong productivity growth and lower oil prices. More recently, why did core inflation not fall less than 2 percent in the depths of the Great Recession? Part of that answer is higher oil prices.

Looking ahead, annualized core PCE inflation probably will rise into the middle of a 2 to 3 percent range. As argued earlier, NAIRU probably has risen closer to a 6 percent unemployment rate versus the 5.2 percent assumed by the CBO. In addition, inflation expectations probably will rise somewhat as unemployment declines and if the Fed is slow to respond adequately to firmer pricing.

How Important Is Finding NAIRU?

As of mid-2014, NAIRU uncertainty was the center of attention for Federal Reserve monetary policymakers and the financial markets. For forecasters, how much wage and price inflation might eventually accelerate as unemployment falls further is a key issue in interest rate and growth projections as we head into the second half of the current decade. In assessing the public discussion of this issue, I think the following points are sometimes overlooked.

First, *an unemployment rate finally going below NAIRU can trigger a mild, rather than a sharp, wage and price inflation pickup*. I always have been suspicious of the so-called "L-shaped" Phillips Curve. It implies a sudden sharp acceleration in wages and prices once unemployment goes below NAIRU. However, that could occur when all labor and product markets are simultaneously operating at full capacity. Instead, a more likely scenario is that different labor and product markets reach full capacity at different points in time. In other words, some markets will tighten sooner than others. In addition, how much price and wage pressures develop in individual markets will depend on the price responsiveness of supplies of labor and products. For instance, it may not take much of an overall wage acceleration to attract discouraged unemployed workers into the labor market.

Second, *an acceleration of wage inflation at low unemployment need not be associated with a commensurate acceleration in price inflation.* That would be the case if there is a pickup in productivity growth, as discussed in Chapter 7.

Key Takeaways

1. The overall consumer price index (CPI) and the core (non-food, nonenergy) personal consumption expenditures chain price index (PCE) are two of the most requested forecast variables.
2. Hard-to-forecast swings in goods and energy prices have become less able to infect much more stable core inflation.
3. Although the money supply is mostly ignored in forecasting inflation, it may start to play a larger role in an environment where the Fed has been engaged in huge quantitative easing (QE) policies.
4. Most economists now believe that there is a diminished Phillips curve trade-off between inflation and unemployment.
5. Inflation forecasters must consider the key role of inflation expectations.
6. The most accurate inflation forecasting models should include shock factors—oil and nonoil import prices and

productivity—along with the more traditional gauges of labor slack and inflation expectations.

7. The nonaccelerating inflation rate of unemployment (NAIRU) probably has shifted to just over 6 percent, versus the long assumed 5 to 5.5 percent range.

8. However, the unemployment rate finally falling to levels at or below NAIRU need not trigger a sharp inflation acceleration, and wages could start rising before prices if productivity growth improves.

Notes

1. Yash P. Mehra and Devin Reilly, "Short-Term Headline-Core Inflation Dynamics," *Federal Reserve Bank of Richmond Economics Quarterly* 95, no. 23 (Summer 2009): 289–313.

2. Jon Faust and Jonathan H. Wright, "Forecasting Inflation," Department of Economics, Johns Hopkins University, Baltimore, Maryland, June 27, 2012.

3. Milton Friedman, "The Counter-Revolution in Monetary Theory," IEA Occasional Economic Paper, no. 33, Institute for Economic Affairs, London, 1970.

4. A. W. Phillips, "The Relationship between Unemployment and the Rate of Change of Money Wages in the United Kingdom, 1861–1957," *Economia* 25, no. 100 (1958): 283–289.

5. Frederic S. Mishkin, "Inflation Dynamics," Annual Macro Conference, Federal Reserve Bank of San Francisco, March 23, 2007.

6. Richard Peach, Robert Rich, and Anna Cororaton, "How Does Slack Influence Inflation?" *Federal Reserve Bank of New York Current Issues in Economics and Finance* 17, no. 3 (2011).

7. Richard Peach, Robert Rich, and M. Henry Linateder, "The Parts Are More Than the Whole: Separating Goods and Services to Predict Core Inflation," *Federal Reserve Bank of New York Current Issues in Economics and Finance* 19, no. 7 (2013).

8. Michael F. Bryan and Brent Meyer, "Are Some Prices in the CPI More Forward Looking Than Others? We Think So," Federal Reserve Bank of Cleveland Economic Commentary, May 19, 2010.

9. Robert J. Gordon, "The Phillips Curve Is Alive and Well: Inflation and the NAIRUI During the Slow Recovery," Working Paper 19390, National Bureau of Economic Research, Cambridge, Massachusetts, August 2013.

10. Henry M. Linder, Richard Peach, and Robert Rich, "The Long and Short of It: The Impact of Unemployment Duration on Compensation Growth," *Liberty Street Economics* blog, Federal Reserve Bank of New York, February 12, 2014.

11. Gordon, "The Phillips Curve Is Alive and Well," 38.

12. Michael T. Kiley, "An Evaluation of the Inflationary Pressure Associated with Short- and Long-term Unemployment," Federal Reserve Board Finance and Economics Discussion Series no. 28, Washington, D.C., March 21, 2014.

13. Gordon, "The Phillips Curve Is Alive and Well," 40.

Chapter 11

Interest Rates: Forecasters' Toughest Challenge

In historical times, credit preceded the coining of money by over two thousand years. Coinage is dated from the first millennium B.C., but old Sumerian documents, circa 3000 B.C., reveal a systematic use of credit based on loans of grain by volume and loans of metal by weight. Often these loans carried interest.

—Sidney Homer, *A History of Interest Rates*, 1977, Chapter 1, p. 17

My first crack at forecasting interest rates was a trial by fire. It began the first weekend of October 1979. I was in my office at the Federal Reserve Bank of New York, preparing

285

my first presentation on credit markets and interest rates for an audience of senior New York Fed officials. As the newly appointed Chief of Financial Markets Research in the domestic research division, I was to brief the officials before they traveled to Washington DC for a regular Federal Open Market Committee (FOMC) meeting. There, the Fed would set the overnight Federal funds rate—a key to the Fed's overall control of interest rates and, by extension, the economy.

The FOMC meeting was slated for October 16, with our internal briefing scheduled the week prior. But on October 6, as I was toiling over my draft, the FOMC was conducting a special, top-secret meeting to adopt a radically new approach to U.S. monetary policy, one that would turn the world of interest rate forecasting upside down. In a hastily called press conference following the meeting, the Fed announced that it was abandoning its Federal funds rate peg in favor of directly controlling the growth of nonborrowed bank reserves.[1]

This breathtaking announcement ushered in a very major reform in the conduct of U.S. monetary policy, one that would present economic forecasters in the 1980s with their toughest challenge. (Note: In Chapter 1, we discussed how very few forecasters in the 1980s could outperform a coin flip in discerning the direction, let alone the magnitude, of interest rate changes.)

This move was truly revolutionary. Up until then, the FOMC had been using its control of the overnight Federal funds rate—the rate banks charge in lending to one another—as its primary tool for influencing overall interest rate levels, the financial markets, and the economy. However, it had become increasingly apparent that this tool was not up to the task. Inflation was surging and the value of the U.S. dollar plunging as global financial markets expressed their rising dissatisfaction with U.S. monetary and fiscal policies.

Though the Federal funds rate was just for overnight interbank loans, it was widely viewed as the anchor for interest rates on longer-term fixed-income securities and longer-term loans, such as home mortgages. Though the spreads of such rates versus the Federal funds rate varied, all were highly dependent on the Federal funds rate, which was especially key to short-term money market interest rates.

Now, with the Fed controlling the quantity of bank reserves that it pumped into the banking system—instead of controlling the overnight interest rate on those reserves—where would the Federal funds rate and other rates head? And, more pressingly for me, what should I tell the senior managers at the New York Fed about the consequences of the seemingly drastic actions they and their colleagues at the Federal Reserve Board of Governors had just taken?

My academic background motivated my initial thinking. I was taught—and I taught students—that interest rates, like any other price, are set by demand and supply. There are many potential determinants of those two drivers. It is the purpose of this chapter to first identify the various potential considerations influencing demanders and suppliers of credit. My experience is that at any point in time the markets are focused on only a particular subset of potential rate determinants. Over time, however, the credit markets can shift their attention to factors that may have been dormant earlier.

For this reason, my approach to interest rate analysis and forecasting begins by understanding the fundamentals driving the credit markets. But when looking beyond the upcoming few quarters, I also want to consider factors that, while not presently important, could regain relevance. When reviewing the information on rate drivers, some explanations naturally make more sense to me than others. But I always want to evaluate how people who accept other explanations will react to developments that I might interpret differently. For instance, although I may not believe that budget deficits are a major longer-run interest rate determinant, I know that many bond market investors regard them as quite important. I therefore shade my interest rate views considering how they, and others who may disagree with me, might behave in response to prospects for the Federal budget deficit.

To put economic and policy developments into perspective when forecasting rates, I find it critical to review past statistical studies that seek to estimate the effects of various determinants (e.g., budget deficits, economic growth, and inflation) on interest rates. Thus, in this chapter we also examine the results of some of these studies and discuss how to interpret them.

Even a strong knowledge of interest rate theories and historical evidence is insufficient for addressing the critical challenges that forecasters will confront in the next decade. With that in mind, this chapter also discusses approaches to evaluating two key questions they face:

1. How will interest rates be influenced when the Federal Reserve reduces its holdings of the around $3.5 trillion in securities that it purchased in order to hold interest rates down during the 2009 to 2014 period?

2. Although the Federal deficit has declined in recent years, what will happen to interest rates when it starts rising again due to widely expected surging Federal entitlement spending?

Figuring the Fed

Forecasting almost any U.S. interest rate begins by projecting the Federal funds rate for overnight interbank loans—the anchor for determining yields on various bond maturities. Indeed, the benchmark 10-year Treasury note yield is more tightly correlated with the Fed funds rate than with any other single explanatory variable, including expected inflation. (Note: Over the 1979 to 2013 period, the benchmark 10-year Treasury note yield had a 94 percent correlation with the Fed funds rate, versus an 89 percent correlation with inflation expectations.)

The Fed funds rate has usually been determined by the open market securities transactions directed by the Federal Reserve's Federal Open Market Committee (FOMC). The exception was the earlier-discussed period in the 1980s, when the Fed controlled the amount of reserves released into the banking system. In that setting, the interest rate on lending those reserves—the Fed funds rate—was determined by the demand for them. In the early 1980s, the Federal funds rate climbed steadily, reaching a calendar-average high of 16.4 percent in 1981, as the Fed struggled to contain rising inflation. As inflation ebbed subsequently, Fed funds rate cycles were characterized by lower cyclical peaks and lower cyclical troughs. (See Figure 11.1.)

Federal Open Market Committee

Decisions about the Federal funds rate are made by the Federal Open Market Committee (FOMC). It meets eight regularly scheduled times

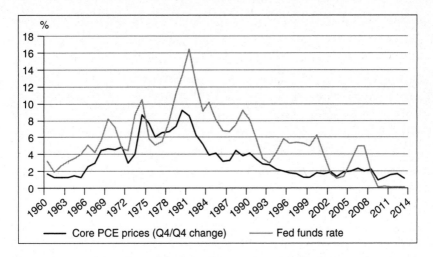

Figure 11.1 The Fed Funds Rate and Consumer Price Inflation
SOURCE: Federal Reserve Board of Governors, Bureau of Economic Analysis.

a year in Washington, DC. (Note: Between formally scheduled meetings, the FOMC can meet to consider issues that must be addressed fairly
immediately—before the next regularly scheduled meeting.) It is com-
posed of the seven members of the Federal Reserve Board of Governors
and the 12 regional Reserve Bank Presidents. The individual Governors are nominated by the President of the United States and subject
to approval by the United States Senate. They occupy Board seats with
staggered 14-year terms, with one of the seven seats' terms ending every
two years. (Note: Individual Governors have rarely occupied a seat for 14
years, and vacancies are filled with newly appointed Governors for the
time remaining for a given seat.) The 12 regional Reserve FOMC Bank
Presidents are selected by the regional Reserve Banks' Boards of Directors. At any point in time, only 12 of the 19 FOMC members can vote
on where to set the Federal funds rate and the volume of securities purchased or sold by the Fed. The seven Governors are permanent voting
members of the FOMC. However, in any year only 5 of the 12 regional
Reserve bank Presidents can vote on FOMC policies, although all of the
FOMC members can participate in policy deliberations before a formal
vote is taken.

A key input in forecasting policy decisions at future FOMC
meetings comes from the various intermeeting public statements by

FOMC members. Public comments (e.g., Congressional testimony, speeches, and media interviews) are routinely scrutinized for clues about the Fed's interpretation of the news and any related policy reactions. *Some FOMC members' public comments clearly have more financial market impact than do others.* At the top of this hierarchy is commentary by the Fed Chair. Next in order of importance are remarks by the president of the Federal Reserve Bank of New York—the only president with a permanent FOMC vote—and the vice chairman of the Board of Governors. They are usually viewed as being more influential than other Governors. Among the 11 regional Reserve Bank presidents who only alternate as FOMC voters, more weight often is given to members voting in any given year. Note, though, that all members—voters and nonvoters—can participate in the FOMC's policy discussions, and some exert more internal influence than others.

Should FOMC members' influence be judged by their perceived forecasting prowess? In selecting which securities analysts' opinions to weigh more heavily in making investment decisions, their recent advice-giving track records can play a key role. Can the same be said for economic commentary by individual FOMC members? In July of 2013, the *Wall Street Journal* published a ranking of FOMC members' forecast accuracy for inflation, economic growth, and jobs[2] (see Table 11.1), drawing on speeches and congressional testimony by FOMC members between 2009 and 2012. It is worth noting that the current Fed Chair Janet Yellen ranked highest, followed by the current New York Fed President William Dudley. (The positions they hold are traditionally the most influential in the FOMC.) It would be a mistake, however, to assess the impact of individual members at FOMC meetings based solely on forecast accuracy: A member's influence on final policy votes will also reflect his or her abilities to reason and persuade. Still, published rankings of individual FOMC members' forecasting records are likely to affect the way those members are viewed by the markets.

What Is the Fed's "Reaction Function"?

Before we can judge how the financial markets will respond to incoming data, we need to understand how the Fed will react to the information. Traditionally,

Table 11.1   Ranking Fed Forecasters (2009–2012)

	Overall Score	Inflation Score	Labor Score	Growth Score
1. Janet Yellen	0.52	0.64	0.64	0.27
2. William Dudley	0.45	0.63	0.50	0.31
3. Elizabeth Duke	0.40	0.50	0.67	0.17
4. Richard Fisher	0.29	0.35	0.50	0.23
5. Charles Evans	0.28	0.72	0.31	−0.67
6. Dennis Lockhart	0.24	0.27	0.72	0.29
7. Sandra Pianalto	0.22	0.44	0.25	−0.03
8. Ben Bernanke	0.29	0.33	0.40	0.14
9. Eric Rosengren	0.21	0.50	0.13	−0.50
10. John Williams	0.14	0.85	−0.50	−0.17
11. Jeffrey Lacker	0.05	−0.03	0.58	−0.15
12. N. Kocherlakota	0.07	−0.1	0.83	−0.50
13. James Bullard	0.00	−0.50	0.20	0.05
14. Charles Plosser	−0.01	0.30	0.56	−0.85

SOURCE: Jon Hilsenrath and Kristina Peterson, "Federal Reserve 'Doves' Beat 'Hawks' in Economic Prognosticating," *Wall Street Journal*, July 28, 2013.

forecasters attempted to quantify the Fed's response by estimating its "reaction function." In this exercise, they correlated the Federal funds rate with potential determinants such as unemployment, inflation, and real economic growth. Their rationale was that studying the Fed's past responses to such data could help in assessing the potential magnitude of future changes. However, *as the Fed has become more transparent in reporting information about those economic variables to which it can respond, historical reaction functions have become less useful in identifying the data that motivates contemporary Fed policy changes, and in gauging by how much.*

Today, investors can stay informed about the Fed's evolving reaction function through the regular post-FOMC meeting public statements and intermeeting public communications. In recent years, for example, the statements have included forward guidance about how long the Fed would maintain its targeted Federal funds rate. In this environment, when the Fed announces no imminent change in its funds rate target, the markets respond to individual economic indicators less than they did previously. Federal Reserve Board Economist Matthew Raskin has studied market responses to economic indicator "surprises" both before and during the Fed's forward-guidance periods. He has concluded that, "date-based guidance led to a statistically significant and economically meaningful change in investors' perceptions of the FOMC's reaction function."[3] In practical terms, market reactions to a lower than expected unemployment rate report are muted if the reported jobless rate remains well over the implied level at which the Fed would raise the Fed funds rate.

What is the normal or neutral Federal funds rate?

The level to which the Fed eventually raises the Federal funds rate reflects the Fed's perception of a neutral or normal real Fed funds rate, adjusted for inflation. The terms *neutral* and *normal* are often used interchangeably to describe the same concept. Fed spokespersons typically define a neutral Federal funds rate as the level at which the Fed's longer-run inflation and unemployment objectives are simultaneously achieved. Neutral does not necessarily mean normal or average, but is sometimes so identified.

Fed Chair Janet Yellen stated at the press conference following the March 18 to 19, 2014, FOMC meeting that a neutral nominal Fed funds rate in the next few years might be around 4 percent. How did she, or how does one, arrive at that judgment? The first step is to select the appropriate inflation rate for calculating the real, inflation-adjusted Fed funds rate. Because the Fed has chosen to target inflation of the core PCE price index, it often is used to illustrate a real Fed funds rate. When Yellen cited an approximately 4 percent neutral Fed funds rate, she stated that it was based on Fed achievement of its longer run inflation goal, which is around 2 percent. How did she arrive at a residual 2 percent real Fed funds rate as being neutral? One way could be to solve for a real Fed funds rate that in a large econometric model would be consistent with the Fed's long-run inflation and unemployment objectives. A more familiar convention is to identify a neutral real Fed funds rate as either its long-term average or what it reached in past cycles when the Fed ceased tightening the nominal Fed funds rate. Performing that exercise often leads to estimates of an approximately 2 percent longer-term real Federal funds rate. (See Figure 11.2.)

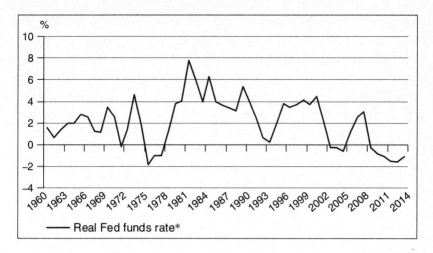

Figure 11.2   Real (Inflation-Adjusted) Federal Funds Rate
*Deflated by core PCE inflation.
SOURCE: Federal Reserve Board of Governors, Bureau of Economic Analysis.

Is the Fed "Behind the Curve"?

When outsiders judge the Fed's performance in coping with various economic scenarios, they sometimes consider it to have been behind the curve. In other words, they believe the Fed has been too slow and too cautious in raising rates to fight the overheating of inflation and credit markets that has preceded recessions, and it has failed to ease the rate sufficiently and quickly enough to moderate recessionary forces once overheating was no longer a concern. As discussed in Chapter 3, the Fed in the 1970s kept the real Fed funds rate too low when a more aggressive posture was required to address accelerating inflation. In the 1980s the Fed failed to adequately use its bank regulatory powers to curb the abuses that culminated in the savings and loan crisis. At the end of the 1990s, the Fed did not foresee the downside in the evolving tech bubble. And the Fed was insufficiently attentive in the past decade to the evolving real estate bubble and its financial implications.

I believe the Fed has ended up behind the curve for a couple of reasons. First, in the regulatory sphere, the Fed has sometimes been cautious, and seemingly concerned about overregulation. Second, *in its monetary policy role, the Fed is prone to be behind the curve because of its dual mandate: to target both inflation and unemployment—two lagging indicators of economic activity.* To be sure, Fed policymakers sometimes state that monetary policy is proactive, because it is based on the Fed's outlook for inflation and unemployment. However, Fed policymakers regularly lament the inevitable difficulties of forecasting, and frequently describe their policies as being data dependent.

Can the Fed "Talk Down" Interest Rates?

Following its mistakes preceding the Great Recession, the Fed has been more open to necessary experimentation. As we discuss later, the Fed's quantitative easing (QE) program has been a very major experiment. *Forward guidance*, a term that describes the Fed's efforts to influence long-term interest rates by shaping expectations through its communications about the possible future course of monetary policy, is another. *If* the Fed can convince the financial markets that it is committed to keeping both inflation and the Federal funds rate relatively low, longer-term interest rates will be lower than otherwise. However, this is quite a challenge, because projecting a low Federal funds rate may come to be viewed as inconsistent with low inflation. As of mid-2014, the jury was still out on reaching a verdict on the success of forward guidance. *My view is that it will be hard to contain longer-term rates with frequent public repetition of the Fed's objectives if and when those objectives begin to appear inconsistent.*

Bond Yields: How Reliable Are "Rules of Thumb"?

Before delving into theories about longer-term interest rate drivers, let us first address two popular rules of thumb for gauging where interest rates are headed. Why do I identify these rules as popular? Because in recent decades, they are the concepts my clients have wanted to discuss most frequently. They're a good introduction to more complex theories about the drivers of longer-term interest rate behavior.

Rule of Thumb #1: The Real (Inflation-Adjusted) Yield on the Benchmark 10-Year Treasury Note Should Return to Its Long-Run Average Level

When I first started my career as a Wall Street economist in 1980, it was often said that the real yield on longer-term Treasury securities should be around 3 percent. Why? That's what it had been in the 1950s and 1960s, before inflation accelerated. Since inflation was decelerating in the aftermath of the deep 1981–1982 recession, investors thought the real rate should return to where it had been before inflation rose in the 1970s. The problem with assuming a real rate of 3 percent, though, is that real rates in the past two decades often have been considerably lower. (See Figure 11.3.)

Note that the real yield in Figure 11.3 is illustrated in two separate ways. In one version, we have subtracted the rate of core PCE inflation from the nominal Treasury yield. As discussed in Chapter 10, the core PCE is often believed to be a better gauge of underlying inflation trends than the overall CPI inflation rate. And the Fed targets core PCE inflation in setting monetary policy. However, there is no hard and fast rule as to which inflation rate should be used to calculate real interest rates.

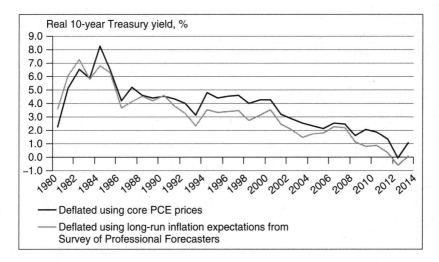

Figure 11.3   Real (Inflation-Adjusted) 10-Year Treasury Note Yield Measures
SOURCE: Federal Reserve Board of Governors, Federal Reserve Bank of Philadelphia, Bureau of Economic Analysis.

From a purely conceptual perspective, the more correct inflation measure should be inflation expectations. Thus, in many interest rate studies, the real rate is estimated using the expected inflation rate reported in the Survey of Professional Forecasters (SPF). (That method is illustrated in Figure 11.3.)

In calculating inflation expectations to be used in depicting real Treasury note yields, how useful is the expected inflation rate implied by the Treasury Inflation Protected Security (TIPS) yields? The implied expected inflation rate is defined as the nominal yield on a Treasury security minus the yield on a TIPS security of the same maturity. It is often referred to as the "break even inflation" (BEI) rate. However, recent research by Federal Reserve Board economists Stefania D'Amico, Don Kim, and Min Wei concludes: "Our results raise caution in interpreting movement in TIPS BEI solely in terms of changing inflation expectations, as substantial liquidity premiums and inflation risk premiums could drive a large wedge between the two, as demonstrated vividly during the recent financial crisis."[4]

Rule of Thumb #2: The Yield on the 10-Year Treasury Note Should Converge to the Rate of Nominal (Current Dollar) GDP Growth

Such a valuation metric makes theoretical sense. Nominal GDP growth is the sum of inflation-adjusted real GDP growth plus inflation. The nominal interest rate should be influenced by inflation, and the real interest rate should partly depend on the growth of real GDP—a proxy for the demand for real investment.

As illustrated in Figure 11.4, the current yield on the 10-year Treasury note need not converge on the nominal GDP growth. (Note: Over the 1979 to 2013 period there was only a moderate 0.69 percent correlation between the annual 10-year Treasury note yield and nominal GDP growth.) That is partly because there is a difference between current inflation and inflation expectations. Also, while real GDP growth may be a decent proxy for business investment needs and associated credit demands, the frequent and sometimes large revisions to real GDP mean that it is a not a timely source of information on business credit demand.

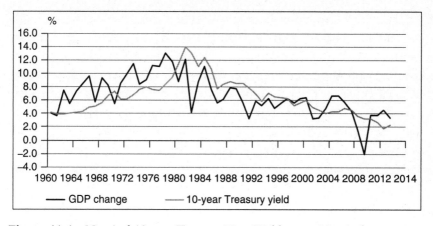

Figure 11.4   Nominal 10-year Treasury Note Yield versus Nominal
GDP Growth
SOURCE: Federal Reserve Board of Governors, Bureau of Economic Analysis.

The problem with simple interest rate rules of thumb—and the reason for their limited forecasting usefulness—is that they ignore other important rate drivers. A valuation metric based on real rates converging to their long-run averages ignores the many fluctuating determinants of those rates. In a similar vein, assumed convergence of nominal yields to nominal GDP growth also ignores many other factors.

Professor Bernanke's Expectations-Oriented Explanation of Long-Term Interest Rate Determinants

A helpful framework for starting to analyze and forecast longer-term interest rate determinants has been provided by former Federal Reserve Board Chair Ben Bernanke.[5] He states: "It is useful to decompose longer-term yields into three components: one reflecting expected inflation over the term of the security; another capturing the expected path of short-term real, or inflation-adjusted interest rates; and a residual component known as the 'term premium'." In other words, longer-term rates depend partly on inflation expectations and on the expected effect of Fed policies on short-term real rates—two relatively familiar and straightforward concepts.

The third element in Bernanke's formulation, the "term premium" concept, may be less familiar than the other two. Bernanke defines it as "the extra return investors expect to obtain from holding long-term bonds as opposed to holding and rolling over a sequence of short-term securities over the same period. In part, the term premium compensates bondholders for interest rate risk—the risk of capital gains and losses that interest rate changes imply for the value of longer-term bonds." Bernanke argues that there are at least two reasons for the term premium's decline in recent years. First, the volatility of Treasury bond yields has been reduced as the Fed-related short-term interest rate component has been depressed to near zero (and the Fed indicated that it would remain there for some time). Second, with the correlation between stock and bond prices becoming increasingly negative, bonds have become more valuable for hedging purposes.[6]

Bernanke's pedagogic explanation of long-term interest rates was not intended to be comprehensive. But it did include the two most important interest-rate determinants: expected inflation and monetary policy. The term premium, however—as a residual that cannot be attributed to these two key determinants—may also represent considerations excluded from Bernanke's analytical framework. These include, for example, variables representing the demand and supply of credit. *The Bernanke framework focuses on various expectations variables that condition the terms on which credit is supplied. But it does not directly incorporate variables that represent the supply of credit itself, which reflects more than just expectations. The demand for credit, including Federal budget deficits, is also omitted.* That said, the framework offered by Bernanke is a useful first step in achieving a broader understanding of longer-run, interest-rate determinants.

When forecasting Treasury note and bond-yield movements over the next year or two horizon, I tend to emphasize the monetary policy-related, short-term, interest-rate component of the expectations framework. In part, this choice reflects the generally stable behavior of longer-term inflation expectations; and it incorporates my belief that term premium considerations play a smaller role in short-run rate determination than they do over longer periods, and they do not change greatly. In addition, I believe that some of the observed interest rate determination attributed to the term premium may simply reflect evolving credit supply and demand considerations.

Supply and Demand Models of Interest Rate Determination

In addition to domestically oriented expectations regarding inflation, and the short-term rates controlled by monetary policy makers, a host of other variables play an important role in U.S. longer-term Treasury yield determination. Among the three most important of these considerations are:

1. Global saving and investment trends.
2. Quantitative easing effects of Federal Reserve securities purchases.
3. Fiscal policy related budget deficits.

Global Savings and Investment as Longer-Run Real Rate Determinants

When thinking about longer-run U.S. real interest rate trends, I focus considerably on the supply and demand for funds. There is considerable evidence of the importance of savings and investment as determinants for both U.S. and foreign interest rates. Consider, for example, the results reported by Bank of Canada economists Brigitte Desroches and Michael Francis.[7] They studied savings, investments, and their determinants over the 1970 to 2004 period for 35 industrialized and emerging economies representing more than 94 percent of 2004 real global GDP.

Desroches and Francis identify the following global savings rate stimulants. (See related saving rate statistical models in Table 11.2.)

- *Real interest rates*: Higher real interest rates motivate more savings.
- *Demographic dependency ratio*: As the working age population has more young and older dependents, the need for workers' savings rises.
- *Life expectancy*: Rising life expectancy raises the need for more savings.

The following factors are said to reduce savings:

- *Real oil prices*: Rising oil prices raise energy spending and make it harder to save.
- *Private credit*: More private borrowing means less net saving by the private sector.

Table 11.2 Global Saving Rate Determinants: Four Models

Variable	Model 1	Model 2	Model 3	Model 4
Constant	0.578***	−0.770***	0.004	−0.410
	(0.182)	(0.208)	(0.026)	(0.270)
Savings (t−1)	0.614***	0.669***	0.818***	0.579***
	(0.124)	(0.122)	(0.062)	(0.124)
World real interest	0.054	0.125*	0.051**	0.016
rate (t)	(0.059)	(0.073)	(0.027)	(0.045)
Retail oil price (t−1)	−0.0001***	−0.00009***	−0.0001***	−0.00005**
	(0.0000)	(0.00003)	(0.0000)	(0.00002)
Private credit (t−1)	−0.001***	−0.001***	−0.001***	−0.001***
	(0.0002)	(0.000)	(0.0002)	(0.0002)
Total dependency ratio	0.003**	0.004***		
(t−1)	(0.001)	(0.001)		
Elderly dependency			1.112***	0.287
ratio (t−1)			(0.295)	(0.388)
Young dependency				0.173
ratio (t−1)				(0.147)
Life expectancy (t−1)	0.006***	0.008***		0.005**
	(0.002)	(0.002)		(0.003)
Real government	−0.181***	−0.110***	−0.126***	−0.197***
deficit (t−1)	(0.030)	(0.036)	(0.035)	(0.021)
Housing price index			−0.0002***	
(t−1)			(0.0000)	

NOTES:
1. Investment data was used for savings in the regressions.
2. All regressors are t−1 unless otherwise indicated. Government deficit excludes Mexico, Turkey, and Russia.
3. Standard errors are in parenthesis.
4. *, **, *** denote significance at the 10 percent, 5 percent, and 1 percent level, respectively.

SOURCE: Brigitte Desroches and Michael Francis, "World Real Interest Rates: A Global Savings and Investment Perspective," Working Paper/Document de travail 2007–16.

- *Real government deficit*: Some factors raising government budget deficits (e.g., lower tax rates and government entitlement programs) reduce the need for private savings. A higher public sector deficit contributes to a reduction in a country's overall net public and private saving rate.
- *Housing prices*: Rising home prices raise household wealth and thus reduce the needed amount of incremental saving out of current income.

Table 11.3   Global Investment Determinants: Four Alternative Models

Variable	Model 1	Model 2	Model 3	Model 4
Constant	0.068***	0.200***	0.127***	0.065
	(0.017)	(0.031)	(0.022)	(0.069)
Investment (t−1)	0.542***	0.176	0.429***	0.335*
	(0.095)	(0.124)	(0.086)	(0.179)
World real interest	−0.175***	−0.164***	−0.102***	−0.163**
rate (t)	(0.039)	(0.146)	(0.019)	(0.073)
Labor force growth	1.452*	0.410**	0.336**	1.656**
(t−1)	(0.867)	(0.170)	(0.148)	(0.817)
Real stock market	0.004	0.011**	0.011***	0.022***
returns (t−1)	(0.003)	(0.004)	(0.002)	(0.005)
Growth industrial	0.151***		0.117***	
production (t−1)	(0.023)		(0.019)	
Stock market volatility		−0.0001***	−0.00003	−0.00009***
(t−1)		(0.00002)	(0.00002)	(0.00003)
Business taxes	−0.018**	−0.016**	−0.016***	−0.005
(t−1)	(0.008)	(0.007)	(0.005)	(0.012)
High tech depreciation	0.396			
rate (t−1)	(0.273)			
Financial liberalization				0.001***
index (t−1)				(0.000)

NOTES:
1. All regressors are t−1 unless otherwise indicated.
2. Standard errors are in parenthesis.
3. *, **, *** denote significance at the 10 percent, 5 percent, and 1 percent level, respectively.

SOURCE: Brigitte Desroches and Michael Francis, "World Real Interest Rates: A Global Savings and Investment Perspective," Working Paper 2007−16, Bank of Canada, Ottawa, Canada, 2007.

Investment, in the study, is positively related to the following variables. (See related investment statistical models in Table 11.3.)

- *Labor force growth*: This helps determine the demand for capital goods required to equip an expanding labor force.
- *Stock market returns*: This is a proxy for expected investment returns that help drive firms' financial investment needs.
- *Industrial production*: Faster industrial production growth raises the demand for capital equipment to be financed.
- *Financial/trade liberalization*: Less regulated financial and trade regulation (i.e., more liberalization) enhance growth and related credit demands.

The following variables are negatively related to investment:

- *Interest rates*: Other things being the same, rising rates reduce investment incentives.
- *Business taxes*: Higher business taxes reduce expected after-tax physical investment returns and related investment funding demand.

Weighing the effects of factors that determine savings and investment and, thus, global real interest rates, Deroches and Francis reached four conclusions:

1. They estimated that global real interest rates fell by around 3 percentage points between 1989 and 2004.
2. They attributed the decline more to weaker investment than to a global savings glut. (Note: Ben Bernanke reached the opposite conclusion two years earlier in 2005.[8])
3. They determined that the declining real global interest rate was mainly the result of the growth and age structure of the labor force—two variables evolving comparatively slowly over time.
4. Projecting from their evidence, they predicted in 2007 that, "the world real interest rate is likely to remain low and to continue to adjust slowly, reflecting long-term trends." This was a correct forecast made before the Great Recession and the exceptionally easy industrial county monetary policies in its aftermath.

One inference of their study, in my opinion, is that low global interest rates were in the works before the Fed's quantitative easing (QE) program was brought into existence in late 2008. Thus, even without QE there are still factors limiting future rises in longer-term real interest rates.

When Will OPEC, Japan, and China Stop Buying Our Bonds?

The potential impact of global savings on U.S. interest rates raises one of the most frequently asked questions of my career. In the 1970s, that question was: When will OPEC countries start to pull their oil export,

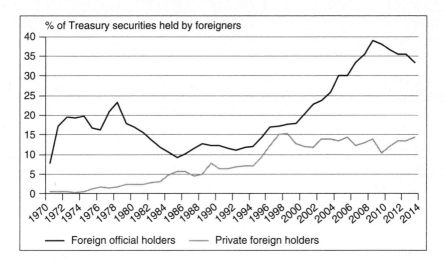

Figure 11.5   Roles of Foreign Investors in U.S. Treasury Securities Markets
SOURCE: U.S. Treasury Department.

dollar earnings out of the U.S. bond market? In the 1980s and 1990s the same question was asked about Japan. In the past two decades China has become the country we worry about. The issue keeps festering, because the markets are aware of the growing role played by foreign-domiciled investors in the U.S. Treasury securities markets. Their holdings as a percentage of outstanding Treasury securities have increased from approximately 5 percent at the start of the 1970s to roughly 25 percent in the mid-1990s to nearly 50 percent near the end of the last decade. (See Figure 11.5 for shares of outstanding Treasury securities held by private and foreign official investors.)

In all these cases, the common denominator was a country running a large international payment surplus with the United States, and uncertainty as to whether the surplus would be rechanneled smoothly into the U.S. financial markets. My answer—which seems usually to have been correct—is that, for various reasons, it has been in these investors' self-interest not to dump their holdings of U.S. Treasury securities. First, unloading these holdings, which had become such a large percentage of the outstanding securities, might significantly depress prices of the bonds in their portfolios. Second, Asian holders of

U.S. securities had accumulated dollar balances that reflected, in part, undervalued currencies, pegged artificially low so that these nations could maintain current account surpluses with the United States. To prevent these excess dollars from appreciating their own currencies, these countries' central banks needed to absorb excess dollars. And the safest place to park them has been in U.S. Treasury securities.

However, *if the large foreign central banks in China, Japan, and Saudi Arabia started to dump their Treasury securities, how might that action influence longer-term U.S. interest rates?* Federal Reserve Board economists Daniel Beltran, Maxwell Kretchmer, Jaime Marquez, and Charles Thomas have estimated that, "if foreign official inflows into U.S. Treasuries were to decrease in a given month by $100 billion, 5-year Treasury rates would rise by about 40 to 60 basis points in the short run. But once we allow foreign private investors to react to the yield change induced by the shock to foreign official inflows, the long-run effect is about 20 basis points."[9] To put these estimates into perspective, it is worth noting that between 1995 and 2010 China acquired just over a trillion dollars in U.S. Treasury notes and bonds. It also is important to note that when foreign official holdings were falling in the late 1970s and early 1980s and again after the Great Recession, there were rises in foreign private holdings, as hypothesized by the authors. (See Figure 11.5.)

What Will Be the Legacy of QE for Interest Rates?

In predicting longer-term interest rates, forecasters have traditionally considered the key independent variables to be the Federal funds rate, inflation expectations, the Federal budget deficit, and foreign securities purchases. Since 2008, a new factor has been added: the Fed's quantitative easing (QE) policy. QE has entailed expansion of the Fed's balance sheet via purchases of Treasury notes and bonds, and mortgage-backed securities. Between 2008 and 2014, Fed holdings of these securities grew by around $3.5 trillion through four separate purchase programs: QE1, QE2, QE3, and the Maturity Extension Program (MEP). Federal Reserve Board economists Canlin Li and Min Wei estimate that the QE1, QE2, and MEP programs lowered the 10-year Treasury yield by about 100 basis points.[10] These cited studies assessed the effects of QE1, QE2, and MEP through 2012. The Fed balance sheet expanded further in 2013 and part of 2014 through QE3. Thus, the cumulative rate impacts from the total QE program from 2008 through 2014 should have been greater than the impact from 2008 through 2012.

To illustrate this point, consider the following regression model in Table 11.4. In this model, the annual yield on the benchmark 10-year Treasury note is related to the Fed's share of outstanding Treasury notes and bonds, the Federal funds rate, inflation expectations, and a binary (i.e., "yes" or "no") dummy variable for the eight-year Paul Volcker era at the Fed, which lasted from late 1979 to late 1987. The positive coefficient on that variable says that, given the other significant rate

Table 11.4 Sample Multiple Regression Model of 10-year Treasury Note Yield

	10-Year Treasury Yield (%)
Constant	3.92
	(7.30)
Survey of Professional Forecasters: Median CPI inflation rate over the next 10 years (% y/y)	0.58
	(2.77)
Fed funds rate (%)	0.38
	(5.01)
Fed holdings of notes and bonds as a share notes and bonds outstanding	−0.15
	−(4.50)
VE*	1.74
	(3.71)
R–Square	0.95
Period	1979–2013

*Volcker era.
NOTE: T-stats in parenthesis.
SOURCE: Federal Reserve Board, Federal Bank of Philadelphia, UBS, and Author's calculation.

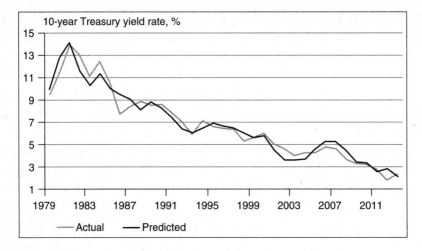

Figure 11.6   Actual versus Model Estimated Yield on 10-Year Treasury Note
SOURCE: Federal Reserve Board of Governors, author's calculation.

determinants, rates were higher than expected. That is probably because, during the Volcker era, investors believed that the Fed would hang tough with its rate policy until inflation had been contained. (Note: The budget deficit/GDP and nominal GDP growth variables were statistically insignificant in this multivariate regression exercise.) This model does a reasonably decent job of explaining the calendar-average level of the 10-year Treasury note yield. (See Figure 11.6)

The negative 0.15 response coefficient on the Fed's share means that each extra percentage point of Treasury notes and bonds held by the Fed lowers the Treasury note yield by 15 basis points (i.e., 0.15 percentage points.) Between 2008 and 2013, the Fed's share rose approximately 10 percent with the just over $2 trillion rise in Fed holdings of overall Treasuries securities during QE1, QE2, MEP, *and* QE3. (See Figure 11.7.) Multiplying the estimated response coefficient by ten suggests that the rise in Fed holdings of overall Treasuries securities could have lowered the 10-year Treasury note yield by around 150 basis points. That estimate is approximately 50 percent higher than the earlier 100 basis point impact cited in the Lin-Wei study through 2012, because there was incremental QE after 2012. According to my model, the negative QE effect on the 10-year Treasury note yield from

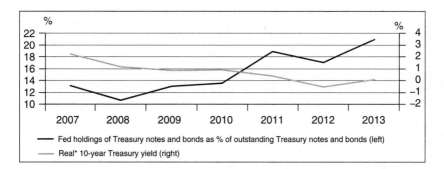

Figure 11.7 Fed's Share of Treasury Notes and Bonds versus Real 10-year Treasury Note Yield

*Adjusted for inflation expectations from Survey of Professional Forecasters.
SOURCE: Federal Reserve Board of Governors, U.S. Treasury Department, and Federal Reserve Bank of Philadelphia.

2008 through 2012 was around 100 basis points—the product of the −0.15 response coefficient and the 6.5 percentage point net rise in the Fed's share. The model estimated that further QE in 2013 subtracted approximately 50 additional basis points from the 10-year Treasury note yield.

If QE has done so much to contain interest rates, how high might rates rise without it? The Fed effectively committed itself to end the QE securities buying program before 2015, unless the economy turned unusually weak. One then asks, if QE programs trimmed almost 1.5 percentage points from the 10-year Treasury yield, would reversing QE (i.e., letting the Fed's balance sheet run down to pre-QE levels) raise the yield by a similar amount? Addressing this question offers some important insights into interest rate forecasting.

First, the *degree to which longer-term interest rates rise once the Fed stops its securities purchases will partly reflect how much advance notice the Fed gives to the financial markets about its plans.* In May of 2013, then Fed Chair Bernanke began speaking publicly about the increasingly imminent end of QE. The month before he spoke, the benchmark 10-year Treasury yield had averaged around 1.75 percent. Three months later, in August, the yield averaged almost a full percentage point higher, at around 2.75 percent. Studies at the time suggested that, through the end of 2012, QE had lowered the 10-year yield by about a full percentage point, so the quick rate rise of approximately 100 basis points was consistent with the notion that the Fed's exiting of QE had been built into bond prices.

Second, *the likelihood of substantially higher note and bond yields in the post-QE environment depends, in part, on whether one subscribes to the "stock" or "flow" view of the way in which the Fed's balance sheet influences interest rates.*

The stock view holds that QE effects on longer-term Treasury interest rates *depend on the share of total Treasury notes and bonds held by the Fed.* As that share rises, bond prices become higher than otherwise (and interest rates lower than otherwise) as more securities are held out of the market. From this perspective, if there are no further QE additions to the Fed's portfolio, there is no further incremental downward pressure on rates. However, if the share held by the Fed is diminished only gradually, the positive impact on rates will be only gradual as well. This is the opinion expressed by most FOMC members.

The flow view holds that QE effects on rates, in any given period, *depend on how much the Fed buys, and not on how much it holds.* Subscribers to this premise argue that trimming Fed purchases, or letting the Fed's balance sheet shrink, raises interest rates. This outlook implies a much larger upward rate impact of ending QE than does the stock viewpoint. In other words, if $50 billion of purchases per month lowers yields by a full percentage point, ceasing such purchases would raise rates by a full percentage point. And selling that much per month would add a further one percentage point to rates.

Which viewpoint will history judge as being closer to correct? As of mid-2014, my thinking was that the 10-year Treasury note yield would rise from its 2.5 to 3 percent trading range in the first half of 2014 to a 3 to 4 percent trading range in 2015 following the anticipated end of QE purchases in late 2014. That conclusion initially might appear more in line with the flow than with the stock school of thought. However, my conclusion is consistent with both the flow viewpoint and an expectations version of the stock point of view. *I believe that the longer-term note and bond markets will reflect not only the Fed's current share of Treasury securities, but also its expected lower share in coming years.*

What Is the Effect of Fed MBS Purchases on Mortgage Rates?

In addition to purchasing Treasury securities as part of its QE programs, the Fed also acquired substantial amounts of mortgage-backed securities (MBS). By the end of 2013, the Fed held around $1.5 trillion in MBS to go along with its $2.2 trillion in U.S. Treasury notes and bonds. The goal was to lower mortgage rates and help stimulate a very weak residential real estate market. Determining how much QE helped to depress mortgage rates is difficult because it is hard to know how much mortgage rates might have changed relative to Treasury yields in the absence of QE-related MBS purchases. Before QE was initiated in late 2008, the spread of conventional mortgage rates versus the benchmark 10-year Treasury note yield was approximately a full percentage point above normal, as investors shied away from MBS while home prices were tumbling. Had the Fed not stepped in during late 2008 to buy MBS, it is hard to say how much more the mortgage spread versus Treasuries yields would have increased. We do know, though, that a year after QE was initiated that spread had contracted by approximately a full percentage point, to around 1.5 percent.

One study by Federal Reserve Board economists Diana Hancock and Wayne Passmore suggests that each $100 billion rise in Fed MBS holdings results in mortgage rates falling by around 5 basis points (0.05 percentage points).[11] By this reckoning, the roughly $1.5 trillion in MBS held by the Fed at the end of 2013 made mortgage rates approximately 75 basis points (0.75 of 1 percent) lower than they would otherwise have been.

Will Projected Future Budget Deficits Raise Interest Rates?

During much of my career, the financial markets focused on budget deficits as a major determinant of interest rates. However, the visual correlation between the U.S. Federal budget deficit as a percentage of GDP and the real (inflation expectations adjusted) 10-year Treasury note yield has been erratic. (See Figure 11.8) Moreover, studies to determine

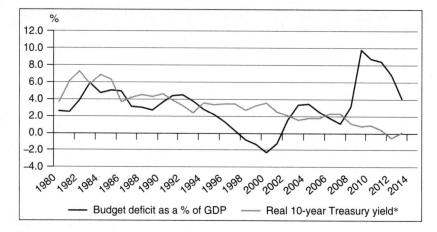

Figure 11.8   U.S. Federal Budget Deficit as a Percent of GDP versus Real Treasury Note Yield

*Nominal 10-year Treasury note yield minus inflation expectations
SOURCE: Federal Reserve Board of Governors, U.S. Treasury Department, Bureau of Economic Analysis, Federal Reserve Bank of Philadelphia.

Table 11.5   Number of Studies Finding Significant/Insignificant Interest Rate Effects of Budget Deficits

Deficit Measure	Mainly Positive Effects	Mixed Effects	Mainly Insignificant Effects	Total
Expected	13	4	1	18
Vector auto-regression	2	2	6	10
Current deficit/debt	14	5	12	31
Total	29	11	19	59

SOURCE: William G. Gale and Peter R. Orszag, "Economic Effects of Sustained Budget Deficits," Urban-Brookings Tax Policy Center, July 17, 2003.

whether U.S budget deficits have had statistically significant impacts on interest rates have been inconclusive.[12] (See Table 11.5.) Note that studies most frequently reporting statistically significant impacts expressed the deficit as either a forecast or a deviation of actual and forecast deficits. More insight into the effects of budget deficits on interest rates can be gained from examining cross-sectional studies that pool data from a variety of countries, instead of just looking at time series results in the United States.

Economists Ari Aisen and David Hauner at the International Monetary Fund (IMF) have studied the effects of deficits on interest rates across 60 advanced and emerging economies in the 1970 to 2006 period.[13] They reported three main conclusions:

1. They found that budget deficits had a highly significant impact on interest rates: approximately 26 basis points (0.26 percent) for each 1 percent of the GDP represented by a budget deficit.
2. The impacts varied across country groups and by the time period examined. The impacts "are larger and more robust in the emerging markets and in later periods than in the advanced economies and in earlier periods."
3. The relationship of budget deficits to interest rates is influenced by other variables. For instance, the impact is greatest when deficits are already high and mostly domestically financed, private debt is high, and openness to foreign capital is low.

Looking ahead, the declining Federal deficit, as a percentage of GDP, is not projected to continue. Unless fiscal policies in place through mid-2014 are changed, the CBO projects that rising Social Security and Medicare benefits for aging Baby Boomers will start to put the Federal deficit/GDP on a sharply higher track by 2020. (See Figure 11.9.)

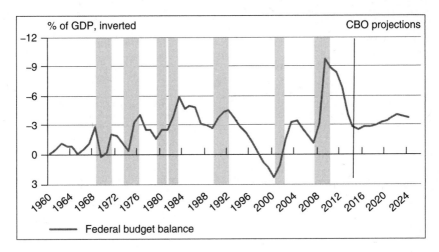

Figure 11.9   CBO Projected Federal Deficit as a Percentage of GDP
NOTE: Shaded areas denote recessions.
SOURCE: Congressional Budget Office.

Most interest rate research, however, indicates that the Federal funds rate, expected inflation, and the eventual unwinding of QE will be far more important than fiscal policy for rate developments.

Key Takeaways

1. The Fed has sometimes been and may occasionally remain reactive (i.e., behind the curve) instead of proactive, partly because its dual inflation and unemployment rate mandated variables can be lagging economic indicators.
2. Predicting the Fed's policy moves entails judging its evolving reaction to incoming economic data.
3. The Fed's success at forward guidance for the financial markets will rest on the credibility and consistency of the inflation and unemployment rate targets that it sets.
4. Unwinding the quantitative easing (QE) program puts potentially significant upward pressure on interest rates, but as of mid-2014 the financial markets had already begun to price in such consequences.
5. Warnings about the effects of budget deficits on interest rates often prove to be false alarms.
6. Real (inflation-adjusted) interest rates remain comparatively depressed in the more integrated global financial markets.
7. Nominal GDP growth is not a strong guide for longer-term interest rate determination.

Notes

1. David E. Lindsey, Athanasios Orphanides and Robert Rasche, "The Reform of October 1979: How It Happened and Why," Finance and Economics Discussion Series, Federal Reserve Board of Governors, Washington, D.C., December 2004.
2. Jon Hilsenrath and Kristina Peterson, "Federal Reserve 'Doves' Beat 'Hawks' in Economic Prognosticating," *Wall Street Journal*, July 28, 2013.

3. Matthew D. Raskin, "The Effects of the Federal Reserve's Date-Based Forward Guidance," Federal Reserve Board Division of Monetary Affairs Working Paper, May 9, 2013.

4. Stefani D'Amico, Stefani, Don H. Kim, and Min Wei, "Tips from TIPS: the informational content of Treasury Inflation-Protected Security Prices," Finance and Economics Discussion Series, Federal Reserve Board, Washington, D.C., January 31, 2014.

5. Ben S. Bernanke, "Long-Term Interest Rates," Remarks at Annual Monetary/Macroeconomics Conference: The Past and Future of Monetary Policy Sponsored by Federal Reserve Bank of San Francisco, San Francisco, California, March 1, 2013.

6. John Y. Campbell, Adi Sunderam, and Luis M. Viceira, "Inflation Bets or Deflation Hedges? The Changing Risks of Nominal Bonds," NBER Working Paper Series 14701, National Bureau of Economic Research, Cambridge, Massachusetts, February 2009.

7. Brigitte Desroches and Michael Francis, "World Real Interest Rates: A Global Savings and Investment Perspective," Working Paper 2007–16, Bank of Canada, Ottawa, Canada, 2007.

8. Ben Bernanke, "The Global Savings Glut and the U.S. Current Account Deficit," The Homer Jones Lecture, St. Louis, Missouri, April 14, 2005.

9. Daniel O. Beltran, Maxwell Kretchmer, Jaime Marquez, and Charles P. Thomas, "Foreign Holdings of U.S. Treasuries and U.S. Treasury Yields," Federal Reserve Board International Finance Discussion Papers, No. 1041, Washington, D.C., January 2012.

10. Canlin Li and Min Wei, "Term Structure Modelling with Supply Factors and the Federal Reserve's Large Scale Asset Purchase Programs," Federal Reserve Board Working Paper No. 2012–37, Washington, D.C., May 30, 2012.

11. Diana Hancock, and Wayne Passmore, "The Federal Reserve's Portfolio and its Effects on Mortgage Markets," Federal Reserve Board of Governors Working Paper No. 22, Washington, D.C., 2012.

12. William G. Gale and Peter R. Orszag, "Economic Effects of Sustained Budget Deficits," Urban-Brookings Tax Policy Center, July 17, 2003.

13. Ari Aisen and David Hauner, "Budget Deficits and Interest Rates: A Fresh Perspective," International Monetary Fund Working Paper, Washington, D.C., February 2008.

Chapter 12

Forecasting
in Troubled Times

When sorrows come, they come not single spies,
But in battalions.

—William Shakespeare, *Hamlet*, Act IV, Scene V

lthough interest rates may be the most difficult *variable* to
forecast, the most challenging *environments* for prognostica-
tion involve unanticipated crises—terrorism threats, natural
disasters, sudden oil price swings, stock market crashes, and foreign
economic turmoil. These events have prompted some major mistakes
by all forecasters—including myself. When they occur, the public is
taken by surprise, the media often overreacts, and our clients demand
fast answers. The world, in other words, is thrown into a bit of a tizzy.
(Figure 12.1 illustrates how crises of the past few decades have affected

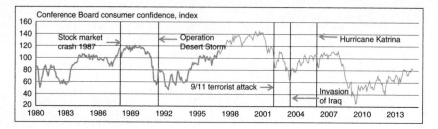

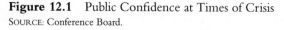

Figure 12.1   Public Confidence at Times of Crisis
SOURCE: Conference Board.

consumer confidence.) Although no one knows when these crises will occur, everyone knows that occur they will. To cite three obvious examples:

1. Spurred by global warming, aberrant weather patterns may spawn more frequent hurricanes and floods.
2. Terrorist threats and attacks on civilian populations are, unfortunately, more than a passing trend.
3. Stock market and oil prices are apt to remain volatile and full of surprises.

Thus, *a successful forecaster must be prepared to address these expected developments.*

Natural Disasters: The Economic Cons and Pros

In recent decades, forecasters have been challenged by the increased frequency of natural disasters. Researchers reporting in the *New England Journal of Medicine* state:

> There were three times as many natural disasters from 2000 through 2009 as there were from 1980 through 1989. Although better communications may play a role in the trend, the growth is mainly in climate-related events, accounting for nearly 80 percent of the increase, whereas trends in geophysical events have remained stable. During recent decades, the scale of disasters has expanded owing to increased rates of urbanization, deforestation, and environmental degradation and to intensifying climate variables such as higher temperatures, extreme

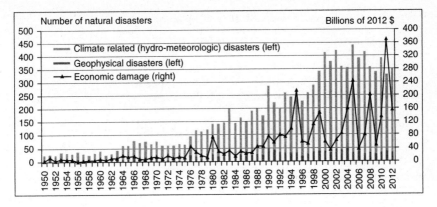

Figure 12.2   Global Natural Disasters

SOURCE: EM-DAT International Disaster database, center for research on the Epidemiology of Disasters, University of Louvain.

precipitation, and more violent wind and water storms.[1] (See Figure 12.2)

Looking ahead, at least some foresee more serious and more frequent natural disasters. David Bennett, for example, wrote in the *New York Times* that, "The population of coastal hurricane zones and cities that sit on or near major seismic faults—from San Francisco to Mexico City to Tokyo—continues to grow, and climatologists warn that climate change could increase the number of extreme weather events in many parts of the world."[2]

How do natural disasters impact an economy? Researcher Carolyn Kousky at Resources for the Future identifies these impacts in Table 12.1.[3]

How much economic damage can be inflicted by natural disasters?

When asked about the potential consequences of an evolving natural calamity, my first response is to look at the economic effects of past catastrophes. Even before the extent of a disaster is known, it helps to establish, via history, the likely upper bounds of its potential costs. As of mid-2014, Hurricane Katrina in 2005 was the most expensive natural disaster in U.S. history. (See Table 12.2.) Its almost $150 billion cost was equivalent to around 1.1 percent of the current dollar GDP that year. (Note: Distinguish between the dollar cost as estimated by the National Climatic Data Center [NCDC] and the disaster's effect on

Table 12.1 Direct and Indirect Impacts of a Disaster

Direct	Indirect
Damage to homes and contents	Business interruption for firms without direct damage
Damage to firm buildings, inventory, and contents	Multiplier effects
Damage to infrastructure	Costly adaptation or utility reduction from loss of use
Mortality and injury	Mortality and morbidity
Environmental degradation	Emergency response and clean-up

SOURCE: Carolyn Kousky, "Informing Climate Adaptation: a Review of the Economic Costs of Natural Disasters, Their Determinants, and Risk Reduction Options," Resources for the Future, Discussion Paper 12–28, Washington, D.C., July 2012.

Table 12.2 Major U.S. Weather/Climate Disasters in Past 25 Years

Event	Estimated Cost in Billions USD	Deaths
Hurricane Katrina, August 2005	148.8	1,833
Hurricane Sandy, October 2012	65.7	159
Hurricane Andrew, August 1992	44.8	61
Midwest flooding, Summer 1993	33.8	48
U.S. Drought/heat wave, 2012	30.3	123
Hurricane Ike, September 2008	29.2	112
Hurricane Wilma, October 2005	19.0	35
Hurricane Rita, September 2005	19.0	119
Hurricane Charley, August 2004	18.5	35
Hurricane Ivan, September 2004	17.2	57
Hurricane Hugo, September 1989	16.9	86
Midwest flooding, Summer 2008	16.2	24
Widespread drought, September 2002	12.9	0
Southern Plains/Southwest drought and heat wave, Spring–Summer 2011	12.4	95
Hurricane Frances, September 2004	11.1	48
Southern drought/heat wave, Summer 1998	10.7	200
Southeast/Ohio Valley/Midwest tornadoes, April 25–28, 2011	10.5	321
Hurricane Irene, August 2011	10.1	45
Midwest/Southeast tornadoes, May 22–27, 2011	9.4	177

SOURCE: National Climatic Data Center.

GDP production. Not all losses are replaced. Some are uninsured, and even insurance proceeds are not always used for physical replacement.)

In 2006, the President's Council of Economic Advisors (CEA) estimated that the combined impacts of Hurricanes Katrina in August of 2005 and Rita the following month reduced the annualized growth of real (inflation-adjusted) GDP by 0.7 percentage points in the third quarter of 2005, and by a further 0.5 percentage points in the year's final quarter.

To gauge the impact of some natural disasters in another way, we can measure the number of housing units lost. In the wake of the 2005 hurricanes, the combined areas of Louisiana, Mississippi, and Alabama—the areas most affected by the storms—lost an estimated 182,000 units.[4] To put that into perspective, it was roughly six-and-a-half times as large as the losses in three of the worst previous U.S. natural disasters. (See Table 12.3.)

Given the size of the United States, storm effects in any one region will have just a limited impact on national GDP. In smaller countries, storms can affect a larger portion of the economy. For instance, analysts at the Inter-American Development Bank studied the impact of 35 natural disasters on 20 Latin American and Caribbean countries between 1980 and 1996.[5] They concluded that the median negative impact on real GDP was almost 2 percent after a year and approximately 3 percent after two years.

What about recoveries from natural disasters?

After a natural disaster inflicts damage, rebuilding efforts help boost growth. For instance, consider what economists at the Institute for

Table 12.3 Structural Damage in Major U.S. Natural Disasters

Year	1906	1992	2004	2005
Natural disaster	San Francisco earthquake/ fire	Hurricane Andrew	Hurricanes Charley, Frances, Ivan, and Jeanne	Hurricane Katrina
Structures/ housing units	28,000 structures	Over 28,000 housing units	Nearly 27,500 housing units	182,000 housing units

SOURCE: American Red Cross, National Association of Home Builders, and Bureau of the Census.

Defense Analysis reported about the impact of the Alaska earthquake of 1964—the most powerful earthquake ever recorded in North America. In evaluating the related grants and loans for rebuilding, they estimated that Alaskans were actually better off financially after the earthquake.[6] In another study of the frequency of natural disasters in 89 countries over a 30-year period, it was concluded that, holding other growth factors constant, nations with more hurricanes and cyclones grew faster than countries with relatively fewer of such occurrences. However, that was not the case for countries with comparatively more earthquakes and volcanic eruptions. Why? The authors speculate that it is easier to prepare for weather-related disasters than for geological catastrophes.[7]

Looking at the aftermath of Hurricanes Katrina and Rita in 2005, analysts at the Congressional Budget Office (CBO) concluded that the net effect was essentially a wash. Following an estimated 0.5 percentage point reduction in annualized real GDP during the second half of 2005, GDP rebounded by a similar amount in the first half of 2006.[8]

Based on this research and my experience, *I believe that the media and financial markets can overreact to initial damage estimates from U.S. natural disasters.* I have observed the largest, albeit understandable, overreactions coming from clients in the affected areas. *However, in setting U.S. monetary policy, the Fed has not overreacted to the potential damage from large natural disasters.* For instance, consider the FOMC statement at the conclusion of its first meeting after Hurricanes Katrina and Rita, when there still was a good deal of uncertainty about the magnitude of their economic impacts. At that meeting on September 20, the Fed voted to raise its Federal funds rate target by 25 basis points to 3.75 percent. In doing so, the Fed stated:

> Output appeared poised to continue growing at a good pace before the tragic toll of Hurricane Katrina. The widespread devastation in the Gulf region, the associated dislocation of economic activity, and the boost to energy prices imply that spending, production, and employment will be set back in the near term. In addition to elevating premiums for some energy products, the disruption to the production and refining infrastructure may add to energy price volatility. While these unfortunate developments have increased uncertainty about

near-term economic performance, it is the Committee's view
that they do not pose a more persistent threat.

**(Press release, Federal Reserve Board of Governors,
September 20, 2005)**

History proved the Fed to be correct. Annualized real GDP growth
did slow from 3.3 percent in the third quarter of 2005 to 2.2 percent in
the fourth quarter, but it then reaccelerated sharply to a 4.9 percent pace
in the first quarter of 2006.

How to Respond to a Terrorist Attack

Natural disasters have been a periodic short-term forecasting problem,
and we have past behavior patterns to enable foreseeing their likely just
temporary growth impacts. However, nothing prepared me—or anyone
else—for what happened on the morning of September 11, 2001. I was
in my midtown Manhattan office when I heard the news of two planes
crashing into the World Trade Center towers. Immediately I went to
my window and gazed downtown. Right before my eyes two of tallest
buildings in the world were burning like candles and quickly melting
down. As I turned away to check the news on my computer screen, I was
even more shocked to learn that another plane had struck the Pentagon.
Soon I recalled what my parents had told me about their reaction 60 years
earlier when they heard on the radio that Pearl Harbor was attacked by
Japan. Seven decades later, I thought I was seeing another Pearl Harbor
and the start of a very major, if not worldwide, war.

Much raced through my mind as that terrible day evolved. Once
assured that my family was safe, my thoughts turned to my job as the
Chief U.S. Economist at a major global investment bank. What advice
should I give to our investor clients? I knew they would depend on
my firm's investment and economic advice, perhaps more than ever. But
how could I tell them what might transpire in a situation that was entirely
new in my lifetime? No one of my generation had ever seen anything
like this happen.

My first instinct was to publicly reassure our clients and urge them
not to panic. That was a challenge. The attacks had temporarily disabled
key elements of the stock market's electronic infrastructure, shutting it

down for several days. When the stock market reopened on September 17, the Dow Jones Industrial Average plunged 684 points—down 7.1 percent in one day. My first opportunity to communicate with our network of U.S. financial advisors was via a conference call in conjunction with senior UBS management. I decided to give an optimistic message of historical adaptability. I reminded these clients that terrorist attacks were not new in other parts of the world (see Figure 12.3), and other countries had adapted to this reality.

Subsequently, our economics team at UBS did say that the 9/11 attack was the proverbial straw that broke the camel's back for the near-term U.S. economy. It had already been on the edge of a recession in the aftermath of the tech bust at the end of the previous decade, which had precipitated a weak stock market and a sharp drop-off in capital spending. However, we also said that the recession would be mild and followed by an economic recovery in 2002.

Most Americans believe there will be more domestic terror attacks.

How to react and forecast in the wake of another terrorist attack should remain a forecaster's ever-present concern. More than a dozen years after the 9/11 attacks, most of the U.S. public remains fearful of further incidents on domestic soil. (See Table 12.4.) As of 2013, a majority believed America was no safer from terrorist attacks than it had been on 9/11/01. And 9 in 10 surveyed Americans believe that Americans will have to live with the risk of terrorism more or less permanently.

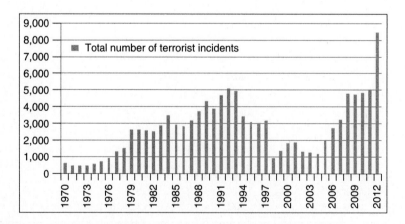

Figure 12.3 Bombing Plus Infrastructure/Facilities Attack Incidents

Source: National Consortium for the Study of Terrorism and Responses to Terrorism (START), 2013 Global Terrorism Database [Data file]. Retrieved from www.start.umd.edu/gtd.

Table 12.4 Public Opinion on Terrorism Likelihood

"Do you think that, as a country, we are more safe, about as safe, or less safe than we were before the terrorist attacks of September 11, 2001?"

	More Safe %	About as Safe %	Less Safe %	Unsure %
9/5–8/2013	39	33	28	—

$N = 1,000$ adults nationwide. Margin of error +/−3.1.
SOURCE: NBC News/*Wall Street Journal* poll conducted by the polling organizations of Peter Hart (D) and Bill McInturff (R), September 5–8, 2013.

"Do you agree or disagree with the following statement? Americans will always have to live with the risk of terrorism."

	Agree %	Disagree %	Unsure %
4/24–28/2013	90	8	2

$N = 965$ adults nationwide. Margin of error +/−3.
SOURCE: CBS News/*New York Times* poll, April 24–29, 2013.

"Which comes closer to your view? The terrorists will always find a way to launch major attacks no matter what the U.S. government does. *Or*, the U.S. government can eventually prevent all major attacks if it works hard enough at it."

	Terrorists Will Find a Way %	Can Prevent All Major Attacks %	Unsure %
4/30/2013	63	32	5

$N = 606$ adults nationwide. Margin of error +/−4.
SOURCE: CNN/*Time*/ORC poll, April 30, 2013.

"How concerned are you about the possibility there will be more major terrorist attacks in the United States? Is that something that worries you a great deal, somewhat, not too much or not at all?"

	A Great Deal %	Somewhat %	Not Too Much %	Not at All %	Unsure %
4/17–18/2013	32	37	20	10	1

$N = 588$ adults nationwide. Margin of error +/−5.
SOURCE: *Washington Post* poll, April 17–18, 2013.

"How concerned are you about the possibility there will be a major terrorist attack in your own community where you live? Is this something that worries you a great deal, somewhat, not too much or not at all?"

	A Great Deal %	Somewhat %	Not Too Much %	Not at All %
4/17–18/2013	13	27	27	32

$N = 588$ adults nationwide. Margin of error +/−5.
SOURCE: *Washington Post* poll, April 17–18, 2013.

Seventy percent of the public is at least somewhat concerned about a major terrorist attack the United States, and a full 40 percent believe that the next attack could be in their own community. A third of those polled felt that the government could eventually prevent all major attacks, but most of the rest believe that determined individuals will always find a way to thwart government antiterrorism efforts.

How have firms and households reacted to terrorist threats?

We can understand how U.S. consumers might respond to future terrorist events by studying their reactions to past crisis periods, such as the immediate aftermath of the September 11 attacks. (See Table 12.5.)

Table 12.5   Changes in Real Consumer Spending in Selected Crises

Monthly % Change	Real Consumer Spending	Durables	Nondurables	Services
Stock Market Collapse*				
Jul–1987	0.5	1.3	0.0	0.6
Aug–1987	0.8	3.6	0.2	0.4
Sep–1987	−0.5	−2.2	−0.2	−0.2
Oct–1987*	0.0	−4.1	0.1	1.0
Nov–1987	0.1	0.9	0.2	−0.3
Dec–1987	0.8	2.9	0.7	0.3
Jan–1988	0.9	2.7	−0.2	1.1
Gulf War*				
Oct–1990	−0.6	−2.3	−0.9	−0.1
Nov–1990	−0.1	−0.5	0.5	−0.3
Dec–1990	−0.4	−1.7	−0.9	0.2
Jan–1991*	−0.8	−5.4	−0.2	−0.3
Feb–1991*	0.5	2.3	0.5	0.2
Mar–1991	1.1	5.6	0.9	0.3
September 11 terrorist attacks*				
Jul–1	0.2	0.1	0.6	0.1
Aug–1	0.3	0.7	0.2	0.3
Sep–2001*	−0.7	−2.5	−1.0	−0.2
Oct–1	2.0	12.9	0.9	0.4
Nov–1	−0.3	−3.8	0.2	0.2
Dec–1	0.3	−2.5	1.4	0.3

*Date of crisis.
SOURCE: Bureau of Economic Analysis.

For example, I based my stated belief in the resilience of the U.S. consumer on studies of Americans' reactions to the Gulf War in the early 1990s and the Cuban missile crisis in 1962. In both cases, a temporary spending decline was followed by a noticeable recovery. And in the case of 9/11, while consumer spending fell sharply during the month of the attack, it rebounded a month later.

During periods of crisis, opinion polls can serve as potential forecast inputs. For instance, consider the polls published prior to the U.S. invasion of Iraq in March of 2003. (See Table 12.6.) Businesses expressed considerable caution beforehand but also expected activity to come back after hostilities and geopolitical uncertainties subsided. As it turned out, the Iraq War was like the Korean and Vietnam Wars, in that it lasted much longer than anyone expected. However, the American economy managed to have some good years even during those wartime periods.

Are we getting used to terrorist and geopolitical threats?

Looking ahead, will U.S. households and firms become less economically sensitive to domestic terrorism or geopolitical crisis episodes? Have they become more resigned to—and more familiar with—these occurrences? One answer in the affirmative comes from the public's immediate reaction to the Boston Marathon bombings on April 15, 2013. A day later, before the suspects had even been apprehended, four of every five people questioned stated that they would not alter their behavior patterns in response to the incident. (See Figure 12.4.)

Why Oil Price Shocks Don't Shock So Much

The longevity of my Wall Street employment reflects, in part, my ability to skirt responsibility for forecasting oil prices. Demand's comparative price insensitivity, coupled with unanticipated supply shifts, have made predicting oil prices one of the most hazardous of all possible forecasting tasks. That said, one cannot ignore oil price swings (see Figure 12.5) when forecasting any economy. Some of my most challenging periods as a forecaster have been caused by unanticipated surges in oil prices, events that surprised me as much as they did the population at large. Over the past four decades, these jolts have occurred frequently enough for us to

Table 12.6 Public Opinion Before U.S. Invasion of Iraq

Pervasiveness: How widespread are geopolitical/terrorism fears?

Question	Percent Responding "Yes"	Survey
Hiring and spending plans in 2003 are being adversely affected by geopolitical uncertainties	40	Federal Reserve Bank of Philadelphia
Concerns about war/terrorism caused your firm to delay or alter business plans for 2003	40	Business Council Survey of CEOs

SOURCE: Philadelphia Fed Business Outlook Survey, February 2003, Business Council.

Degree: If geopolitical uncertainties are having an impact on your hiring and capital spending for 2003, are the impacts:

	Hiring (%)	Capital Spending (%)
Significantly negative	12	36
Slightly negative	79	58
Slightly positive	6	3
Significantly positive	3	3

SOURCE: Philadelphia Fed Business Outlook Survey, February 2003.

Economic Aftermath of a Conflict in Iraq:

Question	"Yes" Response (%)	Survey
Rebound quickly once hostilities subside?	68	National Association of Manufacturers

SOURCE: National Association of Manufacturers.

Once geopolitical uncertainties are resolved, how soon will your hiring and spending increase?

	Hiring (%)	Capital Spending (%)
Immediately	10	8
Within 3 months	28	24
Within 6 months	21	21
After 6 months	13	21
No changes planned	28	26

SOURCE: Philadelphia Fed Business Outlook Survey, February 2003.

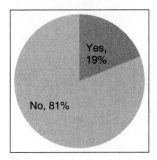

Figure 12.4   Immediate Public Reaction to Boston Marathon Bombing (2013)
"As a result of the Boston Marathon bombing, would you change how you live your everyday life?"
SOURCE: Fox News Poll, April 16, 2003, 619 registered voters nationwide.

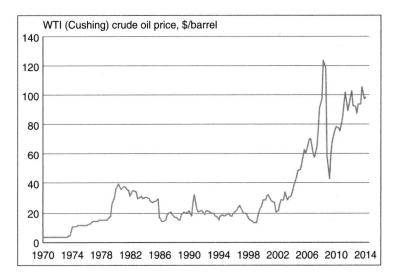

Figure 12.5   WTI Oil Price
SOURCE: *Wall Street Journal.*

establish a historical record that we can consult to judge how firms and households behave when the price of oil suddenly soars or dives.

Americans spent approximately $358 billion on energy in 2013. (See Figure 12.6.) Because the United States is a net importer of oil, rises (declines) in oil prices are usually viewed as unfavorable (favorable) for the economy. If foreign oil–producing nations consumed exactly the same basket of U.S. produced goods and services as consumed by

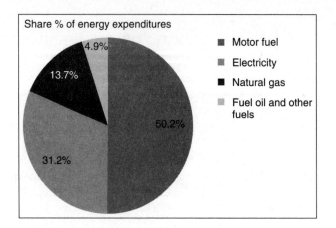

Figure 12.6   U.S. Households' Energy Expenditures (2003)
SOURCE: Bureau of Economic Analysis.

Americans, higher imported oil prices would simply represent a redistribution of income and consumption. However, oil-exporting countries generally have different consumption patterns than does the United States, including a higher national saving rate. As a result, economists typically view higher oil prices as a redistribution of global income that produces higher aggregate global savings. Unless these savings are rapidly redirected into investments, a rise in the price of imported oil can raise the global savings rate and slow worldwide economic growth. For the energy-hungry United States, a rise in imported oil prices can be viewed as an imported-oil tax hike depressing the U.S. economy. Conversely, lower imported oil prices can be seen as a de facto stimulative tax cut. (See Figure 12.7.)

This train of thought ignores the fact that the United States produces at least some of its domestically consumed oil. Unless domestic energy producers consume the same goods and services as domestic energy consumers, the redistribution of domestic income related to changes in oil prices can have at least some disruptive effects on the domestic economy. This became apparent when global oil prices collapsed in the mid-1980s. Although domestic consumers benefited from lower oil-related energy costs, the U.S. economy was providing fewer goods and services to its domestic and international petroleum suppliers. Between 1981 and 1986 when prices West Texas Intermediate (WTI) crude oil prices tumbled by

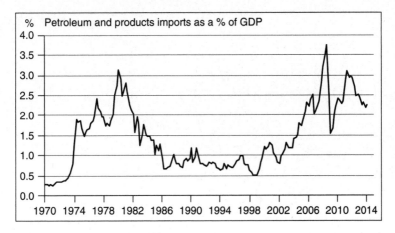

Figure 12.7   Oil Imports as a Percentage of GDP
SOURCE: Bureau of Economic Analysis.

around $50 per barrel, the U.S. petroleum import bill fell by $50 billion. That was a large lift to domestic purchasing power, as a big chunk of funds formerly diverted to petroleum imports now remained in the United States. Between 1982 and 1986, however, when the overall U.S. unemployment rate fell by 2.7 percentage points to 7.0 percent, the unemployment rates in Texas, Louisiana, Oklahoma—three major oil producing states in the United States—rose by between 2.1 and 2.3 percentage points. (The jobless rate in the other major oil producing state—Alaska—rose by 1.2 percentage point.)

Outside of the United States, there also was a plunge in the incomes and purchasing power of the Organization of Petroleum Exports (OPEC) countries. That was a drag on U.S. exports. (Note in Figure 12.8 that the ratio of U.S. exports to OPEC, as a percentage of U.S. imports from OPEC, varies considerably; but at least some of what the United States spends on OPEC petroleum has always been recycled into U.S. exports to OPEC.)

Thus, *the impact of oil price swings on the U.S. economy is mitigated by the related redistribution of incomes and purchasing power between oil-consuming and oil-producing areas.*

Another factor cushioning oil price impacts is whether changes are perceived as temporary or permanent. For example, gasoline prices are volatile. (See Figure 12.9.) If consumers remember this fact, some will be more likely

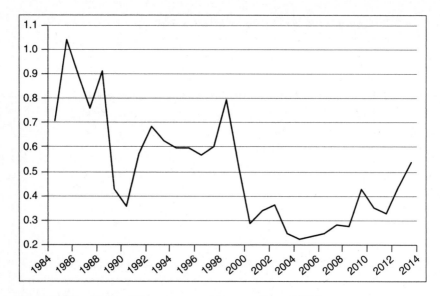

Figure 12.8   Ratio of Exports to and Imports from OPEC
SOURCE: Bureau of the Census.

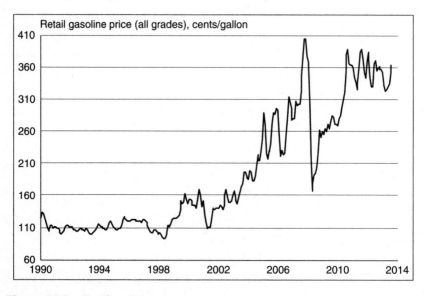

Figure 12.9   Gasoline Prices
SOURCE: Energy Information Agency.

to maintain their consumption patterns despite up and down gas prices. This behavior will likely become more common as credit cards continue to replace cash when paying at gasoline stations. In other words, the ability to borrow on credit cards provides a buffer enabling more households to stabilize their nonenergy consumption patterns when their energy expenses vary. If energy price changes are viewed as being more sustainable in a given direction, they are more likely to affect nonenergy consumption.

Federal Reserve monetary policy has become more likely to cushion, rather than exacerbate, potential oil price swings' impacts on economic activity. As discussed in Chapter 10, core inflation and inflation expectations have become less sensitive to food and energy price swings over time. When oil prices rise, the Fed is less likely to anticipate higher overall price inflation and to tighten interest rates. When oil prices decline, the growing likelihood that such declines may be only temporary should keep the Fed from viewing this as a factor making the economy too strong.

In conclusion, oil price swings are less shocking than in the past. The United States is becoming less dependent on foreign energy supplies. (See Figure 12.10.) Consumers are becoming more familiar with volatile gasoline prices and are better able to utilize credit card debt in coping with the accompanying short-run household budget impacts. And less pass-through from energy price swings to inflation spells a more muted monetary policy response to the broader potential inflation impacts of oil price increases.

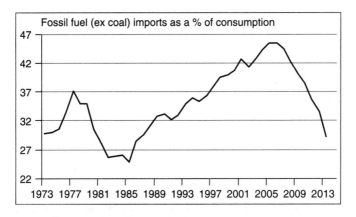

Figure 12.10   U.S. Dependence on Imported Energy
SOURCE: Energy Information Agency.

Market Crashes: Why Investors Don't Jump from Buildings Anymore

The folklore surrounding the 1929 stock market crash includes tales of brokers, traders, and investors so shocked at their sudden ruin that they chose to leave work—and life itself—early, by jumping out of high-story windows. Eighty-five years later, severely disappointed investors, now with access to antidepressants and various other substances, are much less likely to exercise such an option. That said, just about every sharp, sudden stock market decline is accompanied by fears of a major pullback in consumer spending. This, too, can be an overreaction.

It has been almost a half-century since the great American economist Paul Samuelson stated:

> To prove that Wall Street is an early omen of movements still to come in GNP, commentators quote economic studies alleging that market downturns predicted four out of the last five recessions. That is an understatement. Wall Street indexes predicted nine out of the last five recessions! And its mistakes were beauties.[9]

Almost a half-century later, I think it is fair to say that Professor Samuelson was correct. The stock market periodically sounds false alarms about an imminent economic downturn. I learned that lesson the hard way in the autumn of 1987. On October 19 of that year (a.k.a. Black Monday), the Dow Jones Industrial Average (DJIA) plunged 508 points—a 21.6 percent decline that was the largest single-day rout since the Great Crash in 1929. Like just about everyone else, I was shocked. Caught up in the ensuing public panic, on the following day I all too hastily predicted an imminent recession. At least when I caught my mistake, I changed that forecast a few weeks later. What in fact happened was that real overall consumer spending growth did slow substantially to just a 0.8 percent annual rate in the final quarter of 1987 following a fast 4.7 percent growth in the quarter before. And durable goods consumption actually fell at a 10.4 percent pace in the fourth quarter. However, that drop was not sufficient to depress overall real GDP, which posted a strong 6.8 percent annualized growth in the final quarter of the year.

Why can a suddenly declining stock market be a false alarm of recession? There are a couple of reasons. First, evolving trading strategies can engender a market overreaction to negative news. This was the case in 1987 when program trading and portfolio insurance exacerbated what should have been the market's mild negative reaction to a disappointing monetary policy dispute between the United States and its major trading partners.[10] Second, a weaker stock market can trigger an easier Fed monetary policy that helps to cushion the potential blow to the economy.

However, just because a sharp stock market correction need not be followed by a recession does not mean that it is harmless for the U.S. consumer. A commonly cited rule of thumb has been that each dollar decline in households' stock market wealth eventually trims consumer spending by a nickel. As discussed in Chapter 9, though, various consumer spending studies place more emphasis on housing as opposed to stock market wealth effects being a consumption driver. And it is true that stock market wealth is highly concentrated. For instance, in 2012, 83 percent of the net capital gains were reported on just 1 percent of Federal income tax returns: those with adjusted gross income of $250,000 or more.

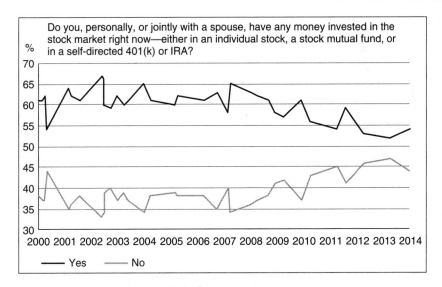

Figure 12.11   U.S. Households' Stock Ownership
SOURCE: Gallup Poll.

Nevertheless, slightly more than half of U.S. households have had money invested in the stock market in recent years, either via individual stock holdings, a stock mutual fund or a self-directed 401(k) or IRA. (See Figure 12.11.) So stock market movements can still have important impacts on consumer psychology. These effects can be amplified by today's enhanced public awareness of market movements. All-day coverage of financial news, on multiple television channels, is one example. In addition, households can now receive daily reports from their financial advisors on the performance of their investment portfolios via the internet.

Contagion Effects: When China Catches Cold, Will the United States Sneeze?

The world outside the United States is full of surprises, and I, like all forecasters, must respond to them quickly. In recent decades, some of the most challenging have been the Asian financial crisis in the late 1990s and the European financial crisis a dozen years later. In both cases, the surprises stemmed from imprudent and often opaque financing practices that eventually impaired the functioning of capital markets and entire national banking systems. Whenever these developments suddenly appear on the radar screen, there are immediate worries that the problems in one part of the globe will be contagious and spread throughout the globe. This is the contagion effect. My experience is that on these occasions, financial markets and many observers overreact with regards to the potential ills inflicted on the U.S. economy.

My initial reaction to foreign financial crises has often been so simple that my audiences are reluctant to believe it. The answer I usually choose is this: *Exports account for only about an eighth of U.S. GDP, and no one region plays a particularly dominant role in U.S. exports.* (See Table 12.7.) Europe purchases about a fifth of U.S. merchandise exports, and another fifth is bought by Canada. Our neighbors to the south of the United States—Mexico, Central America, and South America—account for around a third of what the United States sells abroad. Asian nations purchase just over a fifth of U.S. goods exports. In other words, the

Table 12.7 Selected Shares of U.S. Merchandise Exports (2013)

PARTNER	(%)
Canada	19.0
Mexico	14.3
Europe	20.7
China	7.7
Japan	4.1
NICs*	8.9
South/Central America	11.6
OPEC**	5.4

*Newly industrialized countries
**Organization of Petroleum Exporting Countries
SOURCE: U.S. Bureau of the Census.

United States has a well-diversified mix of global trading partners. This type of initial reaction on my part typically is accompanied by the following question:

"While no one region is a dominant customer of the U.S., what are the consequences if weakness in one area spreads to other U.S. trading partners that do considerable export business with the problem region?"

A way to address this question is to identify a problem region's major suppliers and to determine how closely they are linked to U.S. trade.

Consider the case of China. In 2013, its purchases of goods from the United States represented only about 1 percent of U.S. GDP. (That's the product of China's share of U.S. goods exports and the one-eighth ratio of overall exports to the U.S. GDP.) With a country's imports usually moving in line with its GDP change, a complete halt in Chinese annual growth from the 10 percent in that country's boom years would subtract only a tiny 10th of 1 percent from U.S. GDP growth.

What about the effects of Chinese weakness on its trading partners who also trade with the United States? To answer that question, it is useful to compare a country's exports to China, as a percentage of its GDP, to that country's imports from the United States as a percentage of U.S. GDP. (See example in Figure 12.12.) Consider, for instance, China's largest supplier: South Korea. Its exports to China represent just

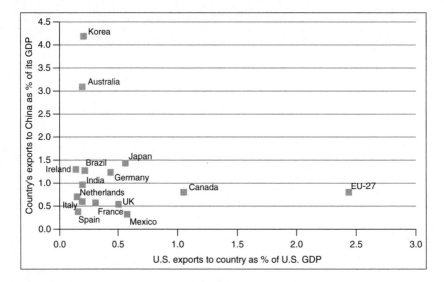

Figure 12.12   Exports to China as a Percent of GDP in 2009
SOURCE: UBS, OECD TiVA, IMF.

over 4 percent of South Korean GDP. However, South Korean purchases from the U.S. represent only a tiny one-quarter of one percent
of U.S. GDP. Considering the spread effects to the U.S. from all of
China's trading partners, I have calculated that a China slowdown would
affect U.S. growth by roughly double the above discussed direct U.S.
growth effect of weaker U.S. exports to China. Thus, even a dramatic
10-percentage point slowdown in Chinese growth would only shave
about 0.2 percentage points from U.S. GDP. (Note: These calculations
are not meant to downplay the potential negative U.S. growth effects
from global economic weakness. Rather, they address potential impacts
on U.S. growth from weakness in a particular region.)

Another, simpler, way to address whether a regional financial crisis is
significantly affecting U.S. growth is to examine the Institute for Supply
Management (ISM) New Export Orders Index. (See Figure 12.13.) Any
index reading over 50 means that U.S. exports are expanding. My experience has been that *the ISM export order growth index is a handy indicator of
near-term export trends. And during past foreign crises, it has—at times—kept
me from overreacting to economic and financial developments in a specific
region.*

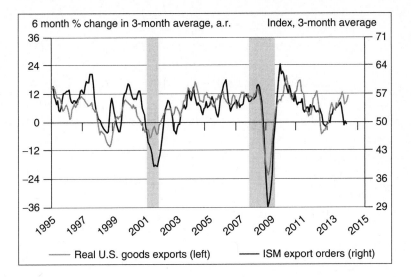

Figure 12.13   ISM New Export Orders Index and U.S. Goods Exports

Export growth (6-month percent change in 3-month moving average), left; ISM New Export Orders Index, right.

NOTE: Shaded areas denote recessions.

SOURCE: Institute for Supply Management (ISM), U.S. Bureau of the Census.

Key Takeaways

1. A successful forecaster must be prepared to react to inevitable but largely unpredictable crises, such as natural disasters, terrorist attacks, oil price swings, stock market crashes, and foreign financial crises.

2. The economic history surrounding past crises provides some guidance on economic behavior in future crises.

3. In developed nations, the initial negative economic impact of a natural disaster is usually followed by offsetting positive impacts from disaster aid and rebuilding.

4. In the United States, the negative economic reactions to international crises and the 9/11 terrorist attack have been short-lived, with these experiences possibly moderating public reactions to such crises in the future.

5. America's sensitivity to oil price shocks has been moderated by a decreasing dependence on foreign energy sources and a lessened tendency to extrapolate swings in volatile energy prices.

6. Although many observers overreact in speculating about the initial adverse economic consequences of a sudden drop in stock prices, more sustained stock price swings remain relevant for consumer spending.

7. Do not overreact to potential contagion effects of foreign crises on U.S. growth: U.S. export markets are well-diversified and exports represent only about an eighth of U.S. GDP.

8. The Institute for Supply Management (ISM) export order growth index is a handy guide in determining whether foreign economic problems are serious enough to materially affect U.S. exports.

Notes

1. Jennifer Leaning and Debarati Guha-Sapir, "Natural Disasters, Armed Conflict, and Public Health, *New England Journal of Medicine* 369 (November 7, 2013): 1836–1842.

2. David Bennett, "Do Natural Disasters Stimulate Economic Growth?" *New York Times*, July 2, 2008.

3. Carolyn Kousky, "Informing Climate Adaptation: A Review of the Economic Costs of Natural Disasters, Their Determinants, and Risk Reduction Options," Resources for the Future Discussion Paper 12–28, Washington, D.C., July 2012.

4. Economic and Statistics Administration, "The Gulf Coast: Economic Impact & Recovery One Year after the Hurricanes," U.S. Department of Commerce, Washington, D.C., October 2006.

5. C. Charveriat, "Natural Disasters in Latin America and the Caribbean: An Overview of Risk," Working Paper No. 434, Inter-American Development Bank Research Department, Washington, D.C., 2000.

6. Douglas Dacy and Howard Kunreuther, *The Economics of Natural Disasters: Implications for Federal Policy* (New York: Free Press, 1969).

7. Mark Skidmore and Hideki Toya, "Do Natural Disasters Promote Long-Run Growth?" *Journal of Economic Inquiry* 40, no. 4 (October 2002): 664–687.

8. Economic and Statistics Administration, "The Gulf Coast."

9. Paul Samuelson, "Science and Stocks," *Newsweek*, September 19, 1966.

10. Mark Carlson, "A Brief History of the 1987 Stock Market Crash with a Discussion of the Federal Reserve Response," Federal Reserve Board Finance and Economics Discussion Series, Washington, D.C., November 2006.

Chapter 13

How to Survive and Thrive in Forecasting

I made a great deal of money in the late 1940s on the bull side, ignoring Satchel Paige's advice to Lot's wife, "Never look back." Rather I would advocate Samuelson's Law: "Always look back. You may learn something from your residuals. Usually one's forecasts are not so good as one remembers them; the difference may be instructive." The dictum "If you must forecast, forecast often," is neither a joke nor a confession of impotence. It is a recognition of the primacy of brute fact over pretty theory. That part of the future that cannot be related to the present's past is precisely what science cannot hope to capture.

—Paul Samuelson, February 1985 lecture at Trinity University

W hen I first started working as a forecasting economist at PaineWebber in 1980, my professional colleagues at the Fed and in academia were wary. How could I publicize economic forecasts when I knew how hard it is to be right even half the time? What would I do when I was wrong? Would I be fired? If so, could I ever get another job as a forecaster? More than three decades later I still am asked this type of question. Except now the typical query is, "How have you survived for so long in such a potentially precarious professional position?"

Part of the answer is that I have tried to apply, diligently, the same best practices that I have advocated throughout this book. Now, in this chapter, I review those practices and concepts, and I share with you some of my on the job experiences. I discuss how to present a forecast and manage a forecasting job. I address questions such as: How do you present a convincing forecast? When do you "hold" and when do you "fold"? What do you say when you are wrong? How can you keep a forecasting job if your forecasts have been incorrect?

I'd like to pass along a few things I've learned along the way:

Making Forecasts: A Dozen Best Practices

1. *Don't reinvent the wheel.*

   A thorough but time-efficient approach is to first review relevant literature. (See discussion in Chapter 2.)

2. *Pay close attention to how data is gathered and processed.*

   (See further discussion Chapter 2.)

3. *Be prepared to supplement statistical model results and quantifiable data points with institutional and historical judgment.*

   Periods with relatively large in-sample statistical model errors are ripe for being supplemented in this way. For forecasting purposes, do not hesitate to adjust statistical model forecasts via judgmental information that is not quantifiable. (For further discussion, see Chapter 2.)

4. *Be cautious in using frequently revised government economic data as a forecast driver.*

   When data is known to be subject to sometimes large revisions, seek other corroborative information. (See further discussion in Chapter 2 and Chapter 5.)

5. *Avoid using hard-to forecast independent variables as major forecast drivers.*

    Instead, it's better to employ lagged independent variables that have already been reported and are not subject to big revisions. (See further discussion in Chapter 2 and Chapter 5.)

6. *For interest rate forecasting, judgmental inputs are critical.*

    (See further discussion in Chapter 2 and Chapter 11.)

7. *Do not adhere too strictly to any particular school of macroeconomic thought.*

    Not enough weight in recent years has been given to monetarism and supply-side theories. (See Chapter 6.)

8. *Take a critical approach to new normal thinking about the next decade.*

    History suggests "normality" is not "the norm." From an analytical perspective, do not ignore the potential dynamism and adaptability of the U.S. economy. (See Chapters 3 and 8.)

9. *Be wary of exuberant multiplier estimates.*

    Both Keynesian and input-output multipliers can easily become unrealistically high. Be skeptical of any Keynesian multiplier much over 1.5. (See Chapter 5.)

10. *Do not base core inflation forecasts on a simple repetition of the Phillips Curve wage-inflation tradeoff in the previous business recovery.*

    This relationship can shift. (See discussion in Chapter 10.)

11. *In forecasting interest rates avoid simple historical rules of thumb about relationships between longer-term interest rates and inflation and nominal GDP growth.*

    These relationships have dramatically changed over time. (See discussion in Chapter 11.)

12. *When projecting Fed policy, respect what policymakers say in public but remember that they, like all forecasters, will have to change their minds when they are wrong.*

    Fed policymakers run the risk of eventually being behind the curve. (See further discussion in Chapter 11.)

Using Forecasts: Ten Critical Guidelines

1. *Forecasters who are more accurate than the average forecaster in predicting extreme events are less accurate in predicting all events that must be forecast.*

    Such forecasters of rare events (e.g., major recessions) can be like broken clocks—rarely changing their outlooks. (See further discussion in Chapter 1.)

2. *Forecasts can be motivated by forecasters' varying loss functions (i.e., perceived rewards and risks from successful or failed forecasts).*

   Independent forecasters are more likely to go out on a limb than forecasters employed in large organizations. (See further discussion in Chapter 1.)

3. *When judging forecasters' track records over longer time intervals, the consensus often is more accurate than any individual's track record.*

   That said, at any point in time be wary of just going with the consensus. Winners of forecasting derbies for any given time period have a history of herding less to the consensus. Moreover, consensus forecasts often fail at critical turning points. (See further discussion in Chapter 1 and Chapter 4.)

4. *A PhD does not increase the likelihood of its holder being a more accurate forecaster.*

   A more relevant gauge of accuracy is the forecaster's proximity to the event being forecast. (See further discussion in Chapter 1.)

5. *More experienced forecasters tend to be more accurate.*

   The evidence is mixed, though, as to whether more experienced forecasters deviate more or less from the consensus than do less experienced forecasters. (See further discussion in Chapter 1.)

6. *Forecasters who mix judgment with their models generally outperform model-driven economic forecasts.*

   (See further discussion in Chapter 2.)

7. *Specific statistics for assessing forecast accuracy depend on the user's particular needs and objectives.*

   The average (mean) error is a measure of directional bias over a number of forecasting periods. The mean absolute error gauges accuracy. If larger mistakes are more costly, proportionately, than smaller mistakes, the root mean squared error is the appropriate guide. To assess forecasters' comparative skills in projecting a variety of variables over a period of time, there are composite metrics. These can reflect the comparative difficulty (e.g., standard deviation) in forecasting individual variables and the internal consistency of forecasts—a key to credibility. (See further discussion in Chapter 2.)

8. *No one school of economic thought has a monopoly on being more correct and relevant than competitive paradigms.*

The followers of Hyman Minsky (aka Minskyites) excelled at predicting the Great Recession but probably overemphasize debt. Although Keynesian economics sometimes is viewed as dated, it remains as a necessary organizational framework for macroeconomic forecasting. Despite its controversial conclusions about taxation, supply-side economics is relevant for evaluating longer-term potential GDP growth. Monetarism has come to be regarded as an oversimplified view of contemporary financial markets and institutions; but monetarists' views on long and variable lags of monetary policies' economic impacts remain relevant in judging the future implications of the Fed's quantitative easing (QE) policies. (See further discussion in Chapter 6.)

9. *While government economic data are assembled in a politically independent manner, forecasts from the Executive Branch have a history of over-optimism.*

   The Congressional Budget Office probably is a more reliable forecaster. The most politically independent macroeconomic analyses are likely to come from economists within the Federal Reserve System. (See further discussion in Chapter 5.)

10. *Input-output studies of potential benefits from specific policies can be wildly optimistic.*

   Caution is warranted in utilizing conclusions of policy advocates utilizing and sometimes abusing this particular technique. (See further discussion in Chapter 5.)

Surviving: What to Do When Wrong

If you want to be a forecaster, you should accept that you'll be wrong at least some of the time. It goes with the turf. Yet you must maintain your audience's support for your services nonetheless. This can be especially challenging for economic forecasters, who have one of the hardest jobs around. In more than three decades as a Wall Street economic forecaster, I have seen some very successful economists and securities analysts enjoying long careers, despite the inevitable blemishes on their forecasting track records. Based on my firsthand observations, I believe survival has more to do with handling oneself when wrong than with being right a relatively high percentage of the time.

Because forecasters know (or should know) that their projections will err on occasion, they should *always* be prepared to be wrong. How one handles mistakes is extremely important in any job, but it is particularly critical for career longevity in forecasting. It is crucial to remember the following, always: *Just because we don't know everything does not mean we don't know anything. We still know a lot.* The forecaster still can be helpful even when a specific forecast has gone awry.

When presenting a forecast, it is important to *outline risks and signposts*. Doing so helps to establish credibility that the forecaster is being diligent and thorough. Also, when a forecast is wrong, the audience will be less surprised than if it had not been warned about risks along the path to a specific projected future outcome.

In assigning *risks* to a specific forecast, a simple approach is to list events that could influence outcomes on either side. For instance, interest rates will be higher than expected if unemployment is lower than assumed, or they could be lower than expected if foreign economic growth is unexpectedly weak. To quantify risks by citing a range of likely outcomes, one approach is to report the standard error from the regression model on which a forecast is based. In providing a formal statistical probability of an outcome, some forecasters find it useful to use probit models to estimate probabilities conditioned on various assumed independent driver variables.[1] Other forecasters will find it simpler but more helpful to report their own subjective probabilities, suggesting the strength of one's conviction. Just be sure to let your audience know whether your stated probability of success is based on a subjective degree of conviction or stems from a specific statistical model.

For *signposts*, be sure that they are leading, and not coincident, indicators of what is being forecast. I sometimes list as signposts assumed values for lagged independent variables in a regression model used to generate a forecast. For instance, rents change with a lag following variation in rental vacancy rates.

It also is important not to overdo the risks and signposts. Bringing up too many caveats can be interpreted as hedging a bet, signaling an unwillingness to take a clear stand. *A forecaster should never lose sight of the end-user's need for decisiveness.* In my experience, forecasters viewed as either indecisive or as bet-hedgers are less well regarded than forecasters who are willing to commit, who are willing to stick their necks out—as their clients must do.

I also find it helpful to *plan responses* to various outcomes. (Going through this exercise can also provide self-feedback as to whether a specific forecast makes much sense in the first place.) When clients such as traders need fast answers, it is very helpful to have a response already planned. For example, if an inflation report is greater than expected, financial sector clients are immediately interested in the interest rate impact. It is critical that the forecaster maintain credibility by not appearing clueless after an unanticipated outcome is reported. I find it helpful in such situations to frame my postresult response in terms of, "Here is what I/we have learned from this surprise." This is a time to remember that you probably know more than the audience. Whatever you can tell them is apt to be more helpful than saying you must go back to the drawing board.

It may be helpful to respond to an unanticipated outcome for an economic statistic by noting that data *revisions* could still make an initial forecast correct. However, to go that route convincingly, be sure to cite typical recent ranges of revisions. And try to avoid being seen as too much of a sour grapes responder when you are wrong.

Should you apologize if you are wrong? It depends. Too many apologies ruin a forecaster's credibility. However, *when a mistake has especially serious adverse consequences for your audience, some humility can be a career saver.* I will never forget the shock of the Enron collapse in the summer of 2001. Virtually all of the securities analysts following this stock were wrong and quite understandably horrified. Clients complained that analysts were so distraught that they would not pick up the phone to at least commiserate with their customers. However, at least one analyst I know did maintain the respect of, and brokerage commissions from, professional investor clients. He phoned them and said, simply, "If you never speak to me again, I understand. However, if you seek my help, I will do everything in my power to be useful." It worked.

Perhaps the most important course of action when wrong is to learn from the mistake. Always examine your personal track record to see where you went wrong and why. If there is a persistent bias in your errors, adjust your forecast for that. Though securities analysts regularly do this with their statistical models, I don't believe they subject their actual forecasts—which reflect the analysts' judgment applied to the models—to the same degree of self-evaluation.

Hold or Fold?

When a critic questioned him about changing a position on a particular issue, John Maynard Keynes is said to have responded: "When my information changes, I alter my conclusions. What do you do, sir?" When forecasters have been wrong, should they still hold on to a forecast awaiting vindication? Or is the evolving best bet to take your losses and change the forecast (i.e., fold)?

Holding: If most of your signposts still point in the direction of your forecast eventually materializing, probably the best strategy is to hold. Your audience should understand why you have made this choice if you have familiarized them with your forecast signposts. In this setting, holding is a good opportunity to communicate conviction. However, before doing so, it is best to see if some variable other than your signpost variables may be exerting a longer-term influence on the behavior of the forecast variable. Also, keep in mind that you don't want to appear unnecessarily stubborn. The consequence could be going out on a limb and sawing it off yourself.

Folding: My experience is that securities analysts and economists are often too fearful of being whipsawed, by folding just when their forecast was about to be right. Although they may also be afraid of being labeled as "capitulating" or "marking to market," those fears must be weighed against the more serious reputational risk of appearing exceptionally stubborn and wrong. If you are wrong and your preassigned signposts are not working, it probably is best to fold, at least for the time being. An audience already informed of your signposts won't be caught off guard.

Whether forecasters hold or fold in a given set of circumstances will naturally reflect their perceived loss function (i.e., perceived cost of loss versus perceived benefit of gain). My advice is to *rid your decisions of your expected psychic comfort or discomfort and focus on the audience's needs.*

In my career as a Wall Street economist, one key consideration in maintaining or abandoning an errant forecast has been a specific audience's investment horizon. Actively managed investment funds, including hedge funds, generally have a shorter time horizon in which to perform than do pension funds and individual investors. With this diverse audience, when wrong about bond yields, for instance, I would change my forecast to go with the unexpected trend over a few months or quarters but usually maintain a multiquarter ahead call unless my signposts had little chance of materializing.

In Chapter 1 we discussed how, in some past studies, forecasters with their own consulting firms were more likely to deviate from the consensus than forecasters employed by larger institutions. The latter organizations are more conscious of potential downside risks for their internal trading and marketing and for their external clients. The former may be influenced by the commercial necessity of publicity. This is not to say that the forecast user should not use independent consulting services, as exploring nonconsensus viewpoints can be very stimulating and helpful in making investment and marketing decisions.

Thriving: Ten Keys to a Successful Career

I have had a reasonably successful three-and-a-half decade career as a Wall Street economist. I have never changed firms and I've been named to *Institutional Investor* All-America Research teams on two dozen or so separate occasions. Also, in 2004, 2006, and 2008, my colleague James O'Sullivan and I were ranked by *MarketWatch* as Forecaster of the Year. In addition, my own teams have received frequent recognition for their forecasting prowess. In 2011, for instance, *Bloomberg* magazine rated us the most accurate of more than six dozen U.S. data forecasters over the 2010 to 2011 period.[2] In the following year, the same publication named me one of the 50 most influential people in the global financial markets.[3] *Everyone has a different specific recipe for their professional successes and achievements but there are some common ingredients.*

1. *Mix judgment with math.*

   I was a much better than average economics student but only an average student in math. That likely has helped me in forecasting because I have been uncomfortable with purely mathematical models. Almost all of my audiences find statistics mixed with historically based judgment and anecdotes to be more believable and convincing than a pure econometric model.

2. *Be neither broken clock nor weather vane.*

Only a few forecasters have long careers being either "perma-bulls" or "perma-bears." Although forecast users may admire such savants' sincere conviction, they do not find them reliable. On the other extreme, there are forecasters who change their views with each blip in the news cycle. From a forecast-user's perspective, I would rather get analytical stimulation from a thoughtful broken clock than a weather vane.

3. *Be brief.*

Important audiences are busy.

4. *Explain "why" succinctly.*

Economists are too often guilty of giving plenty of "what" but insufficient "why." How do you reconcile that requirement with the need for brevity? A few bullet points on one page will usually suffice, followed by one or two exhibits for each of the key "why(s)."

5. *Beware of black boxes.*

Throughout my career I have respected technical analysts (i.e., chartists) and monetarists who use single-variable fundamental monetary models. That said, most forecast users want more "why(s)" than these professionals generally supply. I find it useful to illustrate causality with flow charts, which also help show my train of thought. (See example in Figure 13.1.)

6. *State risks.*

Greater risk sensitivity will be a long legacy of the Great Recession. Useful forecasters often cannot avoid providing either a most likely point estimate or a narrow range of most likely outcomes. However, it always is helpful to state risks framed as second and possibly third most likely scenarios. Be sure, though, to make your most likely scenario clear so that your audience does not depart with the impression that you were just hedging your bets.

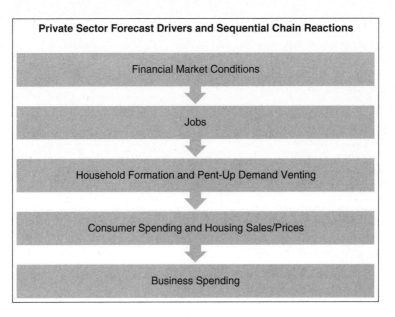

Figure 13.1 Example of Simple Model Presentation
SOURCE: Author.

7. *Educate.*

How do forecasters keep their jobs when they are wrong more often than not? I think the survivors are the ones who provide useful information. Try never to present a client with only a forecast. For instance, I sometimes also like to discuss what I see as exciting new areas where my team is currently conducting research.

8. *Listen.*

Never participate in a discussion without asking questions. Everyone likes to have his opinions solicited. In directing my teams' research agendas toward useful commercial ends, I find it extremely helpful to ask audiences what they want to know that they are not learning from other research providers.

9. *Use humor.*

Humor is handy for more than just pure entertainment purposes. Because economists are teased about not being right all of the time, I sometimes use limericks as a form of self-deprecating humor. (See examples in Figure 13.2.)

According to our foresight
The GDP will be bright
If not, here's our vision
"There will be a revision
And one day we're gonna be right!"

The "hawks" are ready to fight
They think the Fed should be tight
But "doves" demur
They aren't so sure
Who do you think will be right?

A forecast is never "missed"
So says the economist
Who aims with precision
But awaits the revision
And gives the data a "twist."

The GDP was down
The economist said with a frown
"I thought it was higher
They made me a liar
Their data must come from a clown!"

We can't wait to see CPI
We hope it's not too high
But if it is
We'll say in a whiz
"These numbers must be a lie!"

There was an economist named Fred
Whose forecasts were right on the Fed.
Til' the Fed had the nerve
To throw him a curve
And now his face is red.

Figure 13.2 Economist Limericks
SOURCE: Author.

10. *Reiterate your past advice and forecasting record.*

To maintain credibility and good will, I like to review with an audience or individual client what I told them at our previous meeting, even if such advice was not so good. I also find it useful to combine mention of the most recent outcome with some sense of an overall advice-giving track record.

This book aims to improve the reader's ability to make and use forecasts successfully, whether providing advice on the future, building a respectable track record, or simply planning for business needs. By now, however, it should be clear that there is no sure-fire single method that guarantees consistent success. What's critical, however, is to apply a consistent overall approach to forecasting. I believe the five most important elements of that approach are as follows:

1. First, a sense of history is absolutely essential for framing possibilities.
2. Second, the mechanics of prospective economic outcomes should be contemplated in a nonideological fashion, because each of the major schools of economic thought captures at least some relevant behavioral clues to the future.
3. Third, government statistics and studies should always be handled with caution and a healthy dose of skepticism.
4. Fourth, long-term credibility necessitates being willing to change your forecast at times, but not changing your forecasts frequently.
5. Finally, when presenting advice, do not hedge your bets by emphasizing a wide variety of possible outcomes. Instead, to satisfy those asking you about the future, be as decisive as possible, and try not to dump decisions into their laps.

Remember, being wrong at least some of the time goes with the turf when you seek to ordain the future. Despite one's best efforts, there will be inevitable errors and disappointments. How one handles these setbacks is key to longer-term survival as a credible and successful forecaster. Don't hide from mistakes—acknowledge them and explain where you went wrong. And never forget the well-earned satisfaction you feel when you are right. For me at least, the disappointments have been happily outweighed by my exhilaration at successfully forecasting the future and helping others to do the same.

Notes

1. Robert P. Dobrow, *Probability: With Applications and R* (Hoboken, NJ: John Wiley & Sons, 2013).
2. Timothy R. Homan, "The World's Top Forecasters," *Bloomberg Markets*, January 2012.
3. "Most Influential," *Bloomberg Markets*, September 5, 2012.

About the Author

D r. Maury Harris is one of the most experienced economists on Wall Street, with 34 years of service as U.S. Chief Economist at PaineWebber and UBS. Prior to joining PaineWebber, he served on the staffs at the Federal Reserve Bank of New York and the Bank for International Settlements. Dr. Harris has taught and earned his PhD in Economics at Columbia University. As an undergraduate student at the University of Texas, he graduated Phi Beta Kappa.

In 2012, Dr. Harris was selected by *Bloomberg Markets* magazine as one of the 50 most influential persons in global financial markets. A year earlier, *Bloomberg Markets* cited him as the most accurate forecaster of U.S. economic data over a two-year period. In 2004, 2006, and 2008 he and his colleague James O'Sullivan were ranked by *MarketWatch* as Forecaster of the Year, and on seven separate occasions he has been designated in *MarketWatch*'s monthly rankings as Forecaster of the Month. Dr. Harris is a past president of the Forecasters Club of New York. On more than two-dozen separate occasions, he has been selected as a member of *The Institutional Investor* All-America Research teams.

Index